In this careful and thoughtful book, Christian Schnee gets to the heart of the relationship between politicians and their communicators. In his subtle account he challenges conventional wisdom and offers an insightful analysis, based in his own political experience and extensive academic research. A 'must read' for anyone wishing to understand how contemporary politics is communicated

Heather Savigny, *PhD, Senior Lecturer, Bournemouth University, UK*

This is an excellent book that offers a thought-provoking insight into political public relations. The practical experience of the author is combined with their theoretical understanding and empirical data to create a unique and authoritative understanding of how senior politicians communicate.

Dr Nigel Jackson, *Reader in Communication and Persuasion, Plymouth University, UK*

Political Reputation Management

It is widely assumed that a competitive political environment of public distrust and critical media forces political parties to manage communications and reputations strategically, but is this really true? Comprehensive control of communications in a fast-moving political and media setting is often upset by events outside the communicator's control, taking over the news agenda and changing the political narrative.

Based on interviews with leading communicators and journalists, this book explores the tensions between a planned, strategic communications approach and a reactive, tactical one. The interviewees have been instrumental in presenting and shaping the public persona of party leaders and Prime Ministers over the last 15 years, including, amongst others, William Hague, Iain Duncan Smith, Michael Howard, David Cameron, Tony Blair and Gordon Brown. It draws a unique picture of how political reputations are managed and, ultimately, confirms the discrepancy between what political communications management is thought to be, and how communications practitioners actually operate. This book empirically reviews political communications practice in order to analyse to what degree reality matches the concepts of strategic communications management.

This will be essential reading for researchers, educators and advanced students in public relations, communications studies and marketing.

Christian Schnee is Senior Lecturer in PR at the University of Worcester, UK. He began his career as spokesperson for Germany' Christian Democratic Party and later served as director of government communications in Hamburg. He also headed the international media relations for the 2006 FIFA Football World Cup Office in Hamburg.

Routledge New Directions in Public Relations and Communication Research
Edited by Kevin Moloney

Routledge New Directions in Public Relations and Communication Research is a new forum for the publication of books of original research in PR and related types of communication. Its remit is to publish critical and challenging responses to continuities and fractures in contemporary PR thinking and practice, and its essential yet contested role in market-orientated, capitalist, liberal democracies around the world. The series reflects the multiple and inter-disciplinary forms PR takes in a post-Grunigian world; the expanding roles that it performs, and the increasing number of countries in which it is practised.

The series will examine current trends and explore new thinking on the key questions that impact upon PR and communications, including:

- Is the evolution of persuasive communications in Central and Eastern Europe, China, Latin America, Japan, the Middle East and South East Asia developing new forms or following Western models?
- What has been the impact of postmodern sociologies, cultural studies and methodologies which are often critical of the traditional, conservative role of PR in capitalist political economies, and in patriarchy, gender and ethnic roles?
- What is the impact of digital social media on politics, individual privacy and PR practice? Is new technology changing the nature of content communicated, or simply reaching bigger audiences faster? Is digital PR a cause or a consequence of political and cultural change?

Books in this series will be of interest to academics and researchers involved in these expanding fields of study, as well as students undertaking advanced studies in this area.

Public Relations and Nation Building
Influencing Israel
Margalit Toledano and David McKie

Gender and Public Relations
Critical perspectives on voice, image and identity
Edited by Christine Daymon and Kristin Demetrious

Pathways to Public Relations
Histories of practice and profession
Edited by Burton Saint John III, Margot Opdycke Lamme and Jacquie L'Etang

Positioning Theory and Strategic Communications
A new approach to public relations research and practice
Melanie James

Public relations and the history of ideas
Simon Moore

Public Relations Ethics and Professionalism
The shadow of excellence
Johanna Fawkes

Power, Diversity and Public Relations
Lee Edwards

The Public Relations of Everything
The ancient, modern and postmodern dramatic history of an idea
Robert E. Brown

Political Reputation Management
The strategy myth
Christian Schnee

Challenging Corporate Social Responsibility
Lessons for Public Relations from the Casino Industry
Jessalynn R. Strauss

Political Reputation Management

The strategy myth

Christian Schnee

LONDON AND NEW YORK

First published 2015
by Routledge
2 Park Square, Milton Park, Abingdon, Oxon OX14 4RN

Simultaneously published in the USA and Canada
by Routledge
711 Third Avenue, New York, NY 10017

Routledge is an imprint of the Taylor & Francis Group, an informa business

British Library Cataloguing in Publication Data
A catalogue record for this book is available from the British Library

Library of Congress Cataloging in Publication Data
Schnee, Christian, 1973-
Political reputation management : the strategy myth / Christian Schnee.
pages cm. – (Routledge new directions in public relations & communication research)
Includes bibliographical references and index.
1. Communication in politics. 2. Public relations. 3. Strategic planning. I. Title.
JA85.S365 2015
324.01'4–dc23
2014025641

ISBN: 978-1-138-79656-0 (hbk)
ISBN: 978-1-315-75782-7 (ebk)

Typeset in Times New Roman
by Taylor & Francis Books

Contents

1 Strategic reputation management: nothing but a myth? 1

Introducing the argument 1
Introducing the chapters 7

2 Political communications management: understanding the context 9

Political marketing 9
Public relations and the process of reputation management 15
Redefining political public relations 17
The ascendancy of professionalism in politics 26
Why reputation counts: personalization and celebrity politics 32
Reputational objectives: defining the ideal politician 33
Reputational objectives: charisma and the public persona 37
External circumstances: events and charismatic leadership 39
Clarifying the terminology: image and reputation 41

3 The strategic communications management process 45

Analysing the process of reputation building: models of strategic communications management 45
Reviewing professional practice: managing political communications 52

4 Reviewing political communications management practice 55

Media and political communications management practice 55
Agendas and frames in communications management 58
Defining resources: expertise, structures and access 61
Professionalism 61
Resources 63
Internal organization and access 64
Literature reviewed: an afterthought 67

5 Communications management in action 69

Collecting and analysing data 69
Recognizing the relevance of reputation management 72
Using research in reputation management 75
Understanding the ideal public persona 79
Linking personality and reputation management objectives 82
Identifying distinct audiences 86
Positioning politicians 89
Reputation management and the planning process 92
Recognition of strategic options 95
Considerations of timing 101
Linking policies and reputation 102

6 Managing news 107

Comparing communicative styles 107
Journalists, communicators and the shaping of narratives 110
News reporting and its consequences for the public persona 112
Events and their consequences for reputation management 116
Contingency planning and protecting perceptions 119
Managing a politician's communications 121
Controlling the news agenda 125

7 Managing resources 129

Past record: opportunity and burden 129
Reputation management over time 132
Professional advice: quality and implementation 136
Internal communications and management structures 140
Scrutinizing the communicators and their expertise 144
Resources as a quality factor in reputation management 148

8 Debunking the strategy myth: quite tactical after all 150

Findings and discussion 150
Theoretical and managerial implications: a new perspective in political communications management 159
Limitations 162
Conclusion 164
Further research 169

Bibliography 171
Index 191

1 Strategic reputation management

Nothing but a myth?

Introducing the argument

The question I shall be dealing with in this book originates from my professional experience as a communications manager in politics. I spent more than a decade advising candidates and incumbents on their relations with the public in general and the media in particular. My research was driven by an interest in the strategies and techniques that are used by communicators to build up and safeguard a politician's reputation. It was this broad perspective that I adopted when commencing preliminary work on this project in January 2005.

After a number of bends and detours I narrowed my focus and ultimately sought to explore if and to what degree a politician's reputation is being planned and managed strategically. Inspired by my own professional experience, I intended to investigate if what communications advisers and some academics portray as being a planned and strategic process is perhaps more akin to a streak of somewhat haphazard publicity activities as well as reactive and tactical media relations. My findings were a surprise and contrasted with much of what had been published about the subject in the past. The conclusion I arrived at is reflected in the subtitle of this book: *The Strategy Myth*.

I should at this early stage clarify that for practical reasons I decided to limit my attention to the relationship between communicators on the one hand and professional journalism on the other, which turned out to be a complex one, driven by constant rivalry, frequent collaboration and occasional collusion. Gregory (2011) points out that the word 'communication' is the preferred term for all public relations and marketing activities in government, and for this reason throughout this book I refer to communicators, unless there are specific reasons to distinguish between public relations and marketing advisers.

An underlying assumption of this research project implies the centrality of images and reputation, which is shrewdly touched upon by the Spanish philosopher Baltasar Gracian, who reminds us that phenomena cannot be taken for what they are but for what they appear to be (Gracian y Morales, 2005). When we turn to the map of the world we see continents and countries whose location, shape and size seem familiar and plausible to us. However, what we normally look at is a Mercator projection of the world, which for the sake of nautical navigation gives a precise representation of directions and shapes and thereby vastly distorts the sizes of countries, which only vaguely resemble actual world proportions – a factual deficiency most of us will not notice or easily accept, as the traditionally used image of the world looks so appropriate and unquestionable to us (Schechner, 2002).

This example aptly points out how we may be misled by appearances that we take for granted: a lesson politics has learned since the onset of civilization. Leary (1995) details how political leaders throughout history have recognized that their effectiveness and power depends in part on their public persona. Thus, since the early 20th century it has been debated that public opinion may be much less swayed by the electorate's grasp of a factual matter or the candidate's policies (Lippmann, 1997). Instead, politicians have to reckon with public images and reputation (Boorstin, 1992; Eisenegger, 2010). In the view of Eisenegger (2010), the focus on a candidate's or an incumbent's personality has long been used to emphasize and epitomize executive power.

While formerly the party leadership found its support soundly anchored in the party rank and file, nowadays its legitimacy hinges upon the audience's willingness to grant it (Gould, 2002). The British philosopher David Marquand (2004) notes a return of quasi-absolutism in politics. Instead of God, he argues, it is now the mass audience from which the head of government obtains its blessing of legitimacy.

Today it may therefore appear that the individual politician is taking centre stage both in people's perception and media coverage. Already in the 1980s and 1990s findings described the public's attitude towards on-screen political protagonists as highly personalized (Hart, 1998). This in turn raised expectations for a politician's impression management practice (Marquand, 2004). Communications advisers at the time took up the cue, and Ronald Reagan's aide, Michael Deaver, claimed that images of politicians are sometimes as useful as substance: 'Not as important, but as useful' (Deaver, 1987, p.73). Waterman observed that image creation had become a serious business that had critical implications for a politician's success (Denver *et al.*, 2012). Already in 1999 for Plasser *et al.* self-presentation had become a fact of political life and a core concern for any ambitious politician. At the time of Plasser's writing, New Labour exhibited an interest in candidate images that in the view of some observers verged on the obsessive (Rowan, 1998) – an alleged advantage the Conservatives sought to catch up on a decade later with the ascendancy of David Cameron (Shepherd, 2008).

Politicians have adapted to these growing expectations and learned the ropes of public performance in what Sarcinelli (2005) calls a media-representative democracy. Waterman reminds us that 'in politics, candidates and incumbents spend considerable time and money cultivating a preferred image' (Waterman *et al.*, 1999, p.11). In his view the recognition that a politician's image may oscillate between the positive and the negative concedes professional communicators a pivotal role in the political process and makes their expertise in designing images and building reputation indispensable. Thus, the concern with images and the tangible personalization in politics played into the hands of communications advisers who seek to position politicians prominently and present them to specific publics. On television politicians have therefore been portrayed as a clique of individuals who replace policy advocacy with carefully rehearsed sound bites (Maarek, 2011).

When in 2007 Gordon Brown succeeded Tony Blair in 10 Downing Street, *The Economist* launched a poignant criticism against the new prime minister, claiming that what was known about his personality was 'unappetising' (Bagehot, 2007, p.44). The author eerily concluded that 'for Mr. Brown perhaps personality is destiny after all'. Indeed, for many of the preceding months the media had busied themselves with a debate about the new Labour leader's personal strengths and weaknesses. While Gordon Brown's ideological credentials and political visions for the country still appeared to be shrouded in mist, political pundits and the electorate sought to find clues that might help interpret his personality. In the spirit of this debate, Theakston (2010) reminded us that a politician's job specification requires individuals to score well on policy vision, emotional intelligence and communicative competence. In other words, both the media and academic discourses raised the question as to whether Brown's public persona could be related to his fitness to govern the country. In a similar vein, Marquand had argued that the public may not be able to distinguish between the government, the office holder and the private individual, but concentrates its attention on the leader both in his political role and his private life (Marquand, 2004). Brown's case is evidence for the relevance of a candidate's and incumbent's reputation for political success, which has been testified to in interviews that de Landtsheer conducted with 50 marketing experts in various European countries. Respondents agreed that a politician's public profile was a prerequisite upon which political careers might hinge and therefore of 'capital importance' (de Landtsheer *et al.*, 2008, p.218).

In response, politicians seek to ensure that their public persona at least appears competent and appealing. Swanson and Mancini (1996) explored how politicians build up a support structure that helps accommodate and reconcile their respective public persona with the expectations of the media and the electorate. What Swanson and Mancini (1996) describe are instruments and techniques related to political impression management, and tools to alter and adjust a politician's reputation. In a more recent comparative study of political personality public relations (PR) practice, Esser and d'Angelo (2006) insist that candidate selection in the UK is driven by concerns for telegenic criteria, while communications managers are particularly expected to guide politicians' public persona in response to media expectations.

These and similar phenomena in the view of de Landtsheer *et al.* (2008) comfortably fit into concepts of political marketing theory. In this context the candidate is seen as the product and the citizens as consumers who withdraw their support if they are not kept satisfied. It may therefore be argued with some credibility that consumerism has found its way into the political arena and is leaving its mark on democratic processes (Newman, 1999a, 1999b; Lees-Marshment, 2004; Maarek, 1995, 2011). On the surface it would appear that today marketing concepts have become firmly established in a political context and eagerly used by politicians and their advisers to create images of candidates (O'Shaughnessy, 1990; Maarek, 1995; Newman, 1999a, 1999b). Politicians see themselves and are seen by others as performers whose objective it is to influence public perception and gain their audiences' support (Schwartzenberg, 1977; Newman, 1999a; Maarek, 1995, 2011). A reliance on technical expertise and the recruitment of special advisers to fulfil the function of communications professionals – popularly referred to as 'spin doctors' – testifies to this development (Wring, 2004; Negrine, 2007, 2008).

When investigating the contest between political actors and journalists, Negrine found that both sides have become more professional. Moreover the relationship between political communicators and journalists has seen a realignment of power in recent years (Negrine, 2008). In particular, the 1990s witnessed strenuous efforts by New Labour to recruit professional communicators who were tasked not just with advocating the party's cause. Rather, their brief was to emphasize the position of party leaders, help them communicate their messages and gain support among the media (Cook, 1998; Wring, 2004). The journalist Andrew Rawnsley analysed these developments and detailed how improved organizational skills and techniques could potentially give political actors an edge in their personal media relations (Rawnsley, 2010).

Moreover, in their attempts to shape individual politicians' reputations, communications managers have been espousing the notion of planning and strategic management, which writers in marketing and PR defined as a research-based process led by objectives (Grunig and Repper, 1992; Smith, 2012). Planned action and strategic thinking is believed to increase efficiency and effectiveness, as it suggests future action and anticipates developments. Trux (2002) advocates that a strategic plan will bring about better results than reactive and improvised action. This may explain why communicators have sought to create themselves more latitude to manoeuvre strategically by personalizing party political communications, while keeping the respective political party officials at arm's length and relegating the electorate to passive spectators of stage-managed appearances (Swanson and Mancini, 1996; Barkham *et al.*, 2005).

However, when applied to political communications management the case for planned and strategic action starts to appear less feasible. Notwithstanding strenuous efforts in media relations management, it seems fair to say that total control of messages has so far been elusive as events upset the communicators' news agenda, change the political narrative and potentially damage reputation (Smith, 2001). Gould (2002) argued that images in politics are fickle and so is the environment in which politicians and communicators are operating. In his view, campaign objectives and strategies cannot be controlled easily, if at all. Adaptability to constant change is a core requirement for any political communicator. Gould (2002) finds that current literature about communications management does not sufficiently take into account the vulnerability of images as a result of the unpredictable nature of politics and political journalism. Indeed, in his comprehensive survey of strategy making and planning in a communications context, Moss (2011) elaborates on the added challenges posed by a dynamic environment. He contends that across different industries managers tend to have 'little time for planning and abstract strategy formulation' (Moss, 2011, p.30). Already in the mid-1970s some of the management literature called the notion of strategic management a myth, replacing it with an image of evolutionary, reactive action (Mintzberg, 1975). In line with both Moss and Mintzberg, O'Shaughnessy *et al.* (2012, p.357) acknowledge that the media environment in which politicians operate is unpredictable and fluid to a degree that 'defies any attempts at political management'. From this they infer that communications management in politics needs to up its game. Baines (2005) recognized that a volatile environment, sudden shifts in public mood, scandals and eruptions of accusations have to be addressed through more effective and efficient marketing tools and mechanisms.

In these introductory paragraphs I have very briefly touched upon the defining issues that motivate and guide this book. First of all, the centrality of images and personality in political communications explains why individual candidates and incumbents seek to manage their public perception (Smith, 2001). Second, the unpredictability of events and the volatility of the environment challenge intentions to project reputation strategically and to plan communications activities systematically.

Against this backdrop I seek to explore the potential discrepancy between what political communications management purports to be doing (exercising a strategic function), on the one hand, and how communications practitioners in politics actually operate (tactically and reactively), on the other. In Chapters 2, 3 and 4 I shall be reviewing how current research on management and communications has largely ignored this gap. The subsequent empirical part of this book (Chapters 5, 6 and 7) can be understood as a response to Moss (2011, p.40), who insists that this distinction between planned strategy and responsive tactics 'requires closer attention if we are to understand more fully the nature of the managerial role in the communications context'.

This backdrop informs more specific objectives that I am pursuing in this book:

- To explore and identify features that distinguish a planned, strategic communications approach in political reputation management from a reactive, tactical one.
- To consider the resources and circumstances that enable or militate against a strategic approach in political reputation management.

- To understand if, to what degree and under what circumstances we may expect a politician's reputation to be managed strategically.
- To integrate findings into a predictive theoretical framework of strategic personal reputation management in British politics.

To forestall equivocation and misunderstanding, it is worth clarifying that the subject of this book is not primarily the political candidate or incumbent, but instead the collaboration between communications managers and politicians. Together they devise arrangements that allow more or less strategic reputation management activities to take place.

The value of this work is intended to be twofold. Insights drawn from my research should help practitioners advance political public relations practice by identifying prerequisite features for strategic management of reputation in politics. I assume that a strategic approach carries practical advantages in terms of efficiency and effectiveness: thus by constituting a model that assists PR managers in steering personal reputation management more strategically, arguably my findings will help communications advisers in politics to operate more successfully.

Moreover, this book also aims to make a theoretical contribution to the discipline by generating a model that serves as a predictive tool that allows us to identify and forecast the presence or absence of strategic practice in political reputation management.

The data collection and analysis for this empirical study is informed by a research design upon which I would like to touch briefly in order to help the reader understand how I arrived at my findings and conclusions (Mason, 1993). The research for this book is not derived from a hypothesis because of theoretical reasons that are reflected in the following review of literature, which is intended to give an overview of current discourse on political communications practice: I shall be detailing that empirical research about the role of communications management practice in the build-up of a politician's reputation is at an incipient stage. The behaviour of and professional approach taken by communications consultants in the process of political reputation building has so far not been conceptualized within the theoretical frameworks of communications management literature even though the professionalization of political consultants and campaign managers has for years drawn considerable academic attention.

This dearth of a theoretical framework justifies a qualitative, inductive research design, which should lead to the identification of features and patterns within political communications management and concurrently shed light on both internal and external factors that condition how communications management is being practised. I shall present findings that may help us understand if and to what degree strategic reputation management does take place, how it works, who is in charge of and what is instrumental in researching, agreeing and meeting reputational objectives, how and what resources are used to operate effectively, and finally, to what extent reputation management is contingent upon or autonomous from a political party, political decisions or communications management expertise and advice. Eventually, I shall introduce a theoretical model that represents the explicit and underlying variables which shape processes in political reputation building.

Introducing the chapters

Chapters 2, 3 and 4 are intended to provide an overview that illustrates essential themes and current research into this subject area. By choosing a comprehensive, interdisciplinary perspective, I hope to illustrate that academic work on political reputation management is at an incipient stage. I shall be arguing that the practice of individual reputation building in politics so far has not been comprehensively explored in marketing, public relations or political communications studies. In the second part of this book (Chapters 5, 6 and 7) I present data drawn from interviews with communicators and journalists in order to fill these gaps and gain a more complete picture of how political reputation management is practised.

For my initial review of the current and past discourse on political communications management there are two good reasons. First of all, I am trying to discuss political communications strategy and tactics with the intention of establishing features that distinguish a planned, strategic communications approach from a reactive, tactical one. This discussion is broadened by a consideration of the resources and circumstances that enable or militate against strategic practice.

Second, by reviewing the political communications, marketing and public relations literature, I am trying to highlight that the question of whether and to what degree the reputation of political protagonists is being systematically managed has not been raised in academic discourse in either discipline.

In Chapter 2 I start out by presenting the distinguishing concepts of the two disciplines in which this research is grounded: public relations and marketing. Subsequently, I try to analyse how writers on political communications reflect on themes and issues that condition the ascendancy of marketing concepts and techniques in British politics. I shall highlight how an ever more professional communications management and the debate about personalization in politics serve as the context of this book and justify its purpose.

My decision to present a historical overview relates to Negrine's (2007) argument that the professionalization of political communications has been an uneven process, which was accelerated or slowed down both by external and internal circumstances as well as individuals who manage and lead political parties and governments. He goes on to say that election defeats or the sheer willpower of a leader may increase commitment to centralize communications, upgrade technical knowhow and skills, and focus on strategy. In line with Negrine, I draw on arguments to suggest that the professionalization of political communications in the British government and the leading parties proceeded cyclically. In part, this drive for professionalization was a response to politicians' recognition that in an era of mass media-generated images they were increasingly being treated like celebrities and expose to intense scrutiny.

To direct communications management towards an objective, politicians and communicators will need an agreed notion of the type of public persona that should be shaped and presented. This train of thought is echoed in literature about the ideal politician, which in part originates from or culminates in the idea of the charismatic leader (Chapter 2).

Any subsequent discussion of reputation management in politics needs to be based on and grounded in an unequivocal understanding of the key terms 'image' and 'reputation', which in academic writing are at times used interchangeably and confusingly. Following this, I seek to explain how the definition of reputation, its emergence and decline is related to concepts of communications management.

Once we have established how reputation and its emergence are conceptualized across the disciplines, a consideration of strategic management frameworks in Chapter 3 helps us to gauge if and to what degree communicators' approach to and activities of reputation management actually do meet the basic professional and academic conventions of strategic communications processes. Reviewing models of planned strategic communications allows us to discuss, understand and categorize the views and perspectives one encounters when interviewing communications managers.

At a more tactical level, media and communications management are instrumental in a power struggle between journalists and communicators for access to and control over the news agenda. In Chapter 4 I relate PR and marketing literature that presents how tactical and strategic deployment of communications tools allows communicators to frame information. Arguably, evidence of a tussle over the news agenda may testify to a more tactical media relations policy that is short of strategic purpose.

Moreover, in Chapter 4 the communications literature is considered that acknowledges the structural as well as technical conditions and resources needed by communicators to pursue objectives effectively. Centralization, questions of access, numbers and expertise of staff are key issues thought to contribute to or militate against a planned communications perspective.

In brief, Chapters 2, 3 and 4 illustrate how political reputation management is grounded in a number of disciplines, ranging from media relations, political science and social psychology, to management, public relations and marketing. Drawing on these disciplines I aim to define the communication-related strategies and tactics that help establish and manage a politician's public persona. This subsequently allows us in Chapters 5, 6 and 7 to interpret the empirical data generated in practitioner interviews, and eventually to reflect on the existence or absence of a planned strategic approach in political reputation management (Chapter 8).

2 Political communications management

Understanding the context

Political marketing

When individuals, political parties or organizations deploy marketing concepts, theories and approaches to achieve objectives in a political context, we may refer to this activity as political marketing. The fundamental objectives of political marketing are addressing public perspectives and views, the propagation of political convictions, campaigning, winning majorities of the electorate, and finally, legislating with the intention to meet the expectations and hopes of particular segments of the electorate (Newman, 1999b).

Newman (2002) contends that the marketing rationale helps understand why, how and to what purposes candidates, parties and government departments take strategic decisions. Hence marketing concepts appear to offer a valuable framework for a study that endeavours to grasp the degree to which strategic considerations and decisions feed into the political communications process (Harrop, 1990).

Marketing strategy is described as the interface between any entity – political or not – and its surroundings, with particular regard to its key audiences (Mavondo, 2000). Lilleker *et al.* (2006) and Lilleker and Negrine (2006) emphasize the mutual nature of marketing in politics, which promises to satisfy both the electorate's expectations and the organization's needs. For a comprehensive definition I turn to Osuagwu, who conceptualized political marketing as:

> … the systematic and objective analysis, planning, implementation, evaluation and control of political and electoral programmes, policies and processes designed to create, build, sustain and enhance mutually beneficial exchange transactions and relationships between a political party (on one hand) and its relevant audience (such as votes, electorates, party members, funder, etc) for the purpose of achieving efficiency and effectiveness.
>
> (Osuagwu, 2008, p.795)

The academic discipline of political marketing is still relatively young (Baines and Egan, 2001). Only in the late 1960s was the concept of strategic marketing slowly adopted by non-profit organizations and political parties (Kotler and Levy, 1969). At that time Kirchheimer (1965) perceived a change in Western European political communications. He pointed out that political parties had become comparable to branded products. At the time, Kotler and Levy (1969) pioneered research to establish the degree by which marketing and branding expertise could be applied in a political environment.

Newman (2002) reminds us that since then various academic disciplines dealt with political marketing and applied their distinct perspectives. A range of authors with backgrounds in political sciences, communications and marketing have followed Kotler and Levy's example and examined election campaigns to detect evidence of marketing strategy (Newman, 1994b; Bartle, 2002; Kavanagh and Butler, 2005). How marketing style, strategies and tactics have been deployed by parties and candidates in a political context has by now been explored extensively in academic writing (Kotler and Kotler, 1981; Newman, 2002; Ormrod and Henneberg, 2010).

Judging by the amount of literature that has been published on the subject in recent years, we are arguably experiencing the emergence of a new subdiscipline in its own right, which sets itself apart through the use of its own terminology: *political strategy*, *spin*, *political advertising*, *packaging* (Pearson and Patching, 2008). It should be noted that most literature on political marketing has focused on the political system, media channels, the public and their interaction, in either the USA or the UK (Butler and Collins, 1996). A range of writers has also looked into what the strategies of competing parties have in common and where they differ (Wring, 1996, 2004; Wilson, 2011; Cook, 2011; Rennard, 2011).

Newman (2002) points out that political candidates and parties avail themselves of marketing strategy and tactics that hitherto had been widely used in the for-profit sector. Miller, for instance, likens electoral behaviour to economic consumption and thus justifies the presence of marketing in both spheres (Miller, 1997). It has been assumed, therefore, that the classical concepts and principles of marketing as well as the analytical approach to the discipline are informing marketing practice in politics (Lock and Harris, 1996; Henneberg, 2006). This is a phenomenon that Wring (1999) has described as 'colonization' of the field. While some writers still question if marketing should have a role to play in politics (Lilleker, 2005; Savigny, 2012), a majority of scholars and practitioners agree that politics and marketing are closely related. They also consider marketing as instrumental in re-engaging the public with the body politic (Lees-Marshment, 2008), as both disciplines are concerned with facilitating exchange processes and aim to improve quality of life (Kotler and Kotler, 1981, 1999). This optimism is grounded in the assumption that it is through the appropriate application of strategic marketing techniques that the voters' expectations can be readily identified and addressed (Smith and Saunders, 1990; O'Shaughnessy *et al.*, 2012).

To improve the effectiveness and efficiency of an entity's marketing activities, it is mandatory to align their behaviour and offerings with the expectations of its most critical audiences (Fill *et al.*, 2010). Already in 1992, Webster observed that marketing conditions the culture universal to any organization. Osuagwu (2008) concurs and describes marketing as determinant organizational culture both in the for-profit sector and in politics. For years, this has been the rationale for politicians and their consultants to deploy tools and strategies of marketing to propel their efficiency (Bauer *et al.*, 1996).

Marketing's potential role in political communications management has been probed by writers, who have explored if and to what degree concepts and techniques are applicable both in a commercial and a political setting. Lock and Harris (1996) as well as Ormrod (2005) recognize diversity in publics as a relevant feature that political marketing and non-profit marketing have in common. Mauser (1983) set out to identify the similarities between commercial enterprises and politics by suggesting that consumers could be likened to voters while the means of communication are the same in both disciplines. According to Mauser (1983), both candidates and businesses strive to retain voter or customer loyalty, which incentivizes the use of appropriate marketing strategy. However, Mauser's (1983) advice to view the drawing-up of a policy or campaign agenda on the one hand and the designing of a commercial product or service on the other hand as identical processes is not shared unanimously (Maarek, 2011). Still, Mauser's claim does find support in Ormrod and Henneberg (2006), who liken political campaigns to the process of product positioning. Their view of planning and campaigning for votes as being essentially comparable to any marketing communications task appears to be in line with both practitioners' experience and academic literature, such as Busby's (2009) study, which contrasts the promotion of products and services to the electoral campaigns that are stage managed for political candidates.

Marketing strategies in a political context entail activities such as issue-tracking, targeting audiences, image management, formulating agendas and policies, and timing campaign schedules and election days (Smith and Hirst, 2001). A range of marketing tools applied in politics – such as advertising, direct mail or publicity – has long been established in the marketing of the commercial sector (Clemente, 2002). Therefore, the appropriate means to explore and explain the use of communications tools in politics is through a prism of political marketing (O'Cass, 2001).

Rather than producing gimmicks and media stunts, political marketing arguably concerns itself with building up and maintaining a long-term relationship with its publics. It is assumed that this can benefit the electorate as well as the candidates and their respective party. The underlying belief is that this reciprocal benefit can be achieved on the basis of a symmetrical exchange process (Henneberg, 1996; O'Shaughnessy, 2001). Nimmo (2001) and Smith and Hirst (2001) concur in their support of this view, arguing that political marketing is transcending its short-term tactical function, which for years was limited to the processing of data during election campaigns. In their view, political marketing has largely assumed a strategic function, which is evidenced in its long-term managerial involvement with policy formulation. This development acknowledges established marketing knowledge, which is focused on the satisfaction of target audiences (members, voters, funders, media) as the intended outcome of mutual and long-term strategic exchange processes between an organization and its environment.

When talking about political marketing there appear to be recurring misunderstandings, which have to do with diverging definitions of the subject. A fundamental and inconclusive discussion is noted by Walsh (1994), who questions whether marketing helps candidates mainly to communicate their messages or if marketing advice is already involved at a hierarchical level where the policy agenda is developed. Jennifer Lees-Marshment tried to disentangle this debate by suggesting three categories of marketing (Lees-Marshment, 2008, 2001). Her concept is derived from Keith (1960) and his three-stage evolutionary model. First of all there is the product-oriented approach, which suggests that the party develops its policies and afterwards asks the public to support them.[1] Even if public endorsement were to fall short of expectations, the party would stick to its convictions. Second, the sales-oriented option. Here, again, the starting point is the agenda, which is based on the party's political beliefs and ideological outlook. Should public enthusiasm be lacking for what is being offered, the party would embark on a communications campaign to generate public support for its policies. At the heart of this model is the campaign management, which can twist and manipulate voter preferences to align them with the convictions held by the party. Finally, Lees-Marshment (2008, 2001) talks of market-oriented political marketing. This perspective essentially describes how policies are drawn up in accordance with the results of market research. What is being presented is meant to be in line with what the electorate wants (Lilleker *et al.*, 2006; Lilleker and Negrine, 2006; Ormrod and Henneberg, 2006).

Ormrod and Henneberg (2006) emphasize that Lees-Marshment's third option essentially suggests a concentration on client satisfaction. Diamantopoulos and Hart (1991) for good reasons remind us that this pathway has proven its efficiency for organizations that operate in particularly competitive environments. O'Shaughnessy (1990) concurs in this analysis by adding that market orientation should constitute the ideal approach. One fundamental argument in favour of this option was its presumed potential to overcome the divide between what the public expects from their political institutions and representatives on the one hand, and what political parties and candidates plan to do on the other hand (Baines and Worcester, 2002). Another advantage ascribed to market orientation was an increase in the organization's effectiveness and efficiency (Webster, 1992; McKenna, 1991). It is understood that market-oriented marketing in the political context essentially entails the collection of data about the electorate, the spread of this information across relevant organizational units within party headquarters, and the coordination and execution of a strategic campaign plan (Deng and Dart, 1994; O'Cass, 2001; Ormrod, 2011). Lock and Harris (1996) agree with Lees-Marshment that political marketing may only be in a position to guide political actions if a market-oriented strategic framework is adopted. When comparing this to the actual use of marketing by practitioners, we are reminded that often neither a party nor a candidate takes a conscious decision for or against one or the other perspective. Instead, it is suggested that emerging preferences hinge on a party's structural and ideological make-up as well as a multitude of stakeholders whose interests need to be reconciled by the party leadership (Gibson and Römmele, 2001; Mortimore and Gill, 2010).

There appears to be consensus among observers that – at least in the UK – candidates and parties are increasingly espousing a market-oriented stance, while product and sales orientation are having less and less clout with party managers (Smith and Saunders, 1990; Wring, 1996; Henneberg, 2002; Lees-Marshment, 2008; Schneider, 2004). The rationale for this development in Lees-Marshment's (2008) view is expected electoral success that supposedly comes with market orientation. Yet this analysis does not go uncontested. Mavondo (2000) suggests that bringing political messages and content in line with the electorate's expectations does not necessarily guarantee success in the marketplace. Indeed, marketing literature so far has struggled to link market orientation and electoral outcomes (Robinson, 2010). Still, it goes largely undisputed that market-oriented political marketing is in ascendancy and in past decades elevated the discipline from a tactical to an essentially strategic role in party politics and campaigning, which is owed to the acknowledgement in political management literature that organizational efficiency is critical for the achievement of electoral competitiveness (Butler and Collins, 1996; Robinson, 2010; Ormrod, 2011).

A main strand in political marketing writing explores aspects of branding in a business context and enquires how this relates to political practice (Lock and Harris, 1996). Lock and Harris identify political parties as general brands and term specific policies as sub-brands. Butler and Collins (1996) agree, as they liken both political parties and candidates to products in a business context. In line with this, they are suggesting that marketing in politics is a means to extend the brand of a political party and individual candidates. By now there is common agreement that brands are constructs that are instrumental in political communications management and critical for political parties and politicians who engage with stakeholders (Needham, 2005; Smith, 2009).

The use of brands in politics resembles their function in a business context: while commercial enterprises hope to guide consumer preferences, political candidates expect brands to direct voting behaviour (Phau and Lau, 2000; Smith, 2009). More pertinent to the subject under consideration in this book is the article 'The Forces behind the Merging of Marketing and Politics', in which Newman probes the interface between branding and three main candidates in the 1992 presidential race (Newman, 1994a).

Based on this case study, Newman expounds in detail the options politicians have when they strive to turn themselves into a brand. In his view, candidates' brand images are shaped by the perception of their personality, their ability to lead and the messages they disseminate in the mass media, as well as other daily political news by which the voter is surrounded. To this de Landtsheer (2004) adds the significance of visual impressions in the process. These impressions are being transmitted through the politician's physical presence. Newman (1999a, 1999b) also proffers suggestions as to how images are developed and ultimately turned into a brand. One recommended option is through association with celebrities, which has the potential to alter the way in which a politician is perceived. In recent years this strategy has been taken up eagerly by David Cameron, who associated himself in public with the green activist Zac Goldsmith and the campaigner for African poverty relief Bob Geldof (Beckett, 2006). In their accounts of branding Norris (2000) and Palmer (2001, 2004) draw upon examples from the 1980s to remind us of how Prime Minister Margaret Thatcher made tangible changes to her appearance, particularly her way of dressing and her hairstyle. This is interpreted as an attempt to match aesthetical expectations with the prime ministerial persona. In subsequent years the branding of politicians may arguably have become more encompassing and substantive while still invoking the aesthetic. Cameron sought to change his brand with an emphasis on green issues by installing a wind turbine in his garden and visiting and speaking out for fair trade products, while previously William Hague strived to subject his public persona as party leader to a makeover by attending the Notting Hill Carnival and sporting a baseball cap (Smith, 2009). In this context Newman (1999a, 1999b) reminds us that a politician's brand must be condensable to a single sentence that expresses both the individual's assets and at the same time sets them apart from all competitors.

While evidently the concept of marketing and the construct of brands provide useful strategic tools to analyse, understand and guide political communications practice, questions about the suitability and applicability of marketing concepts in politics remain. At a more practical level, the marketing concept espouses features that arguably may not do justice to the democratic process. More explicitly, a marketing strategy demands conformity in message and behaviour, which runs counter to the notion of democratic discourse. At times marketing strategy accepts or even encourages sections of the electorate to abstain from voting (Needham, 2005). While marketing activities usually assist in interpreting highly competitive markets, national politics in the UK for many years appeared to be less competitive than the fast-moving consumer goods markets. Until recently a stable rivalry pitched the two main parties against each other, while the electoral system marginalized smaller and new competitors. This arrangement is typical for what economists would term an oligopoly, for which classical marketing concepts may not fully account (Osuagwu, 2008). Also, some critical aspects of public opinion and voter behaviour such as protest voting are difficult to account for in a marketing framework. Likewise comparative and particularly negative advertising are phenomena that usually are not constitutive of commercial marketing. By contrast, in a political context they do have their place. Lees-Marshment (2008) rightly reminds the reader of the difficulty in indexing the performance of a political party or leader. This, too, sets politics apart from commercial enterprise and deprives marketing in politics of a crucial point of reference that marketers in businesses might be able to exploit in their communications activities.

More critically, marketing's focus on brand building during an election campaign is too narrowly focused on an anticipated exchange process and therefore fails to do justice to the broader concept of an ongoing reputation development plan addressed at a variety of stakeholders (Newman, 1999a; Baines *et al.*, 2002). Political marketing is usually conceptualized in relation to campaigns that ultimately should secure the public support needed to gain or retain political power in democratic electoral systems (Farrell and Wortmann, 1987). This focus limits our perspective and does not account for the practice of reputation management, which is understood to be an ongoing, long-term exercise that transcends the period of an election campaign and is broader than marketing's predominant concern with exchange processes (Ledingham and Bruning, 2000; Watson and Kitchen, 2008).

No less problematic is the failure of marketing to acknowledge the complexities of media relations and to recognize journalists' agenda in the communication of politics as well as the shaping of reputation. While marketing literature treats the news media as yet another channel of communications, it does not give credit to the impact journalists have on setting the agenda and framing messages quite independently from political communicators' intentions (Lees-Marshment, 2009; Maarek, 2011; Savigny, 2012). The repercussions resulting from this conceptual flaw are twofold. It draws into doubt the effectiveness of marketing in generating and managing reputation, which is contingent on the media's third-party endorsement, as I shall try to illustrate in the following section. In other words, its failure to engage with the mechanisms of media relations rules out marketing theory as an interpretative prism to explain and account for processes in political reputation management.

Public relations and the process of reputation management

On the following pages I shall be introducing a PR perspective to the discussion of communications management. This is meant to serve as a prism to assist in interpreting relationships in which individuals or organizations engage with their respective environment in order to build up and safeguard reputation. Economic, social, technological and political factors contribute to dynamics among publics and their expectations. It is widely recognized that a core function of PR is to predict, influence and respond to these changes (Grunig and Hunt, 1984; Broom, 2009). This activity is instrumental in building up and maintaining trust and support among key reference groups. External understanding and support are believed to be vital for an individual in a position of public authority to perform effectively (Ronneberger and Rühl, 1992; Szyszka, 1992; Bentele and Seeling, 1996; Tench, 2009).

Reputation is thought to play a central role in this process of generating trust through its equation to social capital, whose accumulation potentially secures and increases trust. Writers in PR (Faulstich, 1992; Merten, 1992; Morris and Goldsworthy, 2012) attribute to their discipline a pivotal part in the exercise of building trust due to its general association with the construction of image and the management of relationships with critical publics. It is suggested to conceptualize a politician's environment in terms of publics, which are a broad and flexible concept that transcend marketing's focus on the electorate (markets) and do not presuppose the existence of exchange processes.

While both marketing and PR are theoretically grounded in management and communications research, authors in public relations tend to stress the differences between the disciplines, and in particular the limitations of marketing in describing and analysing political communications practice. Cutlip *et al.* (2000, p.8), writing from a public relations perspective, remind us of a core distinction between the two disciplines:

> Marketing focuses on exchange relationships with customers. The result of the marketing effort is quid pro quo transactions that meet customer demands and achieve organisational economic objectives. In contrast, public relations cover a broad range of relationships and goals with many publics – employees, investors, neighbours, special-interest groups, governments, and many more.

Ehling *et al.* (1992) concur by emphasizing that marketing is mainly concerned with furthering the exchange process with customers, in contrast to the public relations function, which is dealing with a wider range of objectives and publics. From a PR perspective, marketing is therefore viewed as the appropriate framework to conceptualize election campaigns and voting behaviour. In contrast, PR emphasizes the use of trust and understanding in order to create goodwill among relevant publics (Gregory, 2007; Smith, 2012). PR stresses not just the persuasive aspects but also the building of quality relationships, which in turn are expected to nurture reputation (Grunig, 2002; Grunig and Huang, 2000).[2] The strategic value of relationship management may arguably be more pivotal in political public relations than in corporate public relations, as the environment appears to be more dynamic, unstable and rife with active and critical stakeholders (Strömbäck and Kiousis, 2011).

A theme that both marketing and public relations have in common is persuasion. An ongoing debate in public relations, in particular, about the role persuasion should play in communications practice, pitches two schools of thinking against each other. On the one hand persuasion is seen as an integrated part of the discipline, while on the other hand it is argued that public relations should be limited to facilitate understanding between publics. These opposed positions are reflected in Grunig and Hunt's (1984) four traditional models of public relations. The Chartered Institute of Public Relations appeared not to advocate the notion of persuasion when it defined public relations as 'the deliberate, planned and sustained effort to establish and maintain mutual understanding, between an organization and its public' (Black, 1962, p.3). This is echoed in Cutlip and Center's (1978, p.31) description of 'mutually satisfactory two-way-communication' which they consider critical for the achievement of goals. It is debatable if a mutually satisfactory two-way communications exchange can ever be directed towards the achievement of strategic goals. A further definition of PR, which offers to reconcile notions of persuasion of publics with the creation of understanding between interrelated systems, is provided by Nolte (1979), who makes explicit reference to PR's role in building reputation (public approval). He describes the discipline as a management function that seeks to adapt an organization (or individual) to the expectations raised by its environment, while concurrently striving for understanding among publics for the organization's (or individual's) behaviour. Ideally, this impacts on senior management's decisions and helps accumulate goodwill and approval among publics.

Grunig and Hunt (1984) remind us of what is problematic with various attempts at defining public relations. In their view, most authors in the field appear to propose too ambitious and comprehensive definitions that entail both expectations of how PR should be practised and the intended effects that are sought. Grunig and Hunt (1984, p.6) therefore suggest that we boil down our notion of PR to the lowest common denominator – in their view, an understanding of PR as 'the management of communication between an organization and its publics'.

Before we can use it any further, Grunig and Hunt's (1984) definition of public relations needs to be adapted to accommodate the objectives of this book. This becomes necessary in response to our investigation's focus on candidates and incumbents rather than organizations. While Grunig talks of communications between an organization and its publics, in this particular case we should consider PR as communication between any entity and its publics. Alternatively – and this is what is being suggested here – we may perceive leading politicians as the hub of human and material resources they hold at their disposal. This interpretation to a large degree reflects reality as politicians at national level do not usually operate as individuals but as senior managers in their own right within smaller or larger supportive structures. Therefore, in terms of communications management processes, the terms 'organization' and 'politician' in this study can be used interchangeably. Equating a political leader with an organization, however, would not suffice to accommodate and account for explanatory variables that are unique to the political context and set it apart from any other organizational – particularly a commercial – environment.

Redefining political public relations

The practice of public relations is thought to have its origin in the early era of mass society, when it had an initial impact on national politics (Le Bon,

1982). Already in the 1920s Edward Bernays, a self-styled founding father of public relations, advocated the use of PR in politics (Bernays, 1955), although decades later he questioned the practice of political consultants whose work he refused to consider PR (Bernays, 1985). While research into political PR is incipient and academic literature only a few years ago was still lacking a monograph on this subject area, most scholarly work to the present day strongly focuses on PR's role in a corporate or non-profit context. Yet, work published in recent years acknowledges a broad consensus about PR advisers' centre stage in British politics. PR's connection with political parties and governments has become part of Britain's political culture (Moloney and Colmer, 2001; Brissenden and Moloney, 2005). Political PR relies on communications techniques to garner support for policies among the media and voters (Froehlich and Ruediger, 2005). McNair's (1995) concept of political PR comprises government information management, internal party communications and reputation management. Of the three categories, the third – dealing with image and reputation – is the most closely related to the research question at hand. Any of these practices should be seen against the backdrop of mounting pressure to communicate and persuade professionally, which is derived from the growing gap between politicians' power to deliver on the one hand, and public expectations placed on incumbents on the other (Cook, 1998).

The PR managers on whose support politicians draw are more specifically categorized as professional political consultants, media experts and party officials with an explicit brief in media relations (Esser *et al.*, 2001). The latter group, whose members are often deeply rooted in the party machine, are more prominent in Europe, while Esser *et al.*'s (2000) findings identify the weakness of political party structures in the USA as a cause for the flourishing of independent consultants who provide their services to candidates. Communications managers' use of media channels is not only aimed at the legitimization of governments: PR practitioners seek to engage with the media on behalf of individual politicians whose respective reputation they are tasked with building. The mutual relationship between senior politicians and journalists emphasizes celebrity protagonists and is said to have propelled consecutive prime ministers to centre stage, which in turn helps them to define the terms of communication (Seymour-Ure, 2003; Heffernan, 2006).

The concern with public profile transcends all areas of British politics and extends from the pinnacle of power right into the constituencies. In a study exploring members of Parliament's (MPs) media relations, Jackson and Lilleker (2004) detail how backbenchers deploy communications tools to build and maintain a public profile with the electorate in their respective constituency. Not only senior ministers, but also the bulk of ordinary MPs have had to recognize that, without consistent communications aimed at the local communities, success at the ballot box is increasingly difficult to achieve (Jefkins and Yadin, 1998). Against this backdrop, Gaber (2000) synthesized the power ascribed to communications management as well as the implications it may have on the trajectory of a politician's career, and concluded that politicians' ascendancy may to a large degree be conditioned by the very message that anticipates their likely ascendancy.

This liaison between journalism and political PR has for years stirred interest among journalists, who have focused specifically on what McNair (2000) terms process coverage, which reflects how in politics messages are created, interpreted, planted and responded to by PR advisers. A decade earlier it was already evident that political PR had become a story in its own right, as Bennett (1992) discovered when analysing the news content during US presidential and congressional elections. In time, suspicion grew among political scientists and journalists alike: some discussed if an emphasis on presentation obscured substance, while others were concerned that the public sphere might be detrimentally affected and the political discourse twisted in favour of those in possession of means to resource communications campaigns (Moloney and Colmer, 2001; McNair, 2007). Weakening portrayals of public relations as *just PR* or pejorative terms such as *spin doctor* for political communications practitioners mirror sceptical views held among academics and many journalists (Turnbull, 2007). While practitioners became widely perceived as a 'malign and evil force at the heart of the body politic' by twisting the truth and manipulating the news (Esser *et al.*, 2000, p.213), the term *spin doctor* itself held no academic significance, nor was it ever adopted by the profession. Instead, it served as journalistic notation to discredit practitioners who were widely seen as media manipulators (Esser *et al.*, 2001). It is hardly surprising, therefore, if political PR managers tend to deny the label (Sumpter and Tankard, 1994). No matter which term is applied, however, the criticism remains, as Mannheim (2011) found, that, in political communications, style may actually trump substance. Indeed, communications managers are recurrently lambasted for their efforts to manufacture public consent by choreographing politicians' statements, gestures and actions (Stockwell, 2007). The interpretation of facts and figures amounts to the claim that communications experts handle the media to a degree that allows them to mould reality (Sitrick, 1998).

These concerns gained particular attention during the years of the Labour governments of 1997–2010, when observers may have wondered if political PR advisers would establish what amounts to a fifth estate (McNair, 2004).[3] This led writers to debate if and to what degree it is acceptable for PR advisers to interfere with policies and ensure a politician's objectives and actions are aligned with public sentiment (Maltese, 1994). This debate was taken further by Gaber (2000), who made the point that political public relations may actually have little to do with imparting information, which takes second place to practitioners' covert machinations. As a result of this discourse the British public came to associate political communications with manipulation, a view that adversely affected advisers' effectiveness to devise messages and implement communications activities on behalf of politicians (Moloney and Colmer, 2001). Voices that sought to defend PR's role as an activity that furthered democracy and public discourse were few and far between (Esser *et al.*, 2001). While this critical debate among political scientists on the image and nature of political public relations shapes a considerable part of the academic discussion, this section will limit itself to reviewing research that explores the managerial angle of political public relations and the work of practitioners.[4] As a starting point one may accept the basic definition proposed by Esser *et al.* (2000, p.218), who conceptualize PR managers as 'key figures through which journalists get access to the candidate'. Further empirical investigation into their practice is expected to encounter a tangible challenge, acknowledged by Johnson (2001), who reminds us that political PR advisers are rarely frank about the technicalities of their job and the means by which they achieve their objectives.

From a theoretical perspective PR practice is conceptualized in models ranging from the one-way public information type, which reflects a persuasive approach, to a symmetrical type, which incorporates a reconciliatory understanding of PR (Grunig and Hunt, 1984). The question addressed here is related to the applicability of these models in a political context: after acknowledging candidates' efforts to create legitimacy by accommodating their electorate's expectations and concerns, Jackson and Lilleker (2004) in their study of constituency MPs argue that the political context offers most opportunities to communicators who subscribe to a two-way symmetrical practice of PR. They argue that the kind of communication may hinge on the distinct situations politicians are in: when speaking on behalf of their respective party or government, they tend to pass on information without provision for feedback. By contrast, when acting as political agents in their own right politicians may be in a position to develop their stance through dialogue with publics (Jackson and Lilleker, 2004). Only a few years later Jackson (2010) returned to his earlier position (Jackson, 2003), thereby disputing political PR's dialogical nature. In a similar vein, Moloney's (2006) definition of political PR as weak propaganda appears to imply a persuasive approach. Xifra (2010) takes a position that potentially reconciles both the persuasive and the dialogic stances, by reminding us of the senior PR manager's strategic responsibility, which comprises both research and planning ahead.[5] Others emphasize an explicit need in politics to understand and accommodate the environment that is if anything even more unpredictable than what communicators deal with in a corporate setting (Liu and Levenshus, 2012). Xifra (2010, p.180) even goes so far as to predict 'communications dysfunctions' if an organization lacks the willingness to understand external expectations. Yet, the ability to adapt to dynamics and adopt appropriate policies requires not just an open culture (Dozier *et al.*, 1995), but also a degree of responsiveness, which arguably runs counter to the widespread assumption that communications efforts are guided by objectives that were agreed in an initial 'campaign planning stage' and subsequent strategy development (Kopfman and Ruth-McSwain, 2012, p.77). Suchman (1995) attempts to reconcile both perspectives by suggesting that, regardless of the increased demand for responsiveness, both persuasion and adaptation are essential in political communications in an attempt to gain support and build legitimacy. This is a view shared by Moloney and Colmer (2001), who found evidence both for the tactical media relations role and the more strategic intention to use personality and content to activate audiences' attention.

The degree to which PR managers are perceptive of environmental changes may arguably depend on their position within an organization's hierarchy: the higher they are – in the view of Xifra (2010) – the more complete their perspective. Regardless of their position in the organizational hierarchy, though, communications managers during recent years have not confined themselves to the role of mere conduits that transport messages on the politician's behalf. Instead, they have assumed the role of advocates who represent a politician's agenda (Oborne and Walters, 2004). This proactive perspective is reminiscent of Esser *et al.*'s (2000, p.212) definition of campaign communications, which is characterized by 'central planning and controlling of all campaign communication activities as part of an integrated communication strategy that follows the patterns of commercial PR'.

This latter model is challenged by Liu and Levenshus (2012), who are not prepared to accept the assumption that efforts to plan ahead could ever sufficiently anticipate and control events in politics.[6] Mannheim (2011, p.32) goes further by suggesting that what he terms 'focusing events' – such as scandals, economic downturns or international crises – may be overriding factors and thus be critical in defining frames of perception. These largely unpredictable external dynamics are arguably compounded by politicians and their media handlers who feed the media unattributable slight with an eye towards discrediting a colleague in their respective party (Heseltine, 2000). Liu and Levenshus (2012, p.104) therefore wonder if perhaps there is 'no point in planning' for issues or crisis situations. Since Martinelli (2012) equates issue management with the strategic planning process, a failure among communicators to scan the environment, monitor publics and anticipate issues suggests that political communications practice by nature has to be reactive. In the view of Martinelli, the lack of forward planning and a reactive approach are the defining nature of political public relations, setting it apart from public relations in the corporate sector. Yet a review of works on strategically planned as well as reactive PR in politics is complicated by academics who show a lack of rigour and precision when using these technical terms. Negrine and Lilleker (2003) as well as Jackson and Lilleker (2004), for instance, appear to minimize the distinction between strategic and tactical by equating the first with PR managers who actively seek media coverage and the latter with non-actively sought media relations. Concepts of strategy and tactics developed in management and marketing literature that help clarify and compare the phenomena are presented and critiqued in Chapter 3.

Moloney and Colmer (2001) found that intense media attention required politicians and their staff to respond by upgrading message delivery speed as well as message variety. In a similar vein Meyer (2002) asserts that the use of

PR techniques in politics merely echoes the mediated nature of politics. In other words, the wary media and a critical electorate force political communicators to resort to promotional tools in order to shape and communicate messages (Moloney *et al.*, 2003). Tony Blair is not the only high-profile politician who is known to have complained about the recurrent media attacks to which he found himself exposed – a phenomenon politicians counter by resorting to instruments of media relations management (Heffernan, 2006). Sampson (2005) recognizes this, but cautions that communicators' display of skill and assertiveness is still countered by unprecedented aggressiveness among journalists, who strive to determine the agenda and thus leave politicians and their staff little alternative to reacting defensively (Page, 1996).[7] In this context Lilleker *et al.* (2002) speak of attempts by the national media to discredit candidates and incumbents, which induces some politicians to prefer contacts with local journalists at the expense of relationships with national newspapers and broadcasters. Others respond by seeking to tighten their control over media relations.

Stockwell (2007) challenges this view: he believes the balance of power tips in favour of communications managers who, through orchestrating political statements, emphasize a specific news angle and thus limit journalists' freedom of action. These endeavours to control the news agenda are arguably more likely to be rewarded with success when large political parties pull their weight, while they become more of an impossible mission for smaller groups with fewer organizational resources and less political clout. The latter are said to be particularly frustrated by their failure to gain extensive visibility in the media at all (Grender and Parminter, 2007). Attempts at news media control by any political PR manager is strongly resented by the media, which at times resort to drastic counter-measures, as occurred when journalists downed their cameras on Blair's campaign bus in protest at what they perceived as unacceptably robust media-handling methods (Moloney and Colmer, 2001). Ruthless media relations involve the expulsion of hostile journalists from the information loop, which is particularly painful for the individuals concerned whose role in a newsroom becomes precarious once they lose their official sources of information (Gaber, 2000; Esser *et al.*, 2000). While specifically Blair's spokesperson Alastair Campbell displayed a preference for intimidating journalists, the full range of media relations tools transcends blunt threats and ranges from wooing and winning over to seducing and misleading. Gaber (2000, p.512) has explored and listed distinct techniques deployed by communications managers to cajole journalists and set the agenda, ranging from efforts to plant a story, to activities of 'firebreaking' aiming to divert the media's attention from a potentially negative story.

In recent years speed in media operations has gained critical relevance, leading parties to institute instant-rebuttal units equipped to respond to an opponent's attacks with instantaneous counter-statements (Stephanopoulos, 1999; Esser *et al.*, 2000). The core of media relations practice often relates to the creation of a positive narrative that ties in with public and journalistic demand. The appeal of a purposeful narrative is judged to be superior to that of shopping lists containing an assortment of policy promises (Grender and Parminter, 2007).

How on aggregate this variety of PR tools and techniques may well help shape the news agenda was detailed by Bentele (1998), who investigated the degree to which PR material was adopted among journalists, who often failed to attribute the sources of their information. Heffernan's (2006) analysis, by contrast, stresses the limitations of PR influence in the agenda-setting process, which in his view hinges on the appropriate balance between performance and substance. He suggests that political PR may not be able to create and sustain images that cut across reality.

Of interest to practitioners and relevant to the specific purpose of this study is Mannheim's (2011, p.36) contention that 'strategic skill' or the lack of it can shift the balance of power in favour of one protagonist or another. This places the skill and ability of website designers, event managers, image consultants, speech and copy writers into an elevated position critical for communications outcomes (Moloney and Colmer, 2001). The ability to apply skill and strategic understanding in daily practice may to a considerable degree be contingent on the politician's communications managers, whose professional expertise and input at times vastly exceeds their modest media relations brief. Seymour-Ure (2003) dedicated a study to their role vis-à-vis the politician, which defined the prime minister's press secretary as adviser on media relations and coordinator of government policies. She argues that these advisers find themselves placed in a powerful position as intermediaries between journalists and politicians, expected to understand both political processes and the media logic (Esser *et al.*, 2001).

Communications managers' power is also related to resources and organizational arrangements (e.g. budget, speaking with one voice, party unity, etc.), which Liu and Levenshus (2012) recognize as a prerequisite for the attainment of communications objectives. The need to bring together otherwise disconnected campaign decisions and integrate them into a single campaign argument is recognized by Mannheim (2011), who calls strategy a medium to align campaigns. In his view, a prerequisite for this to happen is comprehensive self-analysis by the protagonist, careful audience segmentation, ongoing research and outcome evaluation. The use of research in political PR practice has been known since the first polls were commissioned in the early 1930s in the USA (Eisinger, 2000). More recently, electoral surveys have been credited with the repositioning of Bill Clinton and the re-branding of the Labour Party in the UK (Baines and Worcester, 2006). While writers in political communications occasionally challenge the ethical implications and scientific rigour of opinion research, the centrality, availability and accessibility of research data for parties, politicians and their staff is not questioned (Savigny, 2007). In line with this apparent consensus, Grender and Parminter (2007) remind readers that without systematic research message formulation would fail. It is necessary for research and – in a subsequent step – messages to be marshalled in support of overarching objectives. For Seitel (2001) there seems to be no doubt that communications techniques only stand a chance to succeed within a strategic framework and grounded in the data on which the communicator is reliant in order to understand the expectations voiced among key publics in politics. Therefore, the PR planning process in politics requires managers to define both audiences and messages in line with objectives (Gregory, 2000; Jackson and Lilleker, 2004). Leaders or prospective leaders may, for instance, aim to enthral audiences by proving their respective utility and political leverage (Heffernan, 2006). In brief: it is understood that communications led by objectives are viable only if adequate resources are allocated to prevent activities from being reactive, 'haphazard and arbitrary', and instead ensure the strategic implementation of processes in line with communications objectives (Taylor, 2012, p.216).

The functioning and outcomes of communications processes led by objectives are dependent on an infrastructure that either allows for flexible and skilled decision-making processes that enable and ensure strategic action, or (if it slows down or obfuscates processes) militates against it (Mannheim, 2011). An awareness of these structural features partially informs the variables that subsequently help signpost the empirical part of this book and ultimately allow us to understand if, to what degree and under what circumstances planned strategy is likely to occur in political reputation management practice. Largely ignored in texts on communications strategy and tactics but at least touched upon by Brissenden and Moloney (2005) is the notion that an individual's genuine talent for communications or the lack thereof may offset the most carefully choreographed and scripted performance on stage and screen.

Another aspect of political public relations not widely recognized in academic literature is its role in constructing relationships – a concept pioneered by Ferguson (1984) – and the building of reputation.[8] Often the definition used to describe PR in politics is much narrower: Lilleker and Jackson (2011) point out that in the political context public relations are often merely seen as a communications activity in support of marketing. By the same token public relations in politics have been described as media relations. Strömbäck and Kiousis (2011) contend that these reduced definitions are offered by marketers who fail to appreciate the strategic dimension of public relations and consider it instead a technical function and a welcome add-on to marketing. The definitions that have been offered to qualify political public relations have emphasized technical dimensions as well as communications tools (Korte and Froehlich, 2009), or alternatively sinister propagandist scenarios as mentioned above (Brissenden and Moloney, 2005). Only very recently has political public relations' contribution to the building of relationships with stakeholders and managing reputation been acknowledged (Griffin, 2008; Cornelissen, 2008; Strömbäck and Kiousis, 2011). These writers agree that media relations is an unacceptably narrow definition, rooted in the tradition of marketing public relations, which conventionally focuses on generating publicity in support of a new product and is therefore more tactical in nature (Lilleker and Jackson, 2011). In other words, marketers appreciate PR as a means to spice up a product in the eyes of the audience and make its appearance exceed its substance (Moloney, 2006). Lees-Marshment (2001) reminds us that marketing models relegate PR to the implementation phase, preceded by policy design and adjustment.

An integration of political PR into marketing would result in a detrimental restriction of the communicative focus on customers who are intent on engaging in an exchange process (Jackson, 2010). In response to this narrow definition, Martinelli (2012) believes that political communicators lose influence and as a consequence become less effective if their role is curtailed to that of a media relations officer who is neither in charge of the establishment and the maintenance of long-term relationships nor primarily responsible for the creation of a narrative that aligns a politician's strengths with the political messages advocated by party and government (Grender and Parminter, 2007). Ferguson's (1984) advocacy for PR as an exercise in relationship building has been supported by later writers such as Ledingham (2001), who more specifically emphasizes the need to organize relationships around shared interests and goals, which in his view are the source of understanding and thus serve the interests both of the politicians and their publics.

To what degree relationship management calls for external dynamics to be heeded or rejected is conceptualized in contingency theory, which essentially portrays political communications processes as dynamic exchanges between an organization and its publics (Cameron *et al.*, 2008; Reber and Cameron, 2003). Crisis situations politicians encounter in the course of their careers may also be conceptualized in terms of contingency theory. Against this theoretical backdrop Coombs (2000) describes a crisis that threatens a politician's reputation as the result of a breakdown in relationships with publics. Today the establishment and safeguarding of relationships with key publics is not only seen as a core function of PR and a protective tool in crisis situations, but also as conditional in the management of reputation (Ledingham and Bruning, 1998; Grunig and Huang, 2000).

Concepts of reputation feature more prominently in models of corporate public relations (Hutton *et al.*, 2001). The notion of reputation has been taken up by public relations writers in a non-corporate context only recently. By now, the relevance of the concept is little disputed: Liu and Levenshus (2012, p.103) write about the 'debilitating consequences' a damaged reputation may have for public institutions. Evidence of the role reputation management holds with regard to individual politicians appears to be widespread, as Negrine and Lilleker (2004) established in their study, which ascertained that reputation is of concern not just to cabinet ministers and party leaders, but also to many constituency MPs. In national politics, the use of means to build up reputation as a strategy for parties in opposition who seek to re-engage voters and regain power has featured prominently in communications research (Lees-Marshment, 2001). It is important to note that the focus adopted in corporate public relations helps to understand the empirical research presented in this book as it is taking us beyond the boundaries of a specific campaign by analysing reputation management practice as a communications and relational process over a longer timescale (Griffin, 2008; Cornelissen, 2008). This perspective is welcome particularly as it contrasts with political communications writers who focus their attention predominantly on the campaigns in the run-up to election day (Young, 2007). In the view of Young (2007), this emphasis on elections in communication studies is limiting and not reflective of political practice beyond the campaign period. Writing a decade earlier, Saxton (1998) advanced a similar argument by pointing out that reputation is acquired through the course of an extended timeframe. Saxton (1998) goes on to argue that well-managed communications are an effective tool to build up reputation. This suggestion contains the two key terms 'management' and 'communication', which are the constituting elements of public relations and instrumental in reputation building and stakeholder perception management (Carroll and McCombs, 2003). Griffin (2008) reminds us that the very nature of reputation management requires a broader perspective of audiences that transcend the marketers' narrow focus on customers.

This notion of reputation linked to a comprehensive perspective of PR in politics would broaden the marketers' view of the discipline and help to improve our understanding of communications processes in politics. By the same token communications managers are called upon to adopt a more long-term, broader and considered strategic view rather than a merely tactical or technical stance.

We may conclude that, while the marketing paradigm is more widely used to describe communications management in politics, in this study a public relations perspective is adopted that is grounded in the understanding that public relations offers a broader interpretative framework. It incorporates marketing public relations as well as corporate public relations, and thus combines tactical with strategic elements. Political public relations use communications tactics to build relationships as a strategic means to manage reputation. While this perspective may not replace the marketing paradigm, it offers a different model that helps us to analyse and understand communications management processes in a political context.

The ascendancy of professionalism in politics

It has been widely argued – and it is not my purpose to challenge this convention here – that, after Margaret Thatcher's ascension to the leadership of the Conservative Party, political communications in a modern sense gained access to party headquarters (Watts, 1997).[9] The Saatchi brothers are given credit for stirring the Conservative leadership's enthusiasm for ideas of market research and voter targeting – now well-established means of modern political communications (Franklin, 2004; Negrine, 2008; Lees-Marshment, 2008). It nicely fits into the picture that in this period the prime minister's press secretary, Bernard Ingham, was reported to hold tangibly more sway with Thatcher than media relations staff were reported to have had in previous governments (Budge, 2007; McNair, 2003). In her autobiography Thatcher called Ingham her adviser and close confidant (Thatcher, 1993).[10] Issues of access for communicators and clout within the internal decision-making hierarchy are further explored in Chapter 4.

By the end of the 1980s politicians on both sides of the floor recognized the value of publicity and sophisticated communications management to further their careers and their popularity with the public. Matthew Parris is said to have described this phenomenon when he allegedly suggested that politicians were as keen on publicity as horses on oats (quoted in Franklin, 2004).

After the exit of Ingham upon John Major's arrival in 10 Downing Street, three press secretaries succeeded each other in relatively short intervals. None is remembered as a high-profile adviser to the prime minister (Marx, 2008). While it must be admitted that the Major government's divisions over Europe and a succession of sleaze scandals involving members of the cabinet did a lot to shatter the administration's popularity, some of the government's poor standing with the public could probably be blamed on inadequate PR, which failed to respond to the combined assault of a hostile media and a rejuvenated New Labour Party (Major, 2000; Jones, 1999). Major's spokesperson, Sir Christopher Meyer, complained in his memoirs that public relations in Downing Street at this time were handled in the most haphazard way. Apparently, Meyer could not even arrange for the daily papers to be delivered to his home every morning. Meyer gives credit to his successor, Tony Blair's press secretary Campbell, for introducing a much tighter, more efficient and professional structure into the prime minister's public relations operations (Meyer, 2005).

During the 1990s the Whitehall observers became aware that New Labour's communications had become more than just a means of informing and persuading the public. Political communications had developed into a defining and central element of the party (Gaber, 1998; Scammell, 2007, 2008). John Bartle put it succinctly: 'To be in the media is to exist as a politician.' Politicians see themselves as another consumer product and anxiously ask, 'Are they still buying me?' (Bartle, cited by Garner and Short, 1998, p.181).[11] Thus, both Franklin and Scammell may well have a point when they claim that it is hard to exaggerate the role of media and marketing in shaping a politician's public persona (Franklin, 2004; Scammell, 2007, 2008).

The central role that communications gained in the political process in the UK may be seen in the context of similar developments in other Western democracies. In the USA, the UK and Germany, centre-left politicians came to the helm during the 1990s. Incidentally, their coming to power was associated with a consistent use of innovative political communications tools. The trailblazer for this development is understood to have been the Democratic Party campaign of 1992 in the USA, which was able to draw upon financial resources unheard of in other countries and a highly sophisticated political consultancy industry. In the 1990s it was estimated that in the USA about 1,000 freelance consultants and about 40 specialized agencies offered their services in the field of political marketing (Holzer, 1996; Althaus, 1998).

What was particularly remarkable about Bill Clinton's campaign in 1992 was the speed and immediacy of political rebuttals, often within minutes of a competing candidate releasing a statement. Both the rapid response and the concentration on a limited set of core messages were seen as critical tools that contributed to the eventual electoral success (Butler and Collins, 1996). No less attention was given to the set-up of the campaign headquarters, the so- called 'war room' intended to coordinate the campaign, which at the time attracted an unusual amount of attention in the USA and from abroad (Butler and Collins, 1996; Stephanopoulos, 1999; Matalin and Carville, 1994).[12] Clinton's successive election victories in 1992 and 1996 stirred interest and led political communications consultants and campaign managers internationally to adopt some of the techniques used by Clinton's team.

It has been suggested that the US campaigns taught two lessons. The first concerns a more professional approach to political communications, which entails – and this is the second lesson – the direct involvement of communications advice at the decision-making level (Marx, 2008). Tony Blair, upon taking up the Labour leadership in 1994, moved the party headquarters into Millbank Tower in Westminster, where he set up the Labour Party's version of a war room (a large, shared office space modelled on the US example) and his own rapid-rebuttal unit. The party official in charge of the war room was Peter Mandelson, who arranged the office procedures in a way that guaranteed regular barrages of well-sourced press releases in response to any attack by the Conservative Party (McNair, 2003; Jun, 2004; Butler and Collins, 1996; Gould, 1998a, 1998b). It has been reported that a relatively small team of confidants orchestrated Tony Blair's campaign in 1997, guided mainly by the results of opinion polling data. A sample group of 5,000 non-aligned voters was used as the source for continual feedback on policy and presentational issues. Based on these insights the party proposed five clearly identifiable promises, which they had printed on pledge cards and distributed among the electorate. These core messages were meant to be the central themes in all media interviews that the party leadership was invited to give. However, it was not only innovations that set political communications in 1997 apart from prior practices. Blair's communications were also markedly more expensive. While the campaign in 1992 had cost the party £43 million, the 1997 campaign was an investment of about £100 million (Jun, 2004; Butler and Collins, 1996).

Thus, an increase in financial resources and innovative management in combination changed Labour's communications practices, as Blair's pollster Philip Gould summarizes:

> In a campaign, you must always seek to keep the momentum [...] Gaining momentum means dominating the news agenda, entering the news cycle at the earliest possible time, and repeatedly re-entering it, the stories and initiatives that ensure that subsequent news coverage is set on your terms. It means anticipating and pre-empting your opponents' likely manoeuvres, giving them no room to breathe, keeping them on the defensive. It means defining the political debate on your terms.
>
> (Gould, 1998a, p.294)

Once in government, Blair's Labour administration gave its media advisers more operational freedom, curtailing the ideological instincts by which previous shadow cabinets had quite intuitively been guided (Seymour-Ure, 2003). At the same time, the new Labour government went about centralizing communications to an unprecedented degree. The rationale for this was an intention to coordinate and unify messages and to avoid dissenting views. This reorganization echoed earlier calls for change resulting from the Mountfield Report, an investigation into the practice and quality of government communications:

> All major interviews and media appearances, both print and broadcast, should be agreed with the No. 10 Press Office before any commitments are entered into. The policy content of all major speeches, press releases and new policy initiatives should be cleared in good time with the No. 10 private office [...] the timing and form of announcements should be cleared with the No. 10 Press Office.
>
> (Mountfield Report, 1997)

The government tried to ensure that communications were not left to chance. The Mountfield Report (1997) made suggestions for senior policy officers and communicators to meet daily in order to align messages and content. Furthermore, structural changes were introduced to strengthen the government's ability to research and understand publics and their attitudes. A unit was established and tasked to manage, coordinate and advise on policy and presentation, suggest wording to ministries for interviews and speeches, and work with individual departments to make sure that departmental communications staff were aligned and not in competition with each other (Franklin, 2003). Any departmental communicator or cabinet minister who failed to align their respective messages and channels of communications with the guidelines and instructions issued by 10 Downing Street were called on the carpet.

At the same time the style of media management operated by government communicators is said to have changed tangibly. Gaber (1998) accounts how critical journalists were denied interviews with members of government. Alan Rusbridger, editor of *The Guardian* at the time, underlined Gaber's view while adding that government communicators expected him to place specific articles on page one and drop critical coverage altogether. If he refused to comply, it was threatened that exclusive information would in future only be sent to his competitors at *The Independent* (Oborne, 1999). Campbell advised press officers already in 1997 to assume a more assertive stance in their dealings with journalists and to dictate the headline (Timmins, 1997). What this implied is explained by the journalist Nick Cohen, who believes that leading political protagonists and their communicators have the:

> ability to refuse interviews to presenters or journalists who are out of favour. The state has a thoroughly politicised propaganda machine which can swamp reporters with recycled news, diversionary announcements and leaks to the boys and girls who won't bite the hand that force feeds them.
>
> (Cohen, 2001, p.18)

There seems to be agreement that the effectiveness of media management is to a large degree dependent on the assertiveness, insistence and even power to threaten journalists in an attempt to influence coverage, as Pearson and Patching (2008) detailed in their seminal study about spin doctoring in the UK, Australia and the USA.

However, Wolfsfeld (2003) cautions against quick conclusions and reminds us that this tilt in the power balance between journalist and communicator is not inevitable. If the number of prime-time sought-after news programmes is limited and difficult to access, a politician may become dependent on the goodwill of a few gatekeepers, who as a result stand a chance of negotiating on their terms. Notwithstanding this alternative perspective, Franklin is adamant that the strategic impact and managerial powers of government communicators is a legacy of the Blair years that may survive the Labour administration (Franklin, 2004).

Meanwhile, after a bitter and unprecedented succession of electoral defeats, the Conservative Party still found itself in opposition and the party's Central Office decided to follow suit and adopt key features of New Labour's innovations for its own political communications activities. Just as Clinton had done in the USA in the early 1990s, the Conservatives now merged their policy department with their media and PR units and let them work together in close proximity. This innovation for the 2001 general election campaign was the Conservatives' variant of the war room. Furthermore, Conservative leader William Hague put former journalists in charge of presentational matters, just as Blair had entrusted experienced reporters (Mandelson and Campbell) with his media relations. On both political sides professionalism in political communications had reached a hitherto unprecedented level, raising questions of how a sceptical and increasingly cynical electorate would react to a political debate that at times resembled a carefully drafted and choreographed role play (Butler and Kavanagh, 2002; Rawnsley, 2001; Jones, 2001).

This coherent presentation in style and content hinges largely on politicians' decision to permit to some extent their communications advisers access to the policy-making process (Esser *et al.*, 2000, Esser, 2000; Korte and Froehlich, 2009). In Chapter 4 I shall be discussing observations that suggest that communicators have entered centre stage in the political arena and have established themselves squarely at the organizational heart of political parties and government in a way that makes one wonder if there is still a distinction between presentational and policy issues (Blumler and Kavanagh, 1999; Franklin, 2004).

Interestingly, in the 1990s both Clinton's team and New Labour's leadership opened up their communications activities to the public and allowed their communications strategies and tactics to be reported. Parry-Giles and Parry-Giles (2002) see this as part of an effort to create authentic images of the candidates and their teams, which eventually would appear more credible to the audience than reality itself. Parry-Giles and Parry-Giles (2002) point out the need for authenticity in a political era largely made up of images and hyper-reality. They observe that the dividing line between real and fictional images has become blurred to a degree that may already have rendered the distinction between the two meaningless.

Marx (2008) advances a concept that helps us to understand why well-publicized political marketing activities in their own right contribute towards building the images of candidates and political parties. In his view Clinton's war room management as well as New Labour's innovative communications policies in the mid-1990s were deliberately publicized by the respective candidates as an indicator of their management skills and efficiency. The coverage of modern political communications management is seen by Marx (2008) as a kind of meta-communication, intended to help journalists and the wider public predict the degree of efficiency the respective candidates might be expected to deliver when managing an administration.

In this section we have considered how the past three decades have seen a professionalization in political communications, which is grounded in the unprecedented use of communications strategy and tools, as well as resources and structures. Historical and personal accounts suggest that politics is operated with acute and perhaps growing awareness of the strategic role of communications management. Efforts to establish centralized and more efficient communications management processes have institutionally separated and emancipated the function from party structures and led to changes in the government communications unit that I shall explore below.

So far, we have explored how political scientists and contemporary historians detail the development and the techniques of strategic communications efforts that political parties and candidates have been deploying to achieve their respective objectives. We found throughout how it is implicitly taken for granted that political communications are conducted purposefully. Apparently, neither historians nor political scientists appear to explore critically the question of whether the practice of communications and reputation management is planned, active and strategic, or alternatively tactical and reactive. When historians and political scientists do examine this question, it remains unclear how they conceptualize strategic communications, and while they do write about personalization, their concepts of image and reputation remain ambiguous.

As we have seen throughout this section, any writer on professionalization in communications management will need to addressl centralization, access to decision makers, the link between policy making and communications, expert external advice and research. At the same time one needs to bear in mind that the advance in political campaigning seem to be cyclical, depending on the situation of the party or politician, and on whether individuals are ready to espouse expertise and innovation. So far it has not been elaborated if or how the knowledge and availability of strategic communications alters the approach that individual politicians take towards the management of their respective reputation – whether candidates and incumbents in specific cases make use of resources, concern themselves with planning and show willingness to engage with communications strategies and external advice. Up to now, the question of whether a politician's public perception is generated through planned communications management or instead results from tactical responses to external issues has nowhere been systematically addressed.

Why reputation counts: personalization and celebrity politics

What exactly we mean by personalization has not been fully clarified (Papathanassopoulos *et al.*, 2007), and more interestingly it is not even fully agreed if a process of personalization can be observed at all in the political and corporate news coverage. Kaase insists that 'all findings support the notion that personalisation cannot be observed' (Kaase, 1994, p.211), and reminds us that public communication has always placed an emphasis on individual protagonists (Häussler, 2008). This view conflicts with those who explicitly claim that media reporting about corporations, political parties and government is increasingly construed around individual leaders (Imhof, 2010). It is argued that the media are implicitly encouraging both politics and corporations to place individuals at the centre of their messages. A willingness to comply with this expectation leads to a higher degree of media attention and media coverage (Bentele and Fähnrich, 2010).

Since Walter Lippmann's seminal work in the early 1920s it has been attempted to establish the news value of stories. In other words, both practitioners and scholars have been seeking to explain how and why the media select one particular news item at the expense of others (Lippmann, 1997 [1922]; Eilders, 1997). In response, Galtung and Ruge (1965, p.68) suggest that 'the more the event can be seen in personal terms, as due to the action of specific individuals, the more probably it will become a news item'. It is therefore critical for communications managers to adapt their strategy and tools to the criteria the media deploy in their selection of news. Personalization of messages is a tool whose effectiveness is widely recognized (Bentele and Fähnrich, 2010).

Concerns about personalization have been raised mainly by political scientists who fear this development could de-institutionalize democracy and instead establish a direct relationship between leaders and their publics, and thus marginalize parliament and government (Sarcinelli, 2005). While political scientists are concerned with the risks of personalization, research in public relations appears to show stronger interest in opportunities and challenges that come with personalization. Communications managers and writers on the subject have focused on strategies and tactics that can be deployed in support of individuals who have assumed a personalized and visible leadership role (Nessmann, 2009). It has been noted that the strong emphasis that news coverage in politics is placing on prominent individuals can be explained by television's ascendancy as the leading channel of communication, relying on images, movement and emotions, all of which can be found in individual protagonists rather than in organizational structures (Marcinkowski, 1998; Eisenegger and Konieczny-Wössner, 2009).

It has been argued that personalization is playing a critical role in simplifying political messages and procedures in an expectation of rendering politics more accessible and comprehensible for the electorate. Edelman (1964) sets out to analyse the connection between the complexities of the modern world and an avalanche of confusing and at times contradictory information that mass media provides. He goes on to argue that their incapacity to make sense of this situation encourages people to look for personalized leadership that promises to interpret and control the plethora of views, facts and phenomena with which we are confronted every day. Brettschneider (2002) agrees, arguing that the public is unwilling to spend too much time processing political news and therefore seeks to identify politicians' reputation as a shortcut to understanding their policies. This is arguably a way to simplify and emotionalize issues and thus helps citizens to orient themselves in an otherwise confusing political setting. Bromley (1993) elaborates this point, suggesting that politicians should build up a public persona that personifies their values. Rather than finding themselves pressed to take sides in arguably complex political debates, voters may instead choose to rely on the views advanced by politicians whom they trust and support (Brettschneider, 2002).

Reputational objectives: defining the ideal politician

Political marketing literature has sought to discuss ideal traits in a politician and has pointed out how the management of perceptions may contribute to generating a public persona that matches this range of personal features and public preferences (Wray, 1999).

Some characteristics are apparently universally acclaimed, such as honesty, competence and loyalty. These arguably may be part of a public persona that promises something akin to universal popularity. However, a different set of values, preferences and behaviour may appeal to specific audiences only (Leary, 1995). It is the focus of this review to consider what type of person electorates prefer and the values a political contender might want to demonstrate. The notion of ideal traits in a politician arguably constitutes the objectives for any reputation management campaign. We would therefore need to understand how and to what degree political communicators are familiar with desirable personality traits that may be sought in a politician. The absence of this awareness might suggest that long-term intentions to manage and alter reputation have not been discussed or agreed. The findings of this review, therefore, should serve as a framework that helps to focus subsequent interviews, recognize relevant data and understand findings.

Specific attributes assist politicians to appear as the right people for the jobs they are called upon to perform. They may help allow them to appear understanding and sympathetic to the people and their concerns. Darren Lilleker contends that a politician uses political communication to show that he really is a 'rounded, human being, who shares all the emotions with his audience' (Lilleker, 2006, p.79). Bucy (2000) argues that our judgement of political leaders is linked to their ability to show emotions publicly. The argument goes that emotions in politicians help us judge if they are authentic and if we should trust them or not. Lilleker (2006) agrees, and advises the need to emphasize empathy in a politician. He argues that only once the public has access to their emotions can they identify with the individual (Lilleker, 2006). Erikson (1969) draws a similar conclusion in his analysis of inspirational leaders throughout history. He believes that outstanding politicians appear to share essential conflicts, identities and needs with their public, who expect their fears, hopes, experiences and convictions to be echoed in their political representatives (Erikson, 1964). Bucy (2000) agrees and reminds us that the public tends to have a better opinion of leaders who behave in their private lives in the same or a similar way to most citizens. This allegedly allows voters to extrapolate if a politician would share popular views when it comes to taking decisions for the country.

Gardner (1995) takes Bucy's argument further and argues that a politician's apparent ordinariness is most effective if combined with extraordinary charisma and spirituality. Some followers are attracted to physical strength and power, while others like to see originality of ideas in their successful leaders. Politicians may strive to satisfy both groups. Revered leaders such as the US Presidents Franklin D. Roosevelt and Abraham Lincoln visibly possessed a combination of attributes such as flexibility, superior tactics and knowledge, which in the view of Winter (2004) helped earn them great esteem and recognition by the public.[13]

More systematically, Schweiger and Adami (1999) aggregate a range of cases in order to arrive at a definition of attributes voters may look for in a politician. A political candidate in their view needs to display a distinct style, charisma and credibility. Furthermore, they recommend candidates draw up policies and messages that not only mirror these attributes but also appear to be both credible and authentic, and happen to be relevant to the audience. Other researchers, too, recognize authenticity's pivotal role in the management of reputation (Eagly *et al.*, 1991; Tedeschi and Melburg, 1984). More specifically, Schweiger and Adami (1999) place most emphasis on trust as a conditio sine qua non in reputation management. To them, the success of perception management is based on relationships grounded in trust. They therefore conclude that only candidates the public trusts to deliver on their promises stand a chance of maintaining a competitive reputation (Schweiger and Adami, 1999).

How trust and trustworthiness are defined and conceptualized in a political context is addressed by Levi and Stoker (2000). At a practical level, Gomibuchi understands trust as a strategic tool deployed by political leaders to fend off opposition and rally supporters in times of crisis (Gomibuchi, 2004). Williams *et al.* (1991) also speak of trust as a key feature in a politician. However, they argue that, quite apart from trustworthy, voters expect politicians to be dependable, friendly, loyal, reliable, responsible, self-confident, understanding and honest. These were considered the decisive criteria audiences were looking for in candidates (Williams *et al.*, 1991).

Millon (1986) tested what personality traits the public felt suitable for a politician to display. His findings were corroborated in 2002 by Immelman, and in 2004 by Immelman and Beatty. They drew up a list of personality patterns that in the past had been used in experiments of clinical psychology. It was found that the public tended to have more sympathy for extroverted individuals who displayed outgoing personality traits.

In political psychology, personality traits have since been categorized as either a 'Teflon personality' or a 'Velcro personality'. While the former refers to the outgoing extrovert who seems to be impervious to criticism, the latter is defined as an individual who is easily associated with criticism and negative news (Newman, 1999a).

Newman and Davies (2006, p.22) go beyond this catalogue of desirable traits and present criteria that were developed in the 1970s and 1980s during focus group sessions. These are intended as a list of attributes that are most decisive in positive and negative popular judgements of politicians.

- A capable leader
- good in a crisis
- understands world problems
- tends to talk down to people
- rather narrow minded
- too inflexible
- has sound judgement
- more honest than most politicians
- down to earth
- understands the problems facing Britain
- patriotic
- has got a lot of personality
- rather inexperienced

- out of touch with ordinary people.

(Newman and Davies, 2006, p.22)[14]

Rather than looking at politicians in general, the social psychologist Leary focuses on political 'leaders'. He suggests that there are 'five particular impressions' central to any leader's image (Leary, 1995, p.81). They are as follows:

- A leader is typically judged in terms of presumed effectiveness (Leary, 1995). Leaders who are regarded as knowledgeable may be seen as experts, who are trusted and who thus sway more influence (French and Raven, 2001).
- French and Raven (2001) claim that politicians want to be liked while still being viewed as competent. Leary (1995) warns that it may be difficult to blend likeability and the image of competence in a politician, although it has been argued that this conflict can be overcome if politicians are self-deprecating on issues and attributes that are not associated with their leadership qualification (Jones *et al.*, 1963).
- The need to abide by moral and exemplary standards even extends to attributes that bear little relevance to a politician's core professional activities. For that reason US presidents are expected to have an impeccable family life (Klapp, 1964).
- Leaders want to be seen as powerful, calm, decisive and in control, in particular if their constituency or the country at large is under attack in times of crisis or war.
- Leary (1995) suggests that in specific moments politicians even prefer to be seen as intimidating.

It appears that these somewhat general considerations do not sufficiently take into account that popular preferences are transitory and may change over time. Waterman *et al.* (1999) reiterate that images therefore tend to reflect the political concerns of the moment. In the USA throughout the 19th century, voters preferred the *common man* to represent them in the White House. As expectations of a professional government grew, the image of master politician was created. During the 1970s, in the aftermath of the Watergate scandal, the image of the professional insider had become discredited and stood for corruption and deceit. Finally, the notion of the outsider emerged, which suggested that a candidate should not have been tainted by too close familiarity with the machine of professional politics (Waterman *et al.*, 1999; Busby, 2009).

Likewise, themes in election campaigns alter cyclically (Barber, 1980). At times the discourse focuses on conflicts; on other occasions conciliation takes centre stage or conscience is asked for. In line with the respective themes on the agenda a different kind of personality is required in the candidate (Barber, 1980). This led political psychologists to assume that the electorate's appreciation of a candidate's qualities evolves in accordance with the situational context (Winter, 2004). What politicians seem to have in common both in the UK and beyond is a tendency to create a narrative to frame themselves respectively as being modest and of limited material means, who through hard work and against the odds ploughed their way up the political hierarchy (Busby, 2009).

Reputational objectives: charisma and the public persona

Since the early 20th century both sociologists and psychologists have been exploring the origins of reputation. Their research focused on exceptional political leaders and the particular clout they exerted over their followers, which they referred to as 'charisma'. In this section I shall briefly present the main currents in this debate about charisma, which is directly linked to questions of leadership personality and in turn informs images of an ideal politician. The German sociologist Max Weber considers charisma to be 'a certain quality of an individual's personality by virtue of which he is considered extraordinary and treated as endowed with super natural, super human, or exceptional powers or qualities' (Weber, 1978, p.241).

The attention that the charismatic element in a politician's personality seems to attract is perhaps best accounted for by a notion of celebrity culture, which in the view of Franck (1998) is part of a logic that dictates modern news selection and media coverage. Alternatively, it has been speculated that public sympathy for charismatic politicians may be enhanced by situations of national crisis. In particular, problems that are complex and difficult to decipher for the individual give rise to calls for leaders gifted with charismatic personalities who are widely trusted to overcome challenges (Weber, 1978; Abels, 2004). Spinrad (1991) concurs and reminds us that charisma can best be defined as the public's perception of the person who is deemed best equipped to do what needs to be done – politically, morally or militarily. In his view, charisma is accompanied by particular social conditions that generate a demand and support for emergent leadership. Elaborating on this analysis, but taking a psychological perspective, is Aberbach (1996), who tries to explain the unique quality of charisma by describing it as the union between the audience's emotional instability and the leader's particularly developed talents and assets. Ultimately, it has been suggested that the neoliberal notions which dominate society are presenting strong, charismatic leadership as a role model to which both political and business leaders aspire (Imhof, 2010).

Specific sanctity, heroism or the exemplary character of an individual person are in the view of Weber the pillars upon which charisma rests (Weber, 1968). This emotional bond has been referred to as the 'core of charisma' (Froman, 1963). According to Weber the leader's outstanding talents and the audience's extraordinary devotion constitute the unique features of a charismatic individual (Weber, 1968). This view is shared by Schweitzer (1984), who contends that the charismatic concept is founded in the almost worship-like veneration that the public harbours for a leader. However, the German sociologist Weber, who for decades has been the point of reference for any writer on charisma, failed to define charismatic qualities. It therefore remains hard to anticipate whether and when the public detects charismatic features in a leader (Ake, 1966).

Adding to Weber's writing and reflecting on the concept in a managerial context, Bromley (1993) claims that charisma and individuality are powerful factors in the formation of reputation. Charisma, in Bromley's view, depends on a degree of remoteness from the audience. Familiarity, according to Bromley, breeds contempt in the sense that intimate knowledge of another person puts the charismatic aspect of the person into a wider context and diminishes its effect.

An individual who strives to possess charismatic command, in Leary's view, needs to appear highly competent and never at risk of losing the moral high ground. To be genuinely liked by their followers, Leary maintains, it would help if charismatic leaders were to sound as if they were on a moral crusade (Leary, 1995). In Weber's text we encounter this missionary zeal in reflections about a religious or quasi-religious calling, which Weber believes to be one of the two bases on which an individual's charisma rests (Weber, 1978). Not surprisingly, therefore, charismatic leaders have at times been described as superhuman and as saviours, associated with a godlike being (Willner, 1984). In a charismatic leader's audience Bendix (1998) even observed awe, reverence, blind faith and emotions usually associated with religious worship. Since politicians are not normally divine, it would then be open to debate if politicians can actually be endowed with charisma (Friedrich, 1961).

Natural forces and talent are the second basis in which charisma is rooted in Weber's (1978) view. Here charisma is personified by a magician type of individuals who put a spell on their public through extraordinary sentiments. Thus, charisma becomes emotionally charged and adopts a significant role in the political arena (Schweitzer, 1984). In this context Weber talks about a political leader in terms of an ethical prophet, who breaks the power of the demons and cures the victims of hate, anxiety and need (Schweitzer, 1984). Such leaders would be confident of executing a divine mission and their conviction helps them to perform exceptional deeds (Schweitzer, 1984).

We shall now turn to the relationship between charismatic leaders and followers. It has been said before that the particular devotion of followers helps propel the politician into the status of charismatic leadership. Political protagonists at times appear to be generating prophet-like support. No less do leaders in war, in the church or parliament. This suggests that the leader is the tool to carry out a higher calling. Thus, it is not formal position or bureaucratic power that enthuses people, but a strong belief in him (or her) as the saviour and the hero who has come to rescue them, or at least to better their lives considerably (Gerth and Mills, 1958).

Leary (1995) adds that, regardless of competing definitions, charisma certainly is closely related to the leader's image in the followers' perception. It has therefore been suggested that charismatic leadership involves the use of means of communication and the skilful management of impression to help followers see, recognize and pursue their leader's vision (Conger and Kanungo, 1987). However, the concept of charismatic leadership appears to confront reputation management with serious challenges, which are caused by the media's tendency to be instrumental in both the creation of celebrities and their subsequent destruction once the comprehensive belief in their mythical abilities is being questioned (Weber, 1978; Eisenegger, 2010). Insofar as charisma requires deference and devotion, it is not easily compatible with the irreverence of which the British media like to make a point.

External circumstances: events and charismatic leadership

In this discussion on charisma a thought should be directed at the function of *events* and *crisis* in generating charisma. Ratnam (1964) stresses that extraordinary situations call on an individual to show unusual talents. In support of this thesis, Weber (1978) draws on the example of the warlord who turns into a perpetual charismatic leader in a permanent military conflict.

Looking back at the past two centuries of history, we come across a range of significant historical crises, most of which are connected to the name of a charismatic leader. Ann Ruth Willner (1984) defines the charismatic leader in these historical phases as someone who is stretching reality beyond the limits of what hitherto had been thought politically possible.

Maximilien de Robespierre, for instance, was said to be 'remembered at best as an ornament of the Arras bar until the French Revolution propelled him to notoriety' (Roberts, 1978, p.93), and Simon Schama (1989) confirms that prior to the revolution Robespierre's contemporaries thought of him as a marginal civil servant of the *ancien régime*. Not very different was the case of George Washington, who lived the quiet life of a farmer in Virginia before the War of Independence placed him at the helm of the fledgling continental army. Prior to this he had not shown any outstanding talents or professed a burning wish to accomplish something grand in his life. The transformation from provincial farmer to national hero is beyond rational explanation other than that the event constituted a career-changing opportunity (Freeman, 1957).

Quite a number of individuals who in later life were cut out for charismatic greatness had in their earlier years been anything but awe-inspiring figures. Giuseppe Garibaldi was said to have been short, bow-legged and humourless before events conspired to spill him to the helm of Italy's unification army (Hibbert, 1965). Likewise, Abraham Lincoln, who was known for his thin neck, high-pitched voice and ill-fitting clothes, was not a politician likely to have left a lasting, let alone positive, mark on his contemporaries (Brogan, 1935). A range of other examples could be added, not least Mahatma

Gandhi, who, in the words of his biographer Louis Fischer, was mediocre, unimpressive, handicapped and floundering (Fischer, 1982). Probably the most unexpected and dramatic rise from nonentity to charismatic power was that of Adolf Hitler. His youth and young adulthood did not reveal to his friends and neighbours that this man would one day bring continental Europe to its knees. All that was known about him at the time seemed to point to a future of insignificance and mediocrity (Kershaw, 1991).

Only months before his entry onto the Russian revolutionary stage, Vladimir Lenin could have been taken for the local grocer, or so his biographer Ronald W. Clark (1988) wrote. He must have been below average height and 'literally in no way distinguishable from ordinary citizens' (Clark, 1988, p.110). It is widely known that Winston Churchill in the 1930s was considered unelectable, a liability to the Conservative Party, and not only his political adversaries were inclined to diagnose his passionate rhetorical diatribes as early signs of some psychological degradation.

The above examples lead to the conclusion that the crisis – or, in more prosaic terms, the 'event' – is the launching pad for charismatic political figures. It was the crises in Germany and Italy that allowed Otto von Bismarck and Garibaldi, respectively, to emerge. Russia's breakdown in the First World War afforded Lenin with an opportunity he eagerly seized and the Nazi threat in 1940 made British politicians believe that extraordinary times needed an extraordinary politician to face up to them. Upon that admission Churchill became prime minister and by all standards a charismatic leader.

There seems to be evidence that charismatic dimensions become visible under certain circumstances. Or, put in different terms, there need to be events happening that afford individuals with a challenge grand enough to display their talents. If the right opportunities do not arise, a potentially talented and forceful leader may be seen as a less-than-effective politician whose actions were of limited or no consequence.

Yet a charismatic public persona does not appear to hinge exclusively on exogenous factors. Researchers on charisma acknowledge that a particular set of skills and behaviour pertinent to personal communications do help a politician to establish charismatic status (Bass, 1988; Bryman, 1993; Shamir *et al.*, 1993). They recognize a number of skills and behavioural patterns that are believed to contribute to the perception of charisma: rhetoric and speech making (Bryman, 1993); symbols and symbolic communication (Shamir *et al.*, 1993); energy (House and Howell, 1992); creativity (Shils, 1965); and finally, cognition and intelligence (Bass, 1988).

If we turn to political communications research we find a range of other features that may support a politician's charismatic public persona. Literature in this field identified the need for politicians to comprehend and follow operational conditions set by the media (Shoemaker and Reese, 1991): A profound comprehension of what constitutes a strong storyline (Cook, 1996), effective presentational and verbal skills (Mazzoleni and Schulz, 1999), a sense of and some sympathy for dramatization (Gitlin, 1980; Meyrowitz,

1985), skills to manage media opportunities and events (Bennett and George, 2005), and finally, the aptitude and willingness to network intensely with the media community who are the gatekeepers for traditional news channels (Bennett and George, 2005). Thus, sociologists and political psychologists under the headline of political communications have entered a fruitful discourse to explore and define the origins and dimensions of charisma. In conclusion, charisma can be understood as short shrift for a set of behavioural rules, circumstances and skills that allow politicians to mould a public persona that may help them to gain clout over the electorate. We may infer that behaviour, communications and relationship management are implicitly recognized as building blocks for charismatic leaders. The concept of charisma in turn offers a description of public perceptions, preferences and notions of the ideal politician which on aggregate are critical to the strategic management of a public persona.

However, writers on charisma apparently fall short of providing any systematic or comprehensive explanation of how charismatic qualities may be aided or attained through communications management. Neither the strategic approach nor the technicalities or the resources needed to choreograph a public persona are dealt with by writers on charisma. While they conceptualize an ideal, they neither pose nor answer the more mundane question of how politicians technically achieve and protect this intended charismatic reputation.

Clarifying the terminology: image and reputation

I have previously outlined that the assumption about the relevance of reputation serves as justification for this study. The concept of reputation and related terminology with which we are dealing – such as identity or image – is deeply rooted in research that has emerged in a range of disciplines, thereby complicating shared understanding and debate.

As a result, in the literature misunderstandings have been surfacing with regard to the appropriate meaning of terms such as corporate reputation, identity and image. Depending on their perspective and academic discipline, authors treat these concepts either as completely separate, or as overlapping and even at times as identical (Gotsi and Wilson, 2001). Writers in political science, marketing, psychology and sociology all add perspectives to the debate and enrich the discussion, while at the same time appearing to complicate the conceptualization of core issues.

Bromley (2001) points out that the meaning of terms and phrases describing identity, personality, image and reputation tends to be equivocal when disciplinary boundaries are crossed. Shenkar and Yuchtman-Yaar (1997) remind us that the relative standing of an organization or an individual is described in various disciplines in different terms: while sociologists are more familiar with prestige, and economists possibly prefer to talk of reputation, for marketing scholars it is image, and for their colleagues in accountancy and law the appropriate term might be goodwill (see Table 2.1).

Likewise, the questions raised vary according to discipline. Writers in organizational behaviour, public relations, communications, sociology, advertising, organizational strategy and marketing may each apply a different focus. Moreover, each discipline looks at specific aspects of the phenomenon: researchers in communications studies, for instance, investigate the meaning hidden in messages and examine how information is encoded by an organization and decoded by recipients; marketing scholars, meanwhile, tend to strive for an understanding of how consumers react to information about products, services and organizations (Brown *et al.*, 2006).

Over time, each discipline has also built up its own distinct terminology to deal with issues related to the management of organizational communications. It has been rightly noted, therefore, that any interdisciplinary discussion on the subject is likely to be confusing, if not outright incomprehensible (Gioia *et al.*, 2000; Whetten and Mackey, 2002; Pratt, 2003).

Against this backdrop, I use my own professional experience with reputation in politics as guidance, which is best described by Shenkar and Yuchtman-Yaar (1997), who define reputation as an 'uncertainty resolving mechanism'.[15] They suggest that a lack of information about products and services leads people to look for other cues, such as reputation. Their view is shared by Dowling (2008), who in his survey of Australian corporations reminds us of reputation's function to reassure internal and external stakeholders. With regard to its applicability in politics, it is worth noting the decisive impact of reputation on customers in the service industry, where it is understood to be difficult to make judgements on quality as the purchase decision often predates the service (Fombrun and Rindova, 1996; Roper and Fill, 2012). The assessment of quality, therefore, is exceedingly difficult in a service context as there is no tangible product that lends itself to verification before usage. Thus, reputations are often used both to attract and to retain customers (Omar, 2005). It would appear that this perspective links communications management in the service sector to the specific challenges one encounters in politics. Both settings deal with content, quality and promised performance, which customers usually find similarly difficult to measure in advance.

Table 2.1 Usage of terms in various disciplines

Discipline	*Terms used*	*Focal unit*
Sociology	Prestige	Occupation, industry, organization
Marketing	Image	Organization
Law and accounting	Goodwill	Organization, individual
Economics	Goodwill and reputation	Organization, individual
Business	Reputation (image)	Organization

Source: (Shenkar and Yuchtman-Yaar, 1997)

I am siding with authors who argue that image is dealing with current perceptions, while holding the view that reputation encapsulates the aggregation of past and current perceptions and relates them to future expectations (van Riel and Fombrun, 2007). I argue that reputation as used in current business literature appears to be the concept that needs to be incorporated into political practice and terminology, as it helps to shed light on the relationship between politicians and their respective publics, and is instrumental in generating trust and support.

Throughout this book I choose to apply the concept of reputation rather than branding. While the latter is rooted in marketing literature, reputation is widely recognized as defining and guiding the practice of public relations, which – as I argued throughout this chapter – appears to be the suitable prism for an exploration of communications management activities in politics. More specifically, while branding is said to be aimed at generating positive buying decisions among customers, reputation reflects the likelihood of garnering goodwill and receiving support among stakeholders (Fombrun and van Riehl, 2004; Watson and Kitchen, 2008). Evidently, the latter appears to coincide with a politician's concerns about personal public perception.

Notes

1 What in a commercial context would be the product or service, in politics is probably an amalgamation of past performance, party policy, leader image and promises (O'Shaughnessy, 2001). Lees-Marshment (2008) would also consider the party constitution, party conferences, principles, members of the legislature, staff and symbols as part of the party's product.
2 See also the definition of PR by the Chartered Institute of PR, which emphasizes that PR is about reputation, reciprocal understanding and support.
3 Although Brissenden and Moloney (2005) see in the widespread criticism of spin doctoring at the turn of the century an attempt to discredit the Labour government, rather than a genuine weariness with communications techniques.
4 For a comprehensive consideration of PR's role in society and its impact on democratic political discourse, see Pitcher's (2003) *The Death of Spin*.
5 A study by Xifra (2010) suggests that the emphasis on strategy in political PR may be less developed in other countries. Among practitioners in Spain he found the view that PR may well be tactical and seek to support the overall political strategy.
6 Sellers (2010) has portrayed the endeavours by communications managers in US politics to control messages and the news agenda in an effort to build up and safeguard party reputation. He points out that external events and the attacks launched by political opponents are at times insurmountable obstacles that thwart communications plans.
7 Tunstall (1996) details how the British press deploys far more aggressive journalistic methods by comparison to the German media.
8 Liu and Levenshus (2012) emphasize the role of relationship building only as a means to prevent crisis situations. They do not recognize it as an instrument to build up and manage reputation.
9 Brian McNair (2003) mentions that in the 1980s the Conservatives commissioned Saatchi & Saatchi to do value research and psychographics, which to this extent had never been used in the UK before.

10 Bernard Ingham adamantly denies having been an all-powerful quasi-minister of communications (Ingham, 2003, pp.100–20).
11 Erik du Plessis (2008) discusses in his book *The Advertised Mind* rising retention rates through repeated stimuli of synapses in human brains. Repeatedly stimulated synapses allow information to be firmly lodged in the brain. This phenomenon is a rationale for politicians to appear on television regularly.
12 In this context Joe Klein's novel *Primary Colors* (Random House, 1996) reflects on how political marketing in the USA operated at that time.
13 See also Vidal (1984), who gives evidence about the relationship between personal traits and his recognition as a great leader in the case of Roosevelt. Haley (1969) portrays the particularly informing example of Jesus Christ, whose reputation as a unique religious leader directly derived from his personality.
14 Ipsos MORI has used these criteria in their analysis of perceptions of British politicians since the 1980s, even though on occasions some variables were added and others dropped.
15 Shenkar and Yuchtman-Yaar (1997) use the term 'standing', which in their view is interchangeable with reputation, image, goodwill and prestige – all of which are terms that according to Shenkar and Yuchtman-Yaar are used by different academic disciplines to describe a comparable concept. They go on to propose 'standing' as a substitute cross-disciplinary term. However, in the course of this study I subscribe to Westcott Alessandri (2001), who differentiates between image and reputation. This distinction seems to me a useful descriptor of current and time-bound perceptions.

3 The strategic communications management process

Analysing the process of reputation building: models of strategic communications management

It was Edward Robinson who in 1969 declared the death of the *gut feeling* approach to public relations. In his view, communications managers would from then on operate as if they were applied social and behavioural scientists whose decisions and actions were largely based on research. Broom (2009) warns us that even today PR practitioners at times allow themselves to be led by hunches, intuition and individualistic approaches rather than strategic thinking and the data provided by research activity. A growing professionalism and increased competition in political PR generates a need to justify the allocation and expense of resources and to account for processes and outcomes.[1] Forbes (1992, p.32) agrees and comes up with this concise definition of strategic management as 'a process that enables any organisation – company, association, non-profit, or government agency – to identify its long-term opportunities and threats, mobilize its assets to address them, and carry out a successful implementation strategy'.

Insights provided by research feed into planned communications programmes that are designed and carried out as step-by-step processes. In other words the analysis of inputs, the planning of alternatives, the taking of decisions and their implementation are all elements that in their aggregate constitute a sequential management procedure that comprises the entire scale of communications activities. Writers in both communications management disciplines, PR and marketing, have devised a number of paths that detail the course of steps that need to be taken. This begins with the identification and analysis of a problem, leading to the implementation of action and ultimately terminating with an evaluation of the process and its outcomes. While they vary in the sequence and number of steps, the different models share the underlying intention to reflect and schematize what is otherwise a complex plethora of activities and phenomena (Smith, 2012; Tench, 2009).

In the following paragraphs I endeavour to review a limited number of models and critique their contribution to our understanding of communications management practice, as well as their suitability to reflect key phases and variables in political reputation management processes. It makes sense to start with Moss (2011), who from a PR perspective reviewed existing managing frameworks and integrated their core features into findings that were aligned with his observations of communications practice. This led him to generate a management model that assists in organizing and analysing public relations and marketing-related work. He identified a sequence of four principles, (analysis, choice, implementation and evaluation), which he presented as the Communications – hence C – model C-MACIE (Moss, 2011).

Lees-Marshment (2009) reminds us that most communications planning models intended for use in a corporate context fail to recognize that linear decision making is problematic or even unattainable in a party political setting, where the power is located with the lower echelons of activists and any decision maker will have to win over their approval and support. For a critique of communications planning models and their applicability in politics this variable will have to be borne in mind.

In 2006 the British government adopted its own communications management framework, known as ENGAGE. This was seen as a response to the Phillis Review (2004), which had pointed out the weaknesses of government communications practice. The thrust of this criticism pointed out a lack of consistency and failure to support departmental objectives. The framework that government departments were asked to adopt in 2006 intended to strengthen the communications unit's responsibility for conducting stakeholder research and connecting strategic decision and policy making with insights about expectations entertained among key publics. The intention was to organize communications as an activity that is more strategic than tactical and integrated into the policy and administrative process rather than being an add-on and afterthought (GCN, 2010).

The government's ENGAGE model has a comparatively simple structure and consists of four steps. Stage one, called SCOPE, requires the communicators to clarify what they intend to achieve and to specify the research that needs to be done. Stage two is termed DEVELOP, and deals with the question of how the objectives could best be met. This is followed by step three, IMPLEMENT, which refers to the types of arrangements for communications activities available to convey messages. The sequence of steps is completed by an EVALUATION phase to assess how the campaign worked and if it achieved its objectives (GCN, 2010). The ENGAGE model broadly reflects approaches taken towards communications planning by a range of authors in public relations (McElreath, 1997; Austin and Pinkleton, 2006; Smith, 2012). The popularity of this model among political communications planning practitioners appears to be testified to through the interest taken by a number of governments outside the UK, which either intend to introduce or already use it (Gregory, 2011).

A much more detailed analytical device has been developed by Smith (2012, p.10) who in his model splits up the management process in four fundamental phases, which are subdivided into nine individual steps.

- Phase one: formative research
  - Analysing the situation
  - Analysing the organization
  - Analysing the publics
- Phase two: strategy
  - Establishing goals and objectives
  - Formulating action and response strategies
  - Using effective communication
- Phase three: tactics
  - Choosing communication tactics
  - Implementing the strategic plan
- Phase four: evaluative research
  - Evaluating the strategic plan

The disadvantages of a particularly detailed guide are manifold. It may need alterations to adapt it to the requirements in specific environments and situations. Detailed sequences of procedures may be of limited use in a volatile environment that forces all participants to operate under considerable time pressure and in response to external factors that drive actions beyond the control of planned management processes. Broom (2009) warns that a highly detailed communications management process model may not do justice to a dynamic setting, which does not allow a clear compartmentalization of diagnosis, planning, implementation and evaluation stages. Smith (2012) shows awareness of these limitations by reminding his readers that circumstances may require communicators to skip individual steps, evaluate, adapt and simplify planning processes as necessary. One would therefore have to think about a more malleable variation of this chain of actions that allows for opt-outs at specific or all key points in the process. Alternatively, in order to deal more effectively with unpredictable circumstances, one might be well advised to identify a more flexible and broader planning approach that lends itself easily to being deployed in volatile political communications environments. However, Smith's model may arguably prove useful in an attempt to analyse and identify distinct key elements in strategic planning phases. The level of detail is therefore being used in the empirical part of this book as an analytical tool to detect behaviour among communications managers that suggests their engagement in strategic action and planned activity.

A similar level of detail to that in Smith (2012), yet with more consideration of the specific setting of electoral politics, is found in Newman's (1994b) model of political marketing, which is informed by his research on presidential campaigns in the USA. In contrast to Smith (2012), Newman has designed a checklist of steps that echoes the necessities and pressures to which candidates and their staff are exposed in campaigns. To put it differently, Newman is integrating into his communications planning model some of the variables that are specific to a political environment and arguably would have to be taken into account by any customized integrated framework of reputation management. Newman's (1994b, p.42) model is as follows:

Candidate focus
- a) Party concept
- b) Product concept
- c) Selling concept
- d) Marketing concept

The marketing campaign
- Market (voter) segmentation – to:
  - a) assess voter needs
  - b) profile voters
  - c) identify voter segments
- Candidate positioning:
  - a) assess candidate strengths and weaknesses
  - b) assess competition
  - c) target segments
  - d) establish image
- Strategy formulation and implementation
  - a) The 4Ps (product, push marketing, pull marketing, polling)
  - b) Organisation development and control

Environmental forces
- a) Technology (PC, TV, direct mail)
- b) Structural shifts (primary convention and rules; financial regulations, debates)
- c) Power broker shifts in influence (candidate, consultant, pollster, media, political party political action committees, interest groups, voters)

The political campaign
- a) pre primary stage
- b) primary stage
- c) convention stage
- d) general election stage

Newman's (1994b, p.42) model is based on the American experience and features factors we would have to ignore or reconsider in a British context. Some of the formal elements in the political campaign, such as a primary stage and the convention stage, are absent in the British general election calendar. Other building parts of Newman's framework constitute an improvement on Smith's (2012) plan. Clearly, his exploration of the information that feeds into voter segmentation (voter needs, voter profile, voter segments), may help to specify the features I am looking for when interviewing political campaigners about their formative research objectives. It is helpful to recognize, as Newman (1994b) does, the party organization as a force candidates have to reckon with, although it may be fair to argue that in the UK the candidate's political party might not be counted among external 'environmental forces', but instead be more closely associated with the 'candidate positioning'. After all, in the UK the political party conditions candidates' ideological fabric and limits their range of political options.

Newman's view prescribes specific approaches, stages and factors that on aggregate help explain and ideally even predict a candidate's campaign moves. Kotzaivazoglou (quoted in Lees-Marshment, 2009) reminds us that particularly local politicians or any candidate or incumbent with limited resources will find it hard or impossible to follow up the professional and costly research procedure that both standard management models and Newman's (1994b) campaign framework take for granted. Based on his research into Greek politics, Kotzaivazoglou designed a sequence of steps that extends the market-oriented party model to MPs as well as regional and local politicians. He acknowledges that at this level candidates might have to rely on secondary data due to a lack of the resources needed to commission primary research. Yet, Kotzaivazoglou's (quoted in Lees-Marshment, 2009) insistence that candidates address and confine their appeal to niche sections of the market is less than persuasive and perhaps owing to arrangements of the Greek electoral system. A more valuable feature in this framework is entitled 'product adjustment'. Under this heading the section 'reaction analysis' specifies that the candidates' product design might want to be reflective of the ideological fabric of the party they respectively represent. This echoes the notion that the candidates' message content and style are limited by what is acceptable to party officials. Kotzaivazoglou in his framework goes on to recommend a SWOT analysis of the candidate, which is intended to gain a better understanding of his or her strengths, weaknesses, opportunities and threats in comparison to competing contenders. This information will be instrumental in differentiating the political product – that is, the candidate – from rivals.

Both Newman (1994b) and Kotzaivazoglou (as quoted in Lees-Marshment, 2009) analyse election campaigns. Their focus is on the candidate rather than the party, and they discuss objectives of product design with voters' behaviour and the elections in mind. In other words, while the strategic management process used by both authors is informative and feeds valuable insights into considerations of policy and image design in politics, the notion of reputation building in these models appears to be of secondary relevance at best. Furthermore, these approaches that focus on the run-up to election day appear to generate models that rigidly follow through a prescribed sequence of steps that are consistently oriented towards a specific deadline. What may be required to respond to the need for a continuous, day-to-day routine of researching, planning for and adjusting a politician's reputation is a long-term perspective that leads to a more flexible and adaptable framework that exclusively addresses genuinely reputational objectives as opposed to concerns of electoral effectiveness.

These concerns had been taken account of in a much earlier framework suggested by Grunig and Hunt (1984), who advocated a more flexible and theoretically grounded communications model that is sufficiently broad to be used in various contexts. While this would potentially allow for its use in politics, we may find that it is in need of modification to suit specific political communications settings. The design of this model is reflective of a systems theoretical approach. I shall try to give a brief summary of this integrated framework that critically emphasizes the volatility of communications processes, the decisive role of external impacts and the recognition that communications activity may not only be orchestrated around campaigns of limited duration but instead be an open-ended, ongoing management process that needs a long-term perspective and flexibility to adapt to a variety of expectations. The purpose of this framework appears to be to align efficiently both the planning and the actions taken to achieve communications objectives. It lends itself to analysing and guiding communications actions both of organizations and individuals.

The two key terms that need clarifying in Grunig's theory are behaviour and molecule (Grunig and Hunt, 1984). Behaviour is defined here as an individual's or an organization's engagement in a communications activity such as, for instance, the design of a brochure, the organization of a press conference, the writing of a press release or the commissioning of a survey. A molecule is defined as the smallest structural unit that comprises the same features as the larger unit of which it forms a part. For their concept of units and behaviour Grunig and Hunt draw on the framework of Kuhn's systems theory of management (Kuhn, 1975). The behavioural molecule is a model that leads us through the steps of planning and selecting behaviour and in so doing addresses the critical elements of the decision-making process. This approach accommodates a considerable degree of flexibility. It furthermore allows for critical evaluation throughout the process and, if needed, suggests a return to previous planning stages or a restart of the sequence. This model also takes into account two fundamental approaches to public relations, namely efforts to adapt to or control a unit's environment. The sequence of steps suggested in this management model progresses in endless loops and thus reflects the actual sequence of tasks in which managers, candidates or PR deciders engage on a day-to-day basis (Grunig and Hunt, 1984). This latter thought is echoed by Broom (2009), who emphasizes the continuous and overlapping nature of the PR problem-solving process, which he describes as cyclical in nature. Grunig and Hunt's (1984) model is as follows:

- Detect: the manager or candidate identifies a problem, which in the context of this study could be the appreciation that public expectations and candidate reputation are not in line.
- Construct: at this stage within the molecule, managers or candidates through cognitive processes conceive, plan and construct an idea in response to the problem. They devise a solution by defining the problem and choosing an objective (and alternatives) that promises to solve the issue.

- Define: here a strategy is considered and defined. Costs, effects, timescales and other resources are considered. For example, one could decide to explain why particular features or behaviour of a candidate are in the publics' respective interests and therefore correspond with what the situation requires. Alternatively, one could decide to help the candidate alter attributes and align them with public expectations.
- Select: the candidate or manager selects either the original plan or an alternative and is guided by reference criteria that are usually based on past experience, research, or linked to values. If an alternative cannot be selected, they need to return to the construct stage.
- Confirm: although this step is not usually found in management decision-making processes, it seems useful as it allows the manager or candidate a moment to step back and think of consequences, risks and worst possible scenarios of the chosen path. If no overriding concerns are found, the candidate implements by moving on to the 'behave' step. Otherwise, one must return to the segments construct or select.
- Behave: elsewhere this is referred to as tactics and is the actual communications tool used by the candidate or manager, such as a press release, a meeting, a news story, a TV appearance, direct mail campaign or possibly the actual change of the candidate's behaviour to alter public perceptions.
- Detect: the endless loop continues where we started. The candidate and manager analyse the feedback and detect if their objectives have been met or if they need to change the behaviour and return to the construct segment.

This model conceptualizes strategic communications as an open-ended process. It helps to define and describe how individuals take decisions and – more pertinent to this study – is instrumental in analysing managerial practice. These steps will be critical in an exploration of the degree to which reputation management in politics is a planned strategic process.

Reflecting on management models, Smith (2012) makes two valuable observations: he predicts that communications managers may at times be inclined to skip stages of formal planning phases once they are satisfied they have appropriately recognized the problem. Furthermore, he experienced that PR staff may occasionally believe they were not consciously guided by a management plan. Yet he also observed that, when probing further, the ensuing conversation may reveal that these same communicators in fact do go through step-by-step routines that are comparable to variants of planned strategic management processes. While calls for flexibility may collide with Smith's (2012) nine-step communications management model, which arguably appears to be too rigid for a practitioner to follow closely, his detailed exploration may help the researcher identify activities and understand practice that is fully or partially reminiscent of strategic communications processes. Therefore, the steps offered by Smith help to gain awareness of key phenomena in strategically planned communications practice and analyse data.

We may conclude that for it to be used in a political context, any management model that is to reflect strategic communications processes would have to be adapted and expanded by further variables. As mentioned above, the need to find acceptance and support internally for strategy and tactics is critical in a democratically organized structure such as a political party. Related to this is the recognition that ideological preferences and commitments set out by politicians' respective parties may pose limitations to a plan's content and style. Equally, the volatility of the media environment and its power to set an agenda that diverges from or contradicts the politician's intended messages should be considered comprehensively as it may fundamentally militate against a planned approach and instead require an evolutionary perspective. This is a general concern with planning models taken up by Gregory (2011). While she concedes that the planning process in communications management offers guidance and direction, she cautions against the design of a prescriptive formula. Flexibility and the practitioner's professional judgement should allow the model to be adapted to situations. Individual steps may be skipped as long as the framework remains and assists in providing a structured approach, clarity of purpose and a reminder of how relevant it is to be planning ahead (Gregory, 2011).

It was the purpose of these paragraphs to convey a notion of the features that a strategic communications management procedure intended to manage a politician's reputation needs to incorporate. This discussion has provided benchmarks that help to understand and interpret politicians' communications and behaviour, and judge to what degree their approach to reputation management can actually claim to be strategically planned.

Reviewing professional practice: managing political communications

Social psychologists have conceptualized issues related to the creation and communication of a public persona and identified challenges faced by communicators tasked with modelling a politician's reputation. The following paragraphs allow us briefly to touch upon a few aspects of this literature that border on the brief with which a political communicator responsible for a candidate's or incumbent's reputation will be dealing.

Whether on stage or in a broadcast, political protagonists have to reckon with the general necessity to behave in part theatrically and to rely on visual devices that are perceivable in public. In the process, politicians make use of techniques that we would normally expect to see in stagy performances. There is an assumption that the politician's quasi-theatrical self-presentation serves to display convictions and to demonstrate power (Arnold *et al.*, 1998).

The histrionic performance has to help forge, focus and send messages in a nutshell: Greg Jenkins, a former TV producer and charged with travel logistics at George W. Bush's White House, made it clear that he wanted stories to be told in one camera shot rather than stretched out in long-winded commentary (Hujer, 2003). Body language and rhetorical skills are at a premium in any television broadcast, while the print media still tend to stress a story's facts and figures somewhat more (Meyer *et al.*, 2000). Popular media that rely strongly on the power of images portray, for instance, a handshake as a emblementic gesture to demonstrate understanding and trust (Nolte, 2005).

As a consequence, media-savvy politicians appear to be in a comfortable position. Considering the coverage available in the audio-visual media, gifted actors in politics strive to emotionalize, simplify and visualize their performances (Nolte, 2005). Social psychologists speak of impression management tools such as 'ingratiation' or 'exemplification', the latter of which is based on the communication of virtue (Jones and Pittman, 1982). Moral virtues such as honesty, integrity, generosity or dedication and self-sacrifice are apparently conveyed to foster an individual's public image.

Visual, almost theatrical presentations are helped along, justified or even created by events. If events are in short supply, media advisers are known to organize them systematically. These constructed media opportunities come in the disguise of party conventions, press conferences or talk show participation. These are the phenomena for which Daniel Boorstin (1992) coined the term 'pseudo-event'. Some pseudo-events take a much more intimate storyline and reveal aspects of a politician's private life, such as fears, hopes, personal experiences or pastimes.

However, there appears to be a number of constraints that limit the range of options in impression management. The effectiveness of the tools in impression management of which we have heard so far is limited by the audience's attitudes and preconceptions. These preconceived views about a political party or political leader may be stronger than presentational efforts to counter them. Leary (1995) mentions Richard Nixon, who after he was found guilty of having masterminded the Watergate scandal, was widely seen as an unredeemable crook. Any efforts he might subsequently have undertaken to present himself as honest and law-abiding would have been mocked outright. Jones and Pittman (1982) have shown that publicly known or accessible facts about our present and past lives considerably limit our capacity to manage impressions.

Research on impression management confirmed how events have the potential to wreak havoc. Policy failures and adverse news or third-party interference potentially throw a negative light on a candidate or incumbent. Predicaments may make a protagonist look silly, foolish, clumsy, stupid (Edelmann, 1987; Miller, 1992) and may eventually ruin the impression that was originally intended (Schlenker *et al.*, 1990).

Social psychology explores relationships between people or groups and seeks to interpret reactions. However, social psychologists writing about impression management fail to explore the strategic aspect and ignore institutional resources needed to research, project and implement communications techniques. Also, exchanges with the media and the specific institutional setting of political communications are not widely covered by social psychologists.

To be able to understand the specific circumstance in which instruments of impression management are being applied, we now turn to an analysis of the media environment in which political communicators operate.

Note

1 For a description of growing professionalism in political communications in British politics see Negrine's (2008) *The Transformation of Political Communication*, and Negrine's (2007) 'Professionalisation of Political Communication in Europe'.

4 Reviewing political communications management practice

Media and political communications management practice

In the following pages I intend to discuss to what degree the understanding of the media and its mechanisms is critical for the success of communicators who are tasked with managing a politician's reputation by seeking to generate messages and setting the agenda. This set of skills entails the communicator's ability to sense what journalists look for, how they expect to be treated, how they process stories and how they present them in their respective media (Burton, 2007). Tiffen in his 1989 landmark study reminded us how politicians adapt to and use patterns of communications to which journalists react positively. In this context McCombs (2008) detailed how political leaders endeavour to influence the news coverage and how this requires them to understand the relationships of mutual dependency between politics and the media and to engage in agenda-setting mechanisms, which I will be discussing in the following paragraphs.

If the role of political journalism as crucial facilitator of opinion building in the public sphere, authoritative point of reference for the public and leading interpreter of political processes constitutes a core part of democratic society, it may be worth taking a closer look at the underlying rationale that shapes media coverage. A journalist's job description requires them to select and summarize the information that is accessible to them in order to adapt it for their respective audiences (Gans, 1979; Conboy, 2011). Yet, ever since Edmund Burke in the early 19th century described the beginnings of the free press in the UK, it has been questioned if journalists actually confine themselves to reporting events and passing on facts for the sake of educating citizens. Walter Lippmann was under no illusions when he wrote in 1922 that a newspaper is the result of selection processes that determine which story is printed, to what extent and on which page (Lippmann, 1997). While in the decades following Lippmann's writing the debate about media effects remained inconclusive, there was agreement that, through their power to select and interpret information, journalists gain a pivotal function in political communications (McNair, 2003).

As most events and issues in society are outside the grasp of citizens, the news media's pivotal role is not limited to allocating relevance to some issues over others, but it also entails interpreting themes one way or another. Gerstle *et al.* (1991) hold the view that journalists interpret meaning and explore what is relevant in politics. It is this initial interpretative framework that emerges when over time different media interact with their audiences. This framework becomes the reference point and in the long run the agenda for subsequent reporting (McNair, 2003). The power of the media to select issues, define attributes and thus influence public opinion has allowed journalists to exercise a crucial political function (Weaver, 1996; McCombs, 2008).[1]

From a communications manager's perspective the differentiation between setting the agenda and framing issues is critical. By framing we mean attempts to interpret issues, to emphasize as well as de-emphasize particular traits or qualities in an organization or individual, and to highlight selected aspects of a story (Balmas and Sheafer, 2010; Gitlin, 1980). Curtin (1999) and Turk (1986) contend that the practice of PR is intrinsically linked to agenda setting, as the tools deployed by communications managers largely generate information, which in turn is offered to journalists in the expectation that they feed this into the news agenda. This relationship between the media and communications managers is described in competitive terms. While the journalist seeks independent information, the communicators are trying to force their information and interpretation onto the journalist (Ohl *et al.*, 1995; Gans, 1979).

Tedesco (2011) takes this argument further and adds that PR managers not only push themes onto the agenda but also at the same time influence the emphasis of reporting events or individuals. This emphasis may be intended to direct the public's attention to a candidate's qualities such as honesty, competence or compassion (Hallahan, 2011). Framing theory conceptualizes political communicators as sources – or framing strategists – who send information that echoes their preferred interpretation (Hallahan, 1999). The media in turn are referred to in framing literature as intermediaries. Communicators strive to use these media channels to extend their preferred frame (Entman, 2004), although alternatively the media may decide to reject the frame suggested by the public relations manager and re-frame the story or the individual (Kypers, 1997). The notion of framing adds a cultural dimension to the relationship between communicator and journalist that has been likened to a barter trade with an almost businesslike perspective: while politicians try to interpret – or frame – their decisions or their personalities in a favourable way, journalists are seen to accept or decline this frame and instead offer their own, which they expect is more in line with how their audiences interpret phenomena (Ryan, 1991; Scheufele, 1999).

Sufficient financial resources and expertise are, in the view of Wolfsfeld (2003), critical in a politician's endeavour to shape the agenda and control the frame. Once communicators have defined the frame, they engage in impression management activities that shape the public's understanding and images of the politician (Hallahan, 2010). These tactical options range from media stunts and press releases to selecting the right colour of a tie and the organization of pseudo-events. While analysis of communications techniques is not the focus of this study, their power to focus public attention and mould public perceptions of candidates and incumbents needs to be borne in mind (Brewer and Sigelman, 2002). At the same time, Wolfsfeld emphasizes the centrality of real events that are outside the communicator's control. Adverse events that cannot be prevented may be interpreted by communicators to support an existing news frame. In other words, what is being perceived by the publics, but not controlled and guided by the political communicator, may still be interpreted in conflicting ways by a range of political contenders who each seek to use the appropriate frame in an attempt to legitimize and generate support for their respective policies or personality (Wolfsfeld, 2003)

It has been argued that the technicalities of agenda setting are not particularly complex. Zoch and Molleda (2006) detail a step-by-step procedure: They point out that the quality of the relationship between communications manager and journalist is pivotal to the success of agenda setting. In their view it is the mutual recognition of trust, openness and credibility that ensures and determines the effectiveness of the relationship between communications professional and journalist. From the managerial perspective with which we are concerned in this study it is worth stressing this latter point, which is taken up by Howard (2004). In his view, agenda setting hinges more than anything else on the interpersonal relationship between journalists and their sources. This is an observation made and acknowledged by a number of writers in past decades (Delli Carpini, 1994; Wanta, 1991).

The power of well-resourced communicators to set the news agenda is limited by what in communications studies is referred to as 'news value'. Part of media logic dictates that journalists echo what their audiences like to see printed and broadcast (McCombs, 2008). In turn, communicators would have to shape their selection and content of messages to meet these values and interests. If they fail to take this environment into account, they lose the edge their resources would otherwise have given them in their relationship with the media (Schudson, 1991; Palmer, 2000). The relevance of financial and staff resources for the effectiveness of the agenda-setting process will be looked into later on in this chapter.

At this point a final consideration needs to be raised, which helps to understand and to some degree predict a communicator's ability to access the media and potentially affect the agenda: status, reliability and expertise are the characteristics that, in the view of Simons and Jones (2011), add weight to a source in communications processes. Davis (2003) refers to this as media capital or 'legitimate authority' to speak out in public and be listened to. This privilege is usually linked to a formal position in business or politics to represent a constituency or represent issues and thus be taken seriously. Smith (2012) expands this list and emphasizes the need for sources to be credited with charisma, credibility and control. He identified authority as a further fundamental prerequisite for the successful use of persuasive rhetoric.

Yet Broom (2009) cautions us against jumping to conclusions and draws attention to inconclusive research results. In his view the effectiveness of source attributes can be questioned. He views their impact as being contingent on variables such as the specific situation, issue and time. Broom's agreement with his peers appears to be limited to the recognition that, depending on the scenario, sources may have a considerable but varying effect on the initial receptivity to messages.

At this point it should be noted that gaining access to the agenda particularly for senior political figures and relevant institutions arguably might not be the highest priority. Instead, they are thought to aim more explicitly at managing information, which at times requires keeping news off the agenda and hindering journalists' access to critical data (Ericson *et al.*, 1989; Jones, 1999; Pearson and Patching, 2008). However, this also implies that political outsiders, newcomers or dissidents may struggle to gain access to news media. In order to offset this presentational disadvantage, they arguably feel inclined to formulate more radically, propose extreme policies or engage in unique publicity stunts as a means to attract media attention and secure coverage (Wolfsfeld, 2003).

Agendas and frames in communications management

The way in which journalists approach their profession has highly practical consequences for politicians' ability to access media channels in order to convey messages to their publics. Therefore, we shall now briefly look at the literature about political journalism from the politician's perspective.

It was outlined in the previous section that media access hinges on the communicator's appreciation of the media process and an ability to frame messages in a way that is recognized as newsworthy and pertinent to the audience. In other words, politicians are expected to generate news that journalists accept as relevant and gripping (Cook, 1996; Gitlin, 1980; Shoemaker and Vos, 2009).

In the view of Sheafer (2008) there are two categories to differentiate what makes its way onto the news agenda. Category one consists of themes, events or personalities that in a political-cultural context are deemed important to society. A high-ranking government politician who is about to announce a crucial change of policy would therefore provide journalists with two reasons to pay attention (Wolfsfeld, 2003; Bennett and George, 2005). The second category that shapes the news agenda largely reflects the media's own journalistic instinct and economic logic: an interest in the unusual, novel and dramatic, as well as an endemic tendency to personalize and dramatize (Staab, 1990; Wolfsfeld, 1997; Mazzoleni and Schulz, 1999).

These categories constitute the context for a constant and ongoing struggle for attention and dominance. Not represented in Sheafer's (2008) model, however, is a point raised by McCombs (2008), who wondered if journalists limit themselves to reporting facts or instead pursue their respective political agendas. From a politician's perspective the key to access the news agenda is engagement with political events and conflict, which attract media attention and thereby compete with senior political figures over share of media coverage (Schlesinger, 1993; Blumler and Gurevitch, 1995).

Strategic perspectives to succeed in this contest for media attention and positive frames are presented by New Labour's former media manager Peter Mandelson (2011), who details how communications departments regularly use parliamentary lobby journalists to air tentative policy proposals or circulate names of candidates in view to test likely media feedback and potential public support. This practice intended to gauge public reactions suggests that media relations not only are part of a mutual bargaining process between media and communicators, but also require politicians and their staff to be open and responsive to external expectations posed by the environment.

The opportunities for politicians to feed journalists information and see it published or broadcast afterwards is greatly aided not only by an extended number of news channels, particularly in broadcast and online media, but also by the ever more limited financial and personnel resources available to editorial offices, as well as tight deadlines and growing work pressure (Davies, 2008; Morris and Goldsworthy, 2008). It would seem that this mixture of factors makes the ready-to-use media information provided by party and government communications departments appear a welcome shortcut for journalists (Schlesinger and Tumber, 1994; Quinn, 2012). It could be argued that politicians who have the appropriate budget and professional advice may be best equipped to understand media production and then focus their public relations most accurately at the needs of particular journalists. The role of communications officers as information subsidizers was described by Gandy (1982) in the 1980s and a decade later by Manheim (1994), which suggests that the phenomenon predates more recent financial squeeze on journalistic resources. Communications managers who bear this in mind and seek to get the right data as well as the best-prepared sound bites delivered at the right point in time and well ahead of deadlines for the news editions may have an edge over competitors who do not have comparable PR resources at their disposal (McNair, 2003).

While in theory any politician can frame public perception through influencing how the media covers an issue (Fridkin and Kenney, 2005), it has been established that in this struggle over power of interpretation the rules and customs of news making favour incumbents as opposed to challengers (Clarke and Evans, 1983). Incumbents tend to have this advantage due to greater resources to orchestrate the production and dissemination of information (Fridkin and Kenney, 2005). Also, Cook (1989) reminds us that journalists are much more inclined to phone up the incumbent as it is here that authoritative information is produced that a challenger can never claim to have. Graber (1997) adds that, to ensure journalistic success, a news desk is dependent on a good relationship with incumbents and therefore will probably give their message more prominent coverage, while the challenger may have to do with less column space and air time or none at all.

By the same token a party or government job offers individuals a valuable opportunity to demonstrate publicly their skills, talents, knowledge and competence (Leary, 1995). Thus, incumbents seek to use their party or ministerial briefs as a means to generate news which demonstrates their strengths and talents (Baumeister, 1989). Another core skill is said to be their ability to establish cordial relationships with journalists (Graber, 1997). Pearson and Patching (2008) concur that politicians' efforts are aided by journalists' quest for news, which is a prerequisite for the sales of papers or the ratings of broadcasts. Therefore connivance between media and politics arguably reflects the pressure journalists are exposed to in order to fill airwaves and pages (Campbell, 2011).

This also reminds us of how journalists pressure politicians to provide them with newsworthy material (Lloyd, 2004). The reason for these mounting demands appears to be found in the growing competition between broadcasters and publishers for stagnating and dwindling audiences for political news reporting (McNair, 2003).[2] Growing pressure and competition among journalists for political news may also be driven by an increasing speed and turnover rate in news reporting, which is illustrated by Lloyd (2004), who explains how both radio and television run news stories repeatedly until a subsequent news item takes their place. Arguably, politics has earned itself a reputation for having been particularly well placed to satisfy journalists' hunger for events and news (Blumler and Kavanagh, 1999). This craving for news can be seen as an incentive for both sides to engage in mutually beneficial collaboration, which guarantees the journalist information while the politician in return can hope for extensive and positive coverage (Boorstin, 1992).

Even in the early 1960s, this mutual dependence and pressure to produce content had accelerated the emergence of a phenomenon that Boorstin (1992) terms 'pseudo-events'. These are events that do not have intrinsic news value and are intended for communicative purposes only. Pseudo-events in politics may come in the form of a series of carefully orchestrated leaks, verbal attacks, scandals and crisis management (McNair, 2000).[3] It comes as little surprise that the media's parasitic dependence on institutions such as government and political parties to generate news is said to have been growing in recent years (Tiffen, 1989; Davies, 2008; Quinn, 2012).

It has been argued in these past paragraphs that journalists have their very own agenda and aim to dramatize, while politicians may pursue a different set of objectives. This sets the scene for a politician's working relationship with the media as does another perhaps less obvious observation made in these paragraphs, which deserves emphasis. It has been muted that incumbents and candidates are not given the same opportunities to present themselves and their policies in public. The incumbent appears to gain preferential treatment, which clearly may be of use to politicians, who need both media attention and leverage to frame the thrust of their coverage. While writers in communications studies do offer us insights into the mechanisms and motivations of media reporting, they make little mention of the technicalities of strategic media relations and the tactics of presentational policy that we would expect communications managers to pursue in the context of a politician's reputation management.

Defining resources: expertise, structures and access

While journalism has become faster and more aggressive, politicians have responded by professionalizing their public relations. This development in turn has raised concern among observers of political journalism. It is feared that journalists may allow themselves to be guided, if not manipulated, by increasingly well-resourced public relations managers (Michie, 1998; Pearson and Patching, 2008). There is a suspicion that journalists could be too gullible when dealing with political communicators who try to divert them from their critical path of investigation and reporting (Bagdikian, 1984; Davies, 2008).

The following pages intend to explore how political communicators needed to professionalize and draw on the resources necessary to operate effectively. I shall also be drawing on literature about organizational arrangements that define a communicator's role and responsibilities inside a political party or in a government office. It will be seen which organizational structures and arrangements of access to senior deciders would be needed to allow PR-related expertise to be fed into the political decision-making process and inform the policies pursued and implemented.

This discussion is grounded in the assumption that the process of systematic and strategic communications management hinges on the resources that are made available. Some connection may actually be identified between financial and personal resources, as well as organizational structure on the one hand and the ability to conduct research-based communications by objectives on the other.

An increase in resources has created the conditions for more professionalism in communications management practice, which has arguably been formative for political communications in recent decades. In the following section I seek to discuss the growth of professionalism in political PR as an indicator of the degree to which notions of communications planning and strategy are pursued.

Professionalism

Professionalism is a term that sums up a number of features that describe how communications management modernizes its techniques and adapts to a changing environment. For Papathanassopoulos *et al.* (2007) professionalism is grounded in technological, social and political structures in which communications managers have to operate. They list examples such as the use of specially designed campaign headquarters, polls, experts, faster and multi-channel news management, to name just a few. Papathanassopoulos *et al.* (2007) conceptualize professionalization as an ongoing alteration of practices that help to centralize and organize resources with the intention of improving performance. Blumler and Kavanagh (1999) particularly point at the reorganization of political parties and government departments, improvements in data gathering and voter segmentation, more efficient use of communications channels and more sophisticated media management techniques, which they term the professionalized paradigm.

Negrine (2007) describes professionalization through an analysis of change and adaptation to the developments in political communications over time. More specifically, Scammell (1998, p.255) considers technological progress as a sign of 'professionalism'. This latter definition is closer to the common usage of the word and implies a continuous improvement of practice. This contrasts with the discourse held among professions such as medicine and law, whose members meet a catalogue of criteria to recognize their status as a profession (Papathanassopoulos *et al.*, 2007). Negrine (2007) agrees that the interpretation of what constitutes professionalism for those who work in political communications is much looser and does not match the rigid categories – ranging from a code of conduct to a definable body of knowledge – that have been identified by Freidson (2001).

Scammell goes on to argue that in two respects political communications in parties and governments have tangibly become more professional. One entails a higher level of specialization. Largely as a consequence of more generous financial resources being available, communications departments seek to draw on the expertise provided by specialists of a specific communications function, such as polling or online communications (Scammell, 2007, 2008). Second, Scammell points out that political leadership relies more heavily on the views of and advice from professional strategists rather than party officials (Scammell, 2007, 2008). This latter phenomenon has been subject to research by political scientists, who mainly view it in terms of the consequences external advice may have on the power structures of political parties (Mair, 1998). From a communications management perspective, questions about the degree to which communications and marketing specialists find access to the decision-making processes in political parties are probably more relevant. Lees-Marshment (2008) and Farrell and Webb (2002) are zooming in on these issues, which may indicate if and to what extent strategic communications knowledge and skills are drawn upon in reputation management activities. A number of authors appear to suggest that the considerable presence of communications and marketing experts in the planning and implementation of election campaigns in the UK may be indicative of the strategic communications expertise available (Plasser and Plasser, 2002; Thurber and Nelson, 2000).

For a political party to adapt its communications to a changing environment and maintain a competitive advantage, it needs not only the appropriate expert staff but also suitable structures. As has already been pointed out in Chapter 2, from the late 1980s the Labour Party pioneered a campaign headquarters that is external to the political party headquarters. This allowed a nucleus of experts to manage communications with limited interference from party officials, who were kept at a distance at least physically (Gould, 1998b).

Resources

For communications objectives to be achieved, strategies to be developed and tactics to be implemented, politicians in the UK tend to rely on a support infrastructure that is sponsored by either their respective party or various parts of the departmental civil service. The dependency on a well-organized communications department, the expertise of staff and finances is beyond dispute, and has been discussed since political communications became an academically studied phenomenon. Already in 1963 Abrams reminded us that a well-organized political party organization, expert communications department and money were key factors for success in political communications. The same thrust of argument had already been used by Kelley less than a decade before (Kelley, 1956). More recently Plasser and Plasser (2002) asserted that financial resources are critical to any communicator who aimed to draw on professional expertise grounded in research data.

In 1996 Tunstall contended that, at that time, British government communications units in Downing Street and at departmental level were only able to operate in politically calm periods. As soon as issues emerged that led to controversy and perhaps a crisis situation, the government's communications department would flounder due to a lack of staff and expertise. This situation has changed since Tunstall made his observation, as principally the Blair government tangibly increased the resources available to government communications both in terms of finances and staff (Negrine, 2008). Most personnel are at the disposal of the prime minister's office. The political PR functions in ministerial departments are either all covered by a single communications professional, or addressed by various specialists within the minister's office, aided by civil servants, external consultants or agencies (Negrine, 2008).

While Tunstall's argument reminds us of the pivotal role of resources and their impact on the quality of communications services in the mid-1990s and beyond, Negrine (2008) highlights that a dearth of staff still occasionally limits the communicative options in departments today. Yet, quite apart from numbers, the skills and training background of new recruits arguably makes a difference, as both Blair and Alastair Campbell demonstrated when they predominantly drew on former journalists to fill government communications jobs. Their alleged strength appeared to lie in their understanding of the news media logic. They imbued the government's PR activities with the means and approaches usually adopted by journalists. They arranged, for instance, for

Prime Minister Blair to have 166 newspaper articles published with his by-line in the first two years of government alone (Franklin, 2003). This sensitive media relations work that directly aided cabinet members' image was taken care of by special advisers, who in UK politics are traditionally appointed on the understanding that they are completely loyal to the politician and supportive of their respective political objectives. Both responsibilities and numbers of special advisers increased in comparison with civil service press officers (Franklin, 2003; Jones, 2001).

The distribution and balance of resources between the media and communications managers are arguably critical in determining the influence and power in this competitive relationship between politicians and journalists. Aeron Davis accounts how in recent years the resources available to journalists have shrunk, while news sources have tended to increase their efforts to equip communicators with appropriate and growing resources (Davis, 2003). The rebalancing of resources in public relations' favour has in recent years been affecting journalists' editorial autonomy, as they increasingly rely on newsworthy material provided by communicators themselves. In other words, the more human and financial resources a communications department has at its disposal, the more it is likely to invest in media contacts, which in turn strengthens its own position in the agenda-setting process (Miller, 1994; Manning, 2001). However, Davis (2003) cautions against the conclusion that the link between resources on the one hand and the amount of coverage and the quality of media relations on the other is linear.

Internal organization and access

Internal organization and issues of access to the political leadership for professional advisers are critical for effectiveness and efficiency in political communications processes. Negrine (2007) describes how political parties tend to employ external experts to help specifically with campaigns, while party officials tend to stay in overall control.

In government politically neutral civil servants claim to be handling communications. At the same time politicians make ever more extensive use of external political advisers and outside experts, who are tasked to oversee the departments communications operations (Negrine, 2007).

A communications professional's political power and influence within their party or department varies and hinges on formal arrangements. Some may work as full-time political advisers and gain a pivotal role in the politician's entourage, such as Alastair Campbell for Tony Blair, or Andy Coulson for David Cameron. Others may for a variety of reasons be only temporarily employed. The latter are, for instance, experts hired specifically for support during campaigns, but otherwise kept at a distance from issues of content and policy making (Negrine, 2007).

A reason why in government departments communications special media advisers are not always fully integrated into the organizational structure is related to the British notion of an impartial civil service. This tradition is difficult to reconcile with the approach taken by partisan political advisers or experts who are tasked to engineer a politician's or a party's re-election (Phillis Review, 2004).

One may wonder about the consequences of these organizational arrangements and question if they allow for expertise to be offered, taken on board and acted upon. This question gains relevance in view of the notion that communications management expertise is only effective if given access to the decision makers at the top level (Botan, 2006; Hallahan *et al.*, 2007). Strömbäck and Kiousis (2011) therefore warn that communications managers' efficiency is tangibly reduced if they are not granted access to senior decision makers. It is argued that advisers who are not involved at the point of deliberations running up to decisions find it hard to manage relationships with publics on their client's behalf or safeguard their client's reputation. It is not significant, therefore, to hear Andrew Cooper, who was in charge of the Conservative Party's 2001 polling operations, concede that most of the external expert advice was ignored (Cooper, 2002).

Kelley (1956), a pioneer in political PR writing, quotes a practitioner who back in the 1950s detailed that the communications manager is only of value if they 'sit in on all planning sessions and do [their] part in the selecting of issues'. He insisted that 'public relations in a campaign are worthless unless the PR man has at least a voice in selecting, determining and projecting issues' (Kelley, 1956, pp.211–12). Kelley believes that PR managers can only have an impact and shape the relationship with critical publics if they are involved in policy making. This normative perspective often appears not to be echoed in organizational reality. Writers on public relations consider a communications manager who is admitted to meetings with senior management to be an exception (Moss, 2011).

While the exclusivity of access to senior management echelons at the expense of PR advice appears to be the norm in business, a different case may be made for political organizations due to their visibility, as well as the competitive and volatile environment in which they operate (Strömbäck and Kiousis, 2011; Grunig *et al.*, 2002). Castells (2009) and Thompson (2000) remind us that political settings are prone to scandals, which add to the demand for PR to be part of the highest levels of the management structure (Ulmer *et al.*, 2007; Stacks, 2004).

A range of specific internal strategic and tactical briefs as well as distinct reporting and communications tasks suggest that it is perhaps not appropriate to discuss communicators as one homogenous group: in reality, communications professionals have a range of different functions, roles and skills. It could be argued that their respective position and contribution in campaign management dictates and regulates the degree of access to the party leadership or ministerial offices. Against this backdrop, Johnson categorizes communicators and suggests three groups: strategists, who are tasked with developing strategic advice; specialists, whose views are drawn upon for data about polling or speech writing; and finally, vendors – also referred to as technicians – who are briefed to produce or upgrade print material, website content or mailing lists (Johnson, 2000). Of these groups, poll takers tend to be granted access to the most senior decision-maker boards, as they are seen not only as a resource for research information but also as a source of considerate and balanced judgement (Harris, 1963; Gould, 1998a; Mattinson, 2010). However, Harris details that the expert's level of involvement may vary and be dependent on the individual's role, which may allow them to be privy to the most critical strategic decisions. Branigan (2006) concurs with this description and suggests that Philip Gould as New Labour's pollster used focus group research findings as leverage to access the party's dominant coalition and to advocate and bring about the Labour Party's reorganization.

It is partly because of this intense involvement that it is worth asking if and to what degree communicators have a say not only in the delivery of the message, but also in the process of policy selection and content development (Negrine, 2008). Already in 1966 Windlesham pointed out that advisers tasked with effective presentation of political messages may try to mould the message itself. Alastair Campbell, Blair's head of communications at Downing Street, believed that communications objectives and policy objectives should be aligned by communicators. This view required a professional practice with which the civil servants felt deeply uncomfortable (Negrine, 2008). The civil servants in the Government Information Service were ill equipped to support Campbell's active and partisan communications agenda, which at times verged on the aggressive and manipulative. While they may have been relied upon to distribute information, they lacked the strategic and dynamic approach that Campbell had in mind (Seldon, 2005). The quality of support provided by the civil service structure to communicators varied, and was arguably inferior to what sheer numbers and budget figures might suggest.

This becomes evident from findings in the Public Administration Select Committee's Sixth Report, which identifies a lack of interest in communications and presentational issues among senior civil servants involved with drawing up policies (Public Administration Select Committee, 1998). The use of special advisers since 1964 has been a response to deal with this shortcoming, with their brief often including public relations functions, as Blick (2004) details in his study. However, it was found that the presence of individual special advisers until the late 1990s did not compensate for a lack of coordination among departmental communications units, nor was the arrangement conducive to the formulation and implementation of a coherent communications strategy. The analysis of this communicative failure was published in the Mountfield Report, which had investigated the quality of government communications (Mountfield Report, 1997). Seven years later the Phillis Review concluded that government communications still lacked coherence and were in need of modernization, centralization and professionalization. This shortcoming may be largely attributable to the civil service staff in government communications units, who were still adhering to the view that the dissemination of information on the one hand and giving advice on the content of policy decision making on the other were separate functions that should be kept apart (Phillis Review, 2004).

The ensuing centralization comprised both the communications and the policy planning arms of government. It has been argued that this led to a concentration of power in Downing Street, which arguably altered how the prime minister was presented to and perceived by the public. In this context it is perhaps not a surprise that Rose (2001) and Seymour-Ure (2003) saw the prime minister's position and image become to some degree 'presidentialized', while in subsequent years his grip on government communications activities arguably surpassed the control exercised by his predecessors (Negrine, 2008). This centralization allowed Campbell on behalf of the prime minister to control and integrate messages systematically. He carefully aligned the messages and expected press officers in all departments to include in all their communications with the media – and other publics – standardized templates along the lines that the Labour administration was a 'government for all the people' that was 'delivering on its promises' and aimed to pursue a course of 'mainstream policies' (Timmins, 1997, p.2).

In conclusion, resources, internal organization and issues of access appear to provide a framework that determines effectiveness and efficiency of communications professionals. It may be argued that the planning process and the intensity and quality of advice hinge to some degree on the role and organizational position that communicators are allocated, as well as the quantity and quality of financial and personal resources they have at their disposal.

Literature reviewed: an afterthought

While current literature on communications and reputation management may serve as a benchmark to guide and focus the gathering and analysis of empirical data, it is also instrumental in justifying the direction and purpose of research by identifying a gap in the existing knowledge. Admittedly, both personalization in politics and concepts of planned communications management have for years been the subject of broad debate. Likewise, public relations practice and its role in reputation building have been comprehensively explored. Yet, how communicators go about establishing and maintaining the reputation of individual politicians is a question that has not drawn comparable scholarly attention. While this issue is discussed both in political science and communications literature, neither of those disciplines has attempted to clarify empirically to what extent politicians owe their personal reputation to a planned and managed strategy, or alternatively to a blend of tactical media relations and reactions to unpredictable events. This is the gap in the literature that I intend to fill in the second part of this book.

So far, I have explored and identified features that distinguish a planned, strategic communications approach in political reputation management from a reactive, tactical one. I have also presented literature that illustrates the resources and circumstances that militate against or enable a strategic approach in political reputation management. For the second part of this book – Chapters 5, 6 and 7 – I shall present empirical data that link internal and external variables to the presence or absence of strategic reputation management. As outlined previously, my data are grounded in interviews I conducted with journalists and senior communications managers who served successive British governments and political parties in Westminster since 1997. In Chapter 8 of this book I shall integrate my findings in a theoretical framework, which details conditions and circumstances that allow us to predict if reputation management for a politician is more likely to be strategically planned or, in contrast, tactical and reactive.

Notes

1 Greenaway *et al.* (1992) introduce a variant agenda-setting concept, which is more of a collaborative approach between politics and the media. Miller *et al.* (1998) use this approach to analyse the HIV/AIDS campaign that the government ran in the 1980s once the media had alerted the public to the health risks.
2 Apart from CNN and Sky News with their constantly updated 24-hour news cycle, and the BBC with its all-day rolling news programme on Radio 5 and BBC News channel television.
3 With regard to events and pseudo-events, it is worth looking at Kaid *et al.* (1991), who make a valuable distinction between objective, subjective and constructed reality.

5 Communications management in action

Collecting and analysing data

The empirical data I will be presenting in Chapters 5, 6 and 7 originates from interviews I conducted with 21 communications managers and journalists. The kind of complex processes and relationships between politicians, communicators and audiences I came across in the course of this study retrospectively justify the choice of semi-structured interviews as the appropriate method for data collection. Interviews appear to be a suitable tool in studies with explanatory purposes, which seek to produce an understanding of processes and causal relationships between variables. The technique of semi-structured interviews is often used in social sciences in order to develop hypotheses or alternatively to analyse rare societal phenomena and unusual groups (Schnell *et al.*, 2005). They allow for a frank and open-ended conversation, and also give the interviewees the opportunity to vary and emphasize their answers as they see fit. This helped me to gain an insight into personal experiences and encouraged my interviewees to share the professional knowledge they have accrued over many years. These conversations revealed implicit awareness as well as personal perspectives and judgements that impact on actions and decisions.

I specifically selected interviewees whose abilities, knowledge, professional or private backgrounds fit in with particular needs of the study. For these expert interviews individuals had to be identified who could add to the existing knowledge about personal reputation management in politics. I defined an expert to be anyone who holds privileged insights into the reality of political communications management practice. For the purpose of this study the selection included experts in political communications (both external consultants and in-house staff) as well as political journalists. The term 'expert' in political communications is sufficiently broad and allowed me to select a number of individuals who may not hold formal office in a political party or the civil service that would by definition put them in charge of communications functions. In other words, it is understood that a number of participants play only informal roles in their discipline, or did so at a previous point in time. My interviewees were:

- Jason Beattie
  When the interview took place, Beattie held a position as deputy political editor for *The Daily Mirror.*
- Mark Davies
  Davies served Justice Secretary Jack Straw as special adviser for media relations. Since he left politics he has taken up a job with the charity Rethink.
- George Eustice
  Eustice was the Conservative Party's head of press under Michael Howard's and David Cameron's leaderships, until in 2008 he took over an associate directorship at the PR agency Portland Communications. When we met for our interview, Eustice was an MP.
- Shane Greer
  At the time we met, Greer was executive editor for the magazine *Total Politics.*
- Richard Hazlewood
  At the time of the interview, former journalist and BBC correspondent Hazlewood served as special adviser for media relations to the secretary of state for Wales. Previously, he had been in charge of media relations for the Conservative Party in Wales.
- David Hill
  Hill was Prime Minister Tony Blair's last director of communications, a position previously held by Alastair Campbell. When I interviewed him, he was working as communications manager for the London-based Bell Pottinger Group.
- Nicholas Jones
  Jones is an author, former journalist and Westminster correspondent for the BBC.
- Tom Kelly
  Kelly was employed as a civil servant and official spokesperson of Prime Minister Blair until the handover of office to Gordon Brown. When I met Kelly for our interview, he was working for the Financial Services Authority as head of communications.
- Martin Kettle
  I met Kettle in his role as associate editor of *The Guardian* newspaper.
- Spencer Livermore
  Livermore worked as special adviser to Prime Minister Brown both on policy and communications-related subjects. By the time he left Downing Street in 2008, Livermore served as the prime minister's leading strategic adviser. When I met him, he held a post as director of strategy with the communications consultancy Blue Rubicon in London.
- Henry Macrory
  I interviewed Macrory in his function as head of press at Conservative Party headquarters. He had previously served as media relations officer at 10 Downing Street.

- Damian McBride
  At the time of our interview, McBride was working as a teacher at a school in the London suburb of Finchley. Previously he had served as special adviser for media relations to Gordon Brown in his roles both as chancellor and prime minister.
- Andrew Neather
  Neather worked as a journalist for the *Evening Standard*. Previously, he had been a staff member on the Strategic Communications Unit in the prime minister's office and speechwriter at the Home Office.
- Lance Price
  When I met Price, he had retired from politics and was working as a freelance author and columnist. In 1998 he had been appointed the prime minister's deputy director of communications. Between 2000 and 2001 he headed the Labour Party's office of communications.
- Simon Redfern
  Redfern was instrumental as social media strategist in David Miliband's Labour Party leadership contest. He then managed the PR consultancy Pagefield.
- Paul Richards
  Richards is a former special adviser to Labour Cabinet Ministers Hazel Blears and Patricia Hewitt. Later he worked as a political consultant.
- Kiran Stacey
  I met Stacey when he worked as a political correspondent for the *Financial Times*.
- Lord Wilfrid Stevenson of Balmacara
  Lord Stevenson is a member of the House of Lords. He previously worked as director of the Smith Institute and served as communications adviser to Prime Minister Brown.
- Zoë Thorogood
  At the time of our conversation, Thorogood was about to leave her position as head of broadcasting at Conservative Party headquarters.
- Katie Waring
  When I met Waring, she held the position of special adviser for media relations to Business Secretary Vince Cable.
- Nick Wood
  Wood is a former press secretary to the Conservative Party leaders Iain Duncan Smith and William Hague. At the time of our interview, he was chief executive at the PR company Media Intelligence Partners.

The weakness in the analysis of qualitative data generated in my interviews is a function of its flexibility: Gray (2009) contends that there is not one agreed analytical procedure and the smallest common denominator is a somewhat vague recognition that data need coding. The situation is further complicated by notable divisions on the degree to which the researcher should interfere with data in the analytical process. At the one extreme we find Strauss and

Corbin (1998), who contend that researchers should merely present the data (e.g. interview transcripts) and not risk distorting the material through their personal biased attitudes. They expect data to speak for themselves and reach the reader directly without being manipulated by the researcher. Alternatively, Wolcott (1994) portrays data presentation in descriptive terms and advocates storytelling as an appropriate way to relate results. What the variants of qualitative data analysis have in common is the need to break down complex information into smaller units. This is the approach I have chosen in an effort to identify characteristics of behaviour and decision making. Subsequently, it allowed me to identify patterns, reconstruct narratives and develop themes, which contributed to a better understanding of causalities and correlations in political reputation management.

In this and the following two chapters I am presenting the insights – sometimes analytical, often anecdotal – that experts in political communications shared with me. The issues we touched upon in our conversations are organized under headings that are aligned with the core themes of reputation and communications management that I illustrated in preceding chapters. Readers are invited to assess – as I did when first reviewing the material – if and to what degree the insights that experts agreed to reveal to me are reflective of the concepts of strategically planned reputation management that I outlined in the first part of this book.

Recognizing the relevance of reputation management

The starting point of and justification for this study was the recognition of and need for the management of reputation in politics. It therefore appeared critical to see if practitioners agreed with this study's underlying assumption that 'government is all about reputation management, reputation creation, reputation development. I mean, it is all about reputation, everything's all about reputation' (Hill). Hill's is probably the most explicit acknowledgement of this view. Lance Price cautions that the concern with reputation is a comparatively recent phenomenon, or at least its prominence on politicians' minds has become more manifest in recent decades.

It emerged that political communicators are aware of the power reputation has in the making and breaking of a politician's career. While nobody tried to argue that a party leader's or minister's reputation could tip the outcome of a general election, it was made clear that for a politician's career path it was of significance how candidates and incumbents were seen and judged by the party's rank and file, members of Parliament or other key stakeholders. Jones believes this recognition propelled Tony Blair's career early on, when after the sudden death of John Smith the party had to decide who to pick as the new leader. The opportunity to align Blair with values and features that would conform with to popular images and eventually turn him into a public persona stakeholders wanted to see at the helm of the Labour Party and the country may have tipped the balance in his favour, while Gordon Brown's prospects at the time and even more so in subsequent years were constrained by allegations of his obsessions, personality flaws and widely reported anecdotes that mocked his very own terminology of political gobbledygook. Brown's political fortune was also thought to have been hampered by his apparent lack of genuine compassion and empathy – evidenced through the conspicuous absence of a spouse or girlfriend in the initial years of his Westminster career. This latter shortcoming became even more encumbering when Blair was echoing familiar and popular imagery as the beaming family man and caring husband (Jones).

It seems that these considerations of reputation among influential and senior party circles are by no means a feature only of the late 1990s. Richards purports that in the years prior to the Blair era Neil Kinnock had been going through a dramatic image transformation to the point where 'there is nothing left' of Kinnock, who as a consequence could not find his 'own voice anymore'. The advice that was given to him regarded demeanour as well as looks, and it was thought that these were the instruments intended to construct artificially a popular public persona.

In the view of Jones, Michael Howard's resurrection and leadership of the Conservative Party prior to the 2005 election likewise hinged on a necessity to control his reputation. The images Howard was meant to conjure up among voters were reminiscent of what party officials understood to be a safe pair of hands who would put up a solid performance, assuage traditional Tory voters, organize a formidable campaign, hold his own at the dispatch box against Blair and look thoroughly respectable. After the disappointment with the Hague leadership and the disastrous performance of Iain Duncan Smith, the reputation Howard had acquired over years as a minister in Margaret Thatcher's and John Major's cabinets bore just the credentials that matched expectations among key stakeholders. Jones contends that in the Conservative Party there was at the time a strongly felt longing for 'that person, they feel comfortable and secure with and who could be trusted'. It is this reputational profile that, in the view of Jones, propelled Howard into the leader's office.

A more recent case is recounted by Damian McBride, who reminds us that the selection of Gordon Brown's deputy as Labour leader was preceded by extensive opinion polling of potential contenders. The purpose of this exercise was to gauge how each candidate was judged among the electorate and how these views matched the ideal profile the public hoped to find in a future deputy leader. The bottom line of this leadership selection was to understand 'how popular they would be with the public' (McBride). At the time, the preference was for Harriet Harman, as it was found that Gordon Brown had a problem with women, which she might have been able to address.

It appears so far that thoughts about the creation and safeguarding of reputation take centre stage in political communications management activities; however, communicators appear not to spend much time pondering the causes of reputation or its strategic implications. Some of their reasoning is at a rather incipient stage. The journalist Shane Greer admits that, while reputation makes and breaks careers, there is little clarity as to how some politicians' careers are boosted by reputation while others suffer from reputational challenges. He compares Boris Johnson and Ed Miliband in order to highlight the enigma that still awaits an answer: while Johnson may choose to insult entire groups or parts of the country without incurring lasting damage to his public persona, Miliband is prone to draw criticism even though his public announcements and appearances are more carefully calibrated. Hill claims that neither political decisions nor specific policies but the way the electorate views politicians provides a key to understanding why distinct sections of the electorate with distinct interests and aspirations may all agree to support a particular party leader.

Another feature that accounts for the central role of reputation management in politics is related to the media's aggressiveness (Jones, Eustice). It has been observed by communicators – and journalists appear to agree broadly – that while the British media are not the only tool through which reputation can be generated, they are the gravest threat to a politician's public persona and powerful enough to shatter painstakingly constructed images. Eustice ascribes to the media both the power and propensity to 'puff people up and tear them down'. Jones concurs and points out the British media's tendency to personalize politics and to subject contenders to personal scrutiny. The media, he contends, are interested in the public persona and hence this needs careful planning and construction. Therefore, the communicator as reputation manager is widely seen as a key figure on whose contribution the politician's professional survival and success hinges (Eustice).

While reputation's centrality is recognized by former political communicators and journalists, those who are currently advising politicians are not unanimously subscribing to this centrality of reputation. In particular, Henry Macrory's view diverges from the predominant opinion as he points out that, specifically in the case of David Cameron, reputation management is being neither practised nor sought (Macrory). He did admit, though, that taking advice on presentational issues and media training to prepare for TV appearances are popular in Westminster circles. If Macrory adamantly refuses to accept the term 'reputation management' in the context of individual candidates or government members, this may be seen as an effort to disassociate his current party from the notions of spin, which did so much harm to the preceding Labour administration. The line between media training and communications advice on the one hand and reputation management on the other is arguably so fine and flexible that it eludes definition. A case in point is Macrory's account of Cameron accepting coaching when preparing for conference speeches. While he would concede that members of staff discuss and share advice with Cameron on how a speech is best delivered, Macrory insists that communicators would not interfere with how Cameron wears his hair or how he dresses. Arguably, Macrory's unwillingness to accept the centrality of image making and management in the Conservative Party's public relations department may be due to a phenomenon Jones also observed: Cameron's natural skills in self-presentation as well as his genuinely appealing image as a young, caring family father who was visibly afflicted by his child's serious illness quite naturally allowed him to bond with relevant stakeholders.

Jones recalls the 2005 leadership contest when David Davis had been tipped as frontrunner and Kenneth Clarke as likely alternative contender. Jones recalls comments that described Davis as a prickly political loner with a wife who hated media attention. Clarke was seen as an essentially lazy layabout with a penchant for drink and jazz, and finally Cameron was endowed with a range of affable traits described above. This may have allowed Cameron's PR advisers then and in subsequent years to pursue a soft-touch approach to what otherwise was already a suitable reputation. Perhaps this self-imposed limitation to the kind of guidance Conservative Party headquarters proffered to Cameron may not indicate a diminished overarching role of reputation in political communications. It is perhaps more a reflection of the Conservative Party's dismal past experiences when media advisers tried to restyle the then party leader William Hague. At the time it was thought that making him wear baseball caps and jeans and having him drink out of a coconut while attending the Notting Hill Carnival would mould favourably the views people held of him. All my respondents agreed that this mechanical approach to creating image and building reputation backfired and should be avoided.

The verdict in Hague's case in no one's opinion questions the general desirability of a managed reputation. However, communicators make it quite clear that authenticity is a core consideration in their planning. Jones puts this into perspective by pointing out that a politician's public persona at best vaguely resembles the individual's identity, and that the images of a politician are essentially a confection. He reminds us that this 'concoction' is what communicators are expected to fabricate as part of their brief to further the politician's career (Jones).

It appears that the relevance of an individual politician's reputation is a given due to what almost amounts to connivance between communicators and journalists who both treat issues of public persona with great attention. As we shall see in subsequent sections of this and the next two chapters, the centrality of reputation in communications processes encourages communicators and politicians alike to think early on in their careers about issues such as positioning and long-term communications planning (Jones).

Using research in reputation management

The bottom line of my conversations with communicators was that on the whole the resources invested in researching communications issues, environments and stakeholders were meagre. While research is being conducted regularly, it falls far short of the sophisticated polling operation in which some media at times suggest the government broadly engages (Greer).

Number 10 Downing Street or party headquarters provide at their discretion politicians and communicators in government and opposition, respectively, with public opinion data to guide action and help to devise tailor-made communications techniques. It is interesting to note that, even though these polling results may be available, the data may not actually be acted upon. In fact, when asked about the party's means to gauge the electorate's expectations towards leader, Macrory makes it clear that the judgement on who would have the credentials to make a convincing party leader and prime minister hinges on the 'mood' among the parliamentary party and MPs' sense of what their constituency want to see (Macrory). The decision in 2005 to make Cameron leader instead of David Davis was arguably of dramatic consequence for the Conservatives. Yet when selecting a new leader, research findings about popular images of candidates were allegedly not meant to be used as a strategic instrument to guide decisions. If research findings of that kind were used at all, the material served mainly to confront the political opponent (Macrory).

In stark contrast to Macrory, McBride reveals evidence to suggest that political communicators who rely on a hunch and their anecdotal understanding of key publics are ill advised and unable to judge situations appropriately, undermining the effectiveness and efficiency of any campaign message. As evidence, McBride cites polling data about the then Labour Cabinet Minister Alan Johnson, who considered standing for his party's deputy leadership. While Johnson was believed by senior party officials to be popular with the electorate, formal research indicated that Johnson had little credibility with voters, who made it quite clear that they did not trust him. Data related the reason for these critical attitudes to Johnson's habit of wearing shiny suits and sunglasses, which focus groups associated with the image of a used-car dealer. At the same time the party leadership had rightly predicted that focus groups would pick up on Harman's lack of support among male voters. Though it may have come as a surprise when research results revealed that Hilary Benn, who had been considered a rising star in the party, was entirely written off by focus groups.

Perhaps most interestingly, for a long time not even the chancellor's office commissioned polls to understand public perceptions of Gordon Brown. This was allegedly the reason why Brown's staff were largely unaware of the chancellor's deep-running unpopularity with the electorate. This only changed when data commissioned by the prime minister's office were passed on to No. 11 to remind Tony Blair's principal rival of his seriously flawed image (McBride). McBride points out that 'this was the first we really know about sort of some of the image issues that Gordon carried with him' (McBride).

It is somewhat surprising to see how communications strategies and tactics are pursued without a clear idea of how they may resonate with the electorate. At times the discrepancy between their communicative approach on the one hand and public reaction to the new prime minister on the other hand took Brown's communications team by surprise. McBride recounts how in one instance Brown's team was shocked to learn how a focus group thoroughly disapproved of Brown talking publicly about the grief he harboured surrounding the loss of his child. Brown's media team had failed to keep this issue off an interview agenda as they had apparently not been fully aware of the type of negative response they were about to incur.

Interestingly even at No. 10, where resources for formal research are available, anecdotal information gathered at the sidelines of a football pitch on a Saturday afternoon was taken seriously and fed back into Downing Street discussions about policy and communications campaigns (Kelly). Tony Blair, who as prime minister had at his disposal polling expertise, would usually be driven by his instincts, which only in a subsequent phase were corroborated or altered by research findings (Price). At the same time, it is true that Blair decided to intensify polling for highly relevant policy issues as, for instance, he did when the introduction of the euro was being discussed. However, Price affirms that politicians would ultimately not be able to function effectively unless they had a gut feeling for issues, stakeholders and developments to rely on. This view is shared by Richards, who asserts that political communicators are endowed with what he calls 'an alarm bell' or 'an instinctive sort of reaction', which helps them to understand the environment and stakeholders' responses. This intuition blends in with a tendency to rely on anecdotal evidence.

Hill tries to define what research can offer and what it should not be used for. In his view, qualitative stakeholder research should be confined to identifying how relevant publics perceive a policy and not which policy the publics want to see pursued. Eustice concurs in that whichever research tools are used in political communications, the purpose is to improve the communicator's understanding of audiences and to be able to gauge their reaction. While this may be the agreed definition for research used in politics, there appears to be some temptation to push the line further and use research findings as a means to fine-tune policies. Eustice himself emphasizes how research was used by the Conservative opposition to understand public perceptions of Blairism. Findings were fed into a discussion about how Conservative policies should integrate these criticisms of the then government and offer an alternative to Labour's agenda. Still, Eustice insists that the policy content the Conservative Party had to offer was devised independently from any research findings, which were only allowed to help communicators find the right tone and terminology. Eustice highlights Cameron's rhetoric on welfare reform as a case in point, with the presentational issue of policies being informed by research findings. Thus, instead of speaking of welfare cuts for scroungers, one would emphasize the need to help people who are currently stuck in the welfare system (Eustice, Davies).

There seems to be consistent evidence that, outside party headquarters and the prime minister's office at No. 10, systematic opinion polling is not being conducted by any government department. The only exception is occasionally the chancellor's office, which according to some sources – while others dispute it – may have engaged in regular polling in preparation for Brown's takeover of the leadership (McBride, Livermore). McBride summarizes No. 11's rationale for taking up systematic research and opinion polling: 'So, yes, that's something that we did, um, consistently because almost the assumption was, you should be doing that, um, if that's what the leader is expected to do because Tony Blair has been doing it all these years and why not' (McBride).

All other cabinet ministers who are keen to find out what their stakeholders have in mind and expect are usually reliant on polling conducted by the news media (Davies). This source lacked answers to more specific questions that a department or incumbent might have wanted to ask with regard to particular personality traits or political initiatives. News media-generated data are usually too broad for most strategic purposes and therefore do not inform communicative strategy. However, ministers had little alternative. Davies made it quite clear that special advisers who direct cabinet ministers' media relations lack the financial resources and the time it takes to conduct systematic research, the findings of which could then be used to draw up and pursue communications objectives. Richards reminds us that, in 20 years in politics and a decade of work for cabinet ministers, he never had at his disposal the budget needed to conduct opinion polls on a minister's public persona and image generated through their behaviour and policies.

To deal with this Katie Waring, Business Secretary Vince Cable's adviser on media relations, reminds us that she relies on an assortment of random information, titbits and gossip that reaches her. This also implies complaints and hints that someone in the business community may not be happy with a departmental decision. This list of issues does provide Waring with a wealth of information on how the department's and the business secretary's performance are perceived, but none of it is even vaguely representative of the mood or the expectations of specific key publics.

The speechwriter Neather illustrates how much he relied on a hunch of what the audience might want to hear when planning and drawing up speeches for ministers in the Home Office. 'Expectations of the audience are fairly straightforward,' Neather claimed. While he may be right in thinking so, his judgement obviously is not grounded in any kind of formal research. Lacking this, he assumed that audiences of Home Office ministers liked to 'get some sort of feel for the politician as a person' (Neather). Neather would use this approach for all of the hundred or so speeches he wrote for the Home Office in the course of a year. He points out that the only formal research conducted was commissioned by party headquarters and various media. However, it emerges that the kind of data made available by either would not lend itself to gaining a good understanding of specific audiences, nor would it help gauge how politicians are being perceived among individual publics and the attributes ascribed to them.

In conclusion, I realized that interviewees find it easier to talk critically of past political eras and protagonists who have since retired. It is therefore not entirely surprising to see Eustice mention Michael Howard as an example of a politician who fell for the temptation of allowing the public mood as identified in research findings to guide the party manifesto. In this specific case, Howard found that concerns about immigration which his pollsters had raised should be a core theme in the election campaign. It is not the purpose of this research to judge if this approach is ethically acceptable or not. Instead, one needs to acknowledge that Howard apparently allowed the thrust of research results to steer both content and style of his campaign. Without offering any further examples, Eustice believes that a considerable number of politicians concede research findings a pivotal strategic role commensurate with the view taken by Howard. Lance Price made the same observation of Blair, who instinctively supported research for and use of genetically modified food in the UK, but was prepared to change his stance once it emerged that the majority of consumers were much more sceptical and did not wish to see products on the supermarket shelves that had been genetically altered.

In the following paragraphs we will be looking into how communicators describe the ideal public persona and try to establish how this notion is reflected in political public relations processes and the defining of communications objectives. From what we have learned so far, the understanding of what stakeholders consider an ideal reputation may be vague at best and based to some extent on anecdotal evidence. Apart from the prime minister, most leading politicians in the country arguably have only limited interest in and no resources for systematic research and subsequently are unlikely to know what their intended public persona should be, let alone what their current reputation is like.

Understanding the ideal public persona

Apparently, both journalists and communications advisers are aware of the importance of a public persona. It is not the purpose of my research to establish what features and traits this public persona should entail. Of much more interest should be a recognition that, in line with current concepts of reputation management, communications processes need to generate, maintain and safeguard a politician's public image, with a view to create or guarantee a public persona that corresponds with expectations specific publics seem to entertain.

It would seem that there is some confusion as to what in the minds of the electorate constitutes the features of the ideal politician. Price claims that some candidates and incumbents display the looks, rhetoric and gestures that one would expect in a leading politician, and arguably Blair did so at least in his early years. Yet, by contrast, the public also appeared to have given unusual support and sympathy to Mo Mowlam, the Northern Ireland secretary, and Clare Short. These were two politicians whose demeanour was much less in line with the stereotypical description of a serious, strategic-thinking and -acting politician. Price points out this discrepancy and concludes that there is a range of different and at times conflicting personalities and images that seem to be attractive to the electorate and deemed appropriate for individuals who intend to govern the country.

Price clarifies that businesses' public opinion research is difficult to compare with polling in politics, as in the latter issues come up at a high frequency and immediate responses are needed. This state of affairs, in his view, leaves little time for systematic data gathering and analysis, which explains perhaps in part the lack of survey or interview data into what constitutes the ideal image of a politician. Moreover, distinct groups may have different expectations. Particularly, party activists may hope for traits in their representatives that arguably diverge from what the electorate at large asks for. Jones refers to this when he calls William Hague unelectable but 'appealing to the party faithful'.

A more anecdotal route to identifying and describing a politician's ideal reputation is taken by Davies, whose experience as adviser to Jack Straw made him conclude that publics tend to like politicians who speak their mind and appear to be upfront and honest. This, however, is grounded entirely in anecdotal evidence, as is the notion that voters want a 'big personality' (Beattie) – or so insists Beattie when commenting on London Mayor Boris Johnson's apparent ease at retaining public popularity regardless of the policy outcomes he produces and perceived benefits he secures for Londoners. Beattie suspects, therefore, an appetite for 'big personalities'.

In the view of Livermore, being respected was all that was needed for a prime minister and there was no good reason for attempts to generate popularity artificially. Ignoring this counsel, Brown was given advice that a smile on his face when on television would be appreciated by his audiences. Apparently, Brown agreed, as he was unhappy with his lack of popularity and thus conceded to engage in activities and behaviour that endeared him to publics. This led to a trade-off between being liked on the one hand and being respected on the other (Livermore): a tactic that stirred internal controversy. This and similarly hapless attempts to tamper with a politician's perceived personality reveal something about the quality and randomness of political communications in pursuit of an ideal public persona.

Perhaps arbitrary at first glance – though perhaps with some truth in it – is Kettle's speculation that advanced age in party leaders and senior politicians either is actually considered a weakness by the electorate or alternatively party leadership thinks that youth is electorally more viable. The nominations of party leaders in all three major parties suggests that a successful leader is of a comparatively young age set against the backdrop of potential alternative contenders for the leadership. Parties that in the past did choose older leaders saw them ridiculed in the media. Kettle mentions Menzies Campbell, but could also have talked about Michael Foot, who admittedly was also hobbled by his idiosyncratic ideological positions at the time.

Having said this, it appears that, while the leader strives to appear youthful, the leadership team as a whole may well need one older personality to be reflective of the entire electorate (Kettle). Kettle mentions the Conservatives' then Justice Secretary Ken Clarke and the Business Secretary Vince Cable for the Liberal Democrats, who through extended professional experience add 'gravitas' (Kettle) to the perceived credibility and competence ascribed to government or party leadership. He goes on to make the point that as a stand-alone leader Jim Callaghan in the 1970s was apparently the last politician who made advanced age ('you can trust old Jim') a positive trademark in his campaign.

The definition of an ideal public persona is arguably not absolute, but instead relative to a politician's brief. While as defence secretary particular qualities may be considered useful and expected by key publics, we may want a leader of the opposition to speak and act differently. Cabinet ministers may perhaps revel in the management of day-to-day politics, while a prime ministerial personality can afford to and should be above the daily fray and find the right tone to address the nation as a whole rather than fire up his close-knit political supporters (Stacey). Stacey concludes from this that perhaps Brown's public persona was well suited to run the Exchequer, while his style was not adequate for a head of government. By the same token one can argue that Cameron's hands-off approach to managing daily politics might be considered a liability if adopted by a cabinet minister, yet it is a perfectly acceptable stance to be taken by someone who considers him- or herself a chairperson in an almost presidential position. Stevenson makes a similar point by saying that Brown reflected 'a sober and prudent aspect in relation both to policy and person', which for his job at the Exchequer may have been just what the party and the electorate wanted. Stevenson goes on to question if perhaps 'those are not the same characteristics' that are needed as head of government.

Brown may have had an awkward personality and his communication style was somewhat deficient, but he was regarded as a numbers person and a solid administrator who had an impressive track record as chancellor. Livermore takes this up and categorizes politicians in one group who are liked by publics, and another group who are respected, 'almost feared'. Greer wonders if this might have been Brown's selling point as prime minister, regardless of the level of sympathy people entertained for him. Yet he too fears, that the qualities ascribed to Chancellor Brown may not have helped him in the job of prime minister. Livermore concedes this point when he emphasizes that 'the image that he [Brown] sought to create for himself and we sought to reinforce as chancellor was particularly well suited to him as chancellor', which implies that it was an image that perhaps was not best suited to a different portfolio.

Perhaps Alan Johnson's perceived poor performance as shadow chancellor can be understood in this context too. As secretary of state, Johnson was said to have been 'extraordinarily successful', while perhaps he never should have been picked and promoted to shadow chancellor (Beattie). Likewise Davies agrees that publics may want to see qualities in a government politician that are different from traits people accept in a shadow minister. For instance, the home secretary should be trusted to lock away whoever deserves to go to prison and to ensure that no major errors happen in the management of public security. By contrast, in foreign secretaries trust is perhaps a less prominent issue. Instead, they need to be predominantly visible and be 'seen to be part of the big picture' (Davies).

Linking personality and reputation management objectives

From what we have learned so far, it seems apparent that in communicators' minds the public persona and the politician's identity are related, and that one hinges on the other. McBride remembers meeting politicians whom he thought would lend themselves to being portrayed in one particular way only, others were endowed with a media-savvy set of qualities and would likely be able to have according images projected onto them. Richards finds that due to media exposure personality traits are being 'magnified': the more important and visible these traits appear to be, the more attention they will absorb by the communications adviser, who will try to control how they become publicly exposed over time. Richards seems to be making this point when he talks about Hazel Blears, who as a 'down-to-earth, plain-spoken, working-class' politician would by her communications advisers be presented in an environment and with audiences who appreciate these traits.

McBride stresses that attempts to fabricate an image that is unrelated to a person's genuine personality do not usually succeed, as audiences are unlikely to accept an entirely artificial public persona. McBride points out even more explicitly that 'I never, ever saw any attempt to change an image if there was not anything remotely inauthentic about it, I never saw that work and it was always totally destructive in the other way'. It appears that the electorate reacts with considerable aversion in the face of what they consider to be manipulation.

The efforts to shape Gordon Brown's image, in the words of McBride, were designed not to remodel the prime minister's personality, but instead to help publics access Brown's actual identity. The campaign to present Brown as 'not flash, just Gordon' was therefore appreciated both among Labour followers and the opposition as a skilful attempt to shape the prime minister's image within the limits of his actual identity (Eustice). Both Macrory and Thorogood make it quite clear that a complete personality makeover does not work, and it is therefore, in their view, not intended or advisable to make politicians behave or talk in a way that does not reflect their personality.

However, it is understood that, in the case of William Hague, Conservative communicators diverged from this more restrained stance and instead ambitiously sought to model his public persona in a way that did not do justice to his identity (Macrory, Eustice). Michael Portillo, too, appears to have been a politician whose reputation was for a while the result of a skilful makeover, which intended to present him as a Conservative political hard-liner: a public persona that did not match his personality (Jones). Portillo appears to have been unhappy with this rift between who he was and the artificially generated perception. The case of Portillo seems to confirm what we have established so far: in the long run identity and reputation need to be aligned.

Beattie sees a communicator's room to manoeuvre therefore reduced to emphasizing politicians' strengths and hiding their weaknesses. This minimalistic approach to reputation management seems to be widely accepted. It precludes notions that communicators may be able to turn a politician like Iain Duncan Smith into 'the most sparkling, dynamic leader-like person' (Stacey). In the view of Stacey, this is beyond the abilities of communications advisers and is therefore 'just never going to happen'.

With regard to this call for authenticity, Waring points out that Cable genuinely wanted to take part in the entertainment programme *Strictly Come Dancing*, which in her view was an authentic engagement that presented him as a person with a hinterland and interests that transcend politics. Another example of a politician who is genuinely appealing to the public, whom Stacey cites, is Boris Johnson, whose self-effacing humour and ability not to take himself too seriously allows him to get away with controversial actions or remarks that might come back to haunt other politicians. Both cases touch upon an argument Stacey raised by pointing out that audiences find it easier to relate to a politician's positive public persona if it appears to be grounded in charismatic traits that predate and prevail over any communications advice.

Hill concurs with McBride in that the public at some point manages to see through a constructed public persona if it is intended to cover up a personality that is entirely different from the image created. However, he concedes that it is a communicator's legitimate responsibility to emphasize strengths and to ensure that weaknesses are removed from the public focus. However, this does not signify that one can pull 'wool over the eyes of the general public in the modern media war for very long' (Hill). Therefore, Hill and Livermore argue that substance and spin go together, and presentational tools can only work if they are based on the substance that is meant to be communicated. Stevenson concludes that both substance and presentation are relevant for a politician's public persona. This is broadly in line with a claim made by McBride, who argues that individuals in public life can count on PR to present the complexity of their personalities and their strengths to specific publics.

In the view of Hill, what cannot be done with any hopes of succeeding is the entire fabrication of a public persona that does not in the least resemble the politician. This is presumably a recipe that the Conservatives followed when drawing up a communications strategy for Michael Howard in the run-up to the 2005 elections. Eustice remarks that the truth needs to be at the heart of all messages associated with a politician, and should also shape the public persona that is being generated. This is why the Conservatives portrayed Michael Howard as a politician who got things done, which is a perfectly fair description of the former longstanding cabinet minister. However, this would also explain, perhaps, why they did not try to fight an uphill battle against the widespread notion that Howard was anything but charming (Eustice). Jones reminds us that Howard in the run-up to the general election in 2005 would have needed an overhaul of this aspect in his public persona. However, his entrenched reputation for being a 'shifty, untrustworthy, rather unpleasant character' was limiting communicators' options (Jones).

Eustice concludes that attempts to present an individual in any way that diverges from their personality harbours considerable risk. The communicative failure of the Hague leadership is a case in point, illustrating the consequences one had to face when the actual personality of the then Conservative leader was not allowed to guide the communications programme. At the time communicators strove to portray the party as young and stylish, which was probably a reason for taking Hague not only to the Notting Hill Carnival, but also to a theme park, where he was asked to go on a water slide. Eustice argues that the image management of Hague might have worked if the communications had played to his strengths and emphasized that he was a serious man who 'wasn't flash but was sensible'. Hague was then, as now, a serious personality and the books he has published since testify to his intellectual prowess in the eyes of Beattie. Wood's advice to the then party leader William Hague was at the time to play to his ordinary comprehensive school upbringing. It is thought to have been wrong to ignore these features of his background and personality when his public persona was being shaped in the late 1990s (Beattie).

A lack of authenticity may also have been the cause of adverse responses to a brief broadcast by Gordon Brown, who on YouTube was talking about government expenses. During his talk, Brown made a forced effort to smile in between words and sentences. Richards calls this presentational exercise 'completely idiotic and out of character', and comparable to Hague's decision to wear a baseball cap. Kelly advises not to generate an artificial personality or 'bubble', as he calls it, around the political leader, which is likely to burst. Wood concurs and claims that 'most attempts to change it [personality] just don't work or backfire'.

The public persona, in the view of Eustice, must be 'consistent with what they actually are', which is something of which good advisers should ideally have an understanding (Eustice). In a similar vein, Gordon Brown felt uncomfortable having his family used to presentational ends. This is why his communications policy did not envisage roles for his children and indeed the only time he presented himself as a family man for a photo opportunity was on the day he moved out of Downing Street surrounded by his wife and children (Stevenson).

The risk involved with fabricating an entirely artificial public persona that bears little resemblance to the true personality is also described by Stacey, who insists that political correspondents are perfectly able to see and spot these discrepancies, going on to argue that 'you just can't keep up the façade'. Waring agrees by adding that Whitehall correspondents are 'completely immersed in Westminster, and they pick up all the gossip and they see everybody'. This closeness ensures that there is little opportunity to develop a public persona that is at odds with what an individual really is like.

It has been claimed that, if a politician's public exposure staunchly contradicts his or her established public persona, it is particularly damaging for the individual concerned (McBride). Discrepancies between the public image and what is thought to be a politician's personality are damaging when they occur, particularly if an individual's professed values and beliefs turn out to be not in line with their actual behaviour (Greer). These cases may involve politicians who as part of their public persona have taken a particular stance on illegal drugs or family values, which they at some point do not live up to in their respective private lives.

Richards cites John Prescott, the former deputy prime minister, as an example of a politician whose personality as 'a bruiser' could never be hidden or reinterpreted to satisfy publics that might have wished to see different traits in a leading government member (Richards). While Prescott had a tendency to abrasive behaviour and language, former Labour leader Kinnock had an image as someone who after a few drinks and a meal could start a row with the restaurant owner (Jones). Jones notes that Kinnock 'found it very, very difficult to counter that image' (Jones).

Brown's communications team helped over years to frame his bouts of bad temper and abrasiveness, and portray the chancellor instead as a strong personality in the face of adversity (Livermore). The idea was to generate respect for Brown even among those who did not particularly like him (Greer). However, once the public discovered that Brown as prime minister lacked this trait of strength and determination that they had long respected in him, his reputation cracked (Livermore).

The cases above arguably constitute a good reason for George Osborne to keep a low media profile, as he is aware that it would be difficult to hide what Stacey calls his Machiavellian personality and his inclinations to scheme. Likewise, Brown's public persona could not be concealed at will, as journalists sensed and at times knew what was going on behind closed doors in Downing Street, where Brown allegedly threw mobile phones at people and rang up staff at three o'clock in the morning. This and similar behaviour was difficult to hush up, which is why politicians arguably 'tend to end up being perceived in the way that they are' (Richards). This is why Richards finds it hard to think of a politician whose public persona at any point was completely altered.

While Kelly also subscribes to this notion that the public persona cannot be altered easily as it is anchored in an individual's identity, there seems to be evidence of an evolving identity which over time is mirrored in a remoulded public persona. By way of example he reminds us of Tony Blair, who, while fundamentally the same person throughout his tenure in Downing Street, did change insofar as he was increasingly prepared and willing to take on hostile public opinion if he believed his course of action was right. This seems to be a feature in his personality that allegedly was less apparent during his first term.

Identifying distinct audiences

My interviewees on the whole are fully aware of the existence of distinct publics, yet their tools to identify these groups and their methods to address them vary considerably. Stevenson's answer was typical of the responses that emerged. He recognizes the relevance of publics and expects political leaders to engage with them lest their power base erodes. Hill relates the existence of diverse publics to reputation management by describing the sheer range of interests and expectations as a challenge that renders communications more difficult. Colleagues in the cabinet or the shadow cabinet, party members and activists, different political currents within the parliamentary party: all of these count as publics that are viewing the politician in a distinct way and may presumably nurture different expectations.

Redfern elaborates on this by suggesting that the political leader's attention to the electorate and the party activists as key publics is largely sequential. He reminds us that initially aspiring leaders need to play to their respective party's gallery. Once he or she has earned their backing, it is the country at large one needs to address. While doing so, style and selection of content need to be calibrated in a way that ensures the electorate's support without aggravating party activists. In party politics the default position in discussions about market segments and the focusing of limited resources is to direct attention to the marginal seats (Hill). They are geographically easily identifiable and may be pivotal in upcoming elections. More broadly, Hill concurs that the message as well as the approach of party political and government communications is skewed to meet expectations of the electorate even though this diverged from what party activists asked for.

An added challenge is faced by the secretaries for Scotland and Wales, who represent distinct geographical and national interests, which at times are ill aligned with policies pursued by the central government in London. Hazlewood recognizes this and strives to interpret the secretary's statements and decisions as being reflective both of Welsh interests and central government policies.

Davies points out how different target audiences may have conflicting stakes in and contrasting interpretations of specific policies. He cites the currents in the ongoing debate over the wisdom of prison sentences for petty offenders. Politicians may take on board what various publics expect and echo this in their behaviour or style. Likewise, once it had transpired from polling data that Alan Johnson had an image problem, he markedly changed his attire, developed a preference for navy blue suits and made sure that he would no longer be seen in public wearing sunglasses (McBride).

While some politicians make an effort to try to reconcile their public persona with diverse strands of demands and expectations, others decide either for strategic reasons or intuitively not to accommodate a specific public. John Prescott, for instance, was on various occasions mandated by the party convention – a public in its own right – to pursue a specific policy with regard to council house building. Instead of reconciling his personal stance and policy with this demand he habitually ignored the request raised by his party (Davies).

Internal deliberations about the socioeconomic group, gender and the notion of the average – but aspirational – citizen bear testimony to the fact that audience segmentations are not only paid lip service by political parties and candidates but may also play a part in communications strategies. Even though funding to research these publics is limited, there appears to be a basic understanding at party headquarters of how to categorize the electorate (Wood).

The level and sophistication of segmentation are limited by the lack of resources. Therefore, MPs tap into the somewhat random evidence they come across when visiting their constituencies. This rather casual research informs their understanding of what the diverse electorate might need and how groups and interests are distinct. Waring calls it a 'microcosm of society' and details how politicians' visits to their constituents' doorsteps produce 'anecdotal evidence'. This is a strong rationale for community visits. Waring maintains that the business secretary's political behaviour also echoes discussions he is having with his staff about the diversity of his stakeholders, ranging from traders in the City of London to deprived citizens in his constituency. Attempts to keep the balance between these two extremes exemplify awareness of distinct publics and an understanding that they need to be accommodated.

McBride clarifies that neither as chancellor nor as prime minister did Gordon Brown invest in intense audience research that would have allowed him to gauge the different publics and give him directions as to how their expectations overlapped or conflicted. Nor was Brown given data to illustrate how his own self-perception diverged from their respective views. As a result, views and suggestions among communications advisers about the most appropriate messages and channels of communications were not grounded in reliable data. Yet Stevenson insists that the tools of communication with key publics are selected in accordance with the targeted audience's media behaviour. Women's magazines, to name an example, were considered an appropriate communications channel for Brown to address female voters, who appeared to be even more sceptical about him than the electorate at large (McBride). McBride also mentions Lord Stevenson's idea to publish a book allegedly to portray Brown the way he really is. This suggestion was cautioned against by colleagues, who felt that the relevant audience of young and not particularly politicized voters arguably might not be too excited by the idea of a book authored by the prime minister (McBride). A practical rather than research-based approach to selecting communications tools and channels was taken in Conservative Central Office too. With specific segments of the electorate in mind, Cameron was advised, for instance, to agree to an interview with *GQ* magazine and to appear on the *Jonathan Ross Show* (Macrory).

Newspapers likewise offer themselves as a distinct channel and Beattie explains how pivotal the role of the *Daily Mirror* can be for communications between the Labour leadership and its supporters, many of whom read this newspaper. Communicators also need to show awareness of how a political pundit's attention span and level of interest differs from the average newspaper or TV audience's patterns of media consumption. Beattie subscribes to Alastair Campbell's view that, once the political activist gets tired of a piece of policy information, the media-consuming public just about starts to notice something has been said. In this respect the people who make the media and those who consume them are quite distinct audiences for any political communicator to deal with.

Redfern observes a tangible difference between corporate and political communications with regard to the amount and intensity of stakeholder research. He details that business clients would survey their supposed stakeholders, organise data in diagrams, and plan communications strategy according to their findings. By contrast, to compensate for a lack of audience data, political communicators make use of generic polling results commissioned by publishers and broadcasters (McBride). These publicly accessible data helped to explain, for instance, how Brown was seen in his native Scotland and how his alleged attempts to act as more English were being perceived and interpreted north of the border.

Redfern suggests that another reason for a lack of market segmentation and opinion research into the electorate may be communicators' deep-running familiarity with the audiences. Redfern refers to the Labour leadership contest in 2010. He clarifies that in the campaign team that was organizing David Miliband's bid for the party leadership there was a good understanding of the distinct publics that would sway the result. Particular attention was dedicated to party constituents with an intention to favour the right of the party as opposed to the left. Specific union chapters were being targeted, as were individual MPs. The strategy deployed envisaged wins with specific moderate and conservative publics and anticipated comparatively poor showing with others: MPs, unions and party activists at the same time were aware of who their favourite candidates were and what they stood for. In the view of Redfern there were no doubts about what David Miliband represented.

In this array of media-consuming and -generating audiences Kelly accepts that the electorate is the ultimate target audience for any politician. However, he contends that newspapers are both an important channel and a critical audience that cannot be bypassed – either through television or social media. He particularly advises communicators not to challenge the print media because 'there was only one winner in that' (Kelly).

Beattie is implicitly pointing at the discrepancy in judgement that distinguishes the electorate from journalists by detailing the cases of Alex Salmond and Boris Johnson. Beattie contends that the public is prepared to forgive and accept individuals and their failings. Journalists may not. Beattie would also argue that journalists are more critical individuals who tend to get bored and as a consequence cover a politician or a policy less favourably. In their dual function as target audience and as channel, journalists play a central role in political communications, which seems to be echoed in the way communicators treat reporters, editors and entire news desks. Messages are being passed on selectively to specific papers and their correspondents. This allows communicators to build up working relationships with sympathetic media and cut out adverse papers that would potentially have used information against the source (Beattie).

One powerful tool of communication with distinct publics is the party leader's conference speech, which is drawn up with a similar awareness of the distinct audiences to which it will be addressed. Neather details that the party faithful nurture interests and expectations that may be different from those of television audiences. Jones adds that particularly the tabloid newspapers traditionally were on the mind of the politician who was about to face the conference. McBride details how Gordon Brown at party conferences would direct chunks of his speech at the party members whom he needed to reassure that their concerns were being listened to and that their apprehension about Tony Blair's previous policies were being responded to. In McBride's view, this was of only limited relevance to the media in the room or the audience that followed events on the evening news channels. In the years preceding Brown, Blair had inserted into his scripts at party conferences passages that were exclusively aimed at the TV audience and other elements that had been integrated to satisfy party members (McBride).

This ability to engage the public at large and not just his own party activists constituted, in the view of Hill, the recipe for Blair's success over many years. Even though it was obvious that particular publics entertained distinct interests and expectations, Blair is reported to have tailored only his style, but not bent his messages to respond to different demands in the audience (Hill, Price). Price maintains that it was allegedly his 'emotional intelligence' that allowed Blair to be in tune with the mood of the conference. It is not the purpose of this investigation to corroborate the actual quality of leaders or their respective leadership speeches at conferences. In the context of this study I take the above narrative about conference speeches as an indicator to suggest that audience segmentation is at least being considered and acted upon in personal reputation management, even though perhaps not very systematically.

Positioning politicians

In this section interviewees are addressing the notion that politicians are being perceived by their publics in a specific way that is relative to the standing of their peers. In other words, an individual's perceived strengths and weaknesses may amount to qualities that are teased out, hidden or emphasized as publics compare politicians. It is the purpose of the following paragraphs to consider if this process of positioning is systematically guided and influenced by communicators.

In the view of Price, Prime Minister Blair was fortunate insofar as the successive leaders of the opposition by whom he was challenged took tactical approaches to attacking the government. Rather than presenting themselves as alternatives to the prime minister, they tried to criticize details in the daily management and implementation of politics. This allowed Blair to echew petty point-scoring and claim that he was the only politician around who had the country's best interests at heart and who genuinely cared about the nation's long-term prospects. Price reminds us that the positioning of politicians in the public perception and associating them with a particular narrative distinct from those to which their political competitors subscribe is critical both in times of government and opposition. The opposition is, in his view, disadvantaged as they cannot create associations with the same ease as incumbents do who align themselves with values resulting from actions and decisions they take. Instead, a challenger's tool to claim and defend a position in the field of competing political issues and contenders is largely symbolic.

In an attempt to position himself within the Labour Party hierarchy, John Reid was driven by his advisers to pick rows with Gordon Brown just for the sake of the confrontation itself. His advisers allegedly wanted to present Reid in public as a politician influential enough to challenge Blair's presumptive successor. Apparently, the gravitas of his adversaries – or so his advisers are believed to have reasoned – may have added to Reid's own standing (McBride). Waring made the same observation during the campaign for electoral reform when fights were picked as an instrument that aimed to clarify one's position and make it visible to a wider public. Apart from using conflict with colleagues or even the head of government to make one's own position known and distinct from anyone else's, there may be alternative and smoother ways that allow cabinet members to conform with government policy and the prime minister's directives, while at the same time using the little flexibility left to them to develop their respective images and shape the perception the public entertains of them. Price names David Blunkett as education and later home secretary as a politician who managed to carve out his own position while still toeing the government line.

When identifying and consolidating public perceptions of a politician, advisers may take into account how the respective individual is being seen and what their strengths and weaknesses are perceived to be. Richards, who at different times advised cabinet ministers Patricia Hewitt and Hazel Blears, remembers how Blears, due to her working-class background, felt patronized and underestimated by her cabinet peers in some situations, while in meetings with trade unionists she gained confidence and could demonstrate her good rapport with the audience. Richards's understanding of her abilities allowed him to arrange public engagements with the intention of positioning Blears favourably. By the same token, Hewitt was known to be a highly intellectual personality who would be able to make a mark in interviews that required one to develop and pursue complex trains of thought (Richards). If politics requires different talents and abilities in different situations, and if politicians are being seen and judged by their respective publics in different ways, political advisers thus may make use of this diversity of expectations and situations and position their clients accordingly.

Gordon Brown's long wait to succeed Tony Blair at the helm of government was interspersed with questions about his suitability for the top job. Clearly, his abilities and personal traits were being discussed in the context and compared to the qualities of other potential contenders. Price points out that Brown's strength was considered to be his management of the economy, which supported his claim to the premiership and gave him an edge over other cabinet ministers who could not necessarily as confidently command authority in their respective department or claim competence in their subject area. However, both the fact that Brown was Scottish and his arguably difficult personality may also have fed into the overall perception and raised doubts about the wisdom of the impending promotion. Price claims that these issues, which affected Brown's public positioning vis-à-vis his cabinet colleagues, were being dealt with systematically by his communications staff.

One might wish to speculate, for instance, if Brown's mantra of Britishness in his public statements was a rhetorical device to associate himself with national values that he by birth and nature lacked – very much to the detriment of his political ambitions. Before Brown became prime minister he went on a tour across the country and agreed to be interviewed by local radio stations whose journalists, in the words of McBride, saw this as an opportunity to present to their listeners the man who was tipped to become the next head of government. In these settings Brown talked about local issues and themes beyond his normal remit of the economy and public finances. This intentionally set him apart from the incumbent at 10 Downing Street, Tony Blair, who, in the words of McBride, at the time had lost his rapport with the public and appeared to care more about his legacy and his standing as an international statesman. His apparent weakness opened up a niche in the political arena for someone who was 'down to earth and listening to ordinary people' (McBride).

Livermore suggests that positioning Brown for a while was reasonably successful as he was seen by the public as the 'antidote' to Blair, whose alleged interest in presentational issues damaged his image and undermined his popular appeal. Brown was taking a different stance, which distanced him from his predecessor.

Once Brown had taken over the premiership, this strategy was taken further: occasions were seized by him and his staff to portray the new incumbent as different from the predecessor, who stood accused of having entertained a hands-off approach to a number of issues and to delegating challenging problems instead of dealing with them personally (McBride). To demonstrate this repositioning of the prime minister, a major visible task was needed that could focus public attention on Brown's qualities. The second outbreak of foot and mouth disease among cattle in the course of only a few years afforded this opportunity, as it allowed Brown to illustrate how firmly he was in control of crisis management and, through detailed attention and active problem-solving strategies, avoided mistakes and oversights in which Blair had become engulfed when the epidemic struck the first time. Brown was positioned as hard working and serious – two features Blair never considered his core disciplines (McBride).

Greer believes that Brown's public perception deteriorated once his advisers began to steer him away from the initial claim that, while the prime minister may not be the most popular politician, he was at least a safe pair of hands with the economy. To present Brown as friendly and smiling was evidently an attempt to reshape the position he held in people's perceptions, though arguably not a very successful one.

At about the same time, repositioning the Conservative Party was one of David Cameron's main activities after he took over the leadership in 2005. This entailed, in particular, the selection of themes and the advocacy of issues that reflected values with which the Conservatives intended to be associated with. Among other things, these included Cameron's engagement with environmental issues, which Greer calls an act of positioning but nothing the Conservatives genuinely cared about.

Positioning oneself and attacking or questioning the position the political opponent claims are flip sides of the same coin. Richards points out how the Labour Party tried to undermine Cameron's core claim of being firmly positioned in the centre of the political spectrum. They argued instead that the Conservatives' reformed agenda was not genuine and there was no proof that the party had seriously undergone a political transformation. It was alleged by Labour that at heart their Conservative adversaries were still the acolytes of Thatcher and her ideas. It was this train of thought that explains the Labour Party's efforts to position Cameron unfavourably by describing him as a chameleon (Richards).

Reputation management and the planning process

Redfern asserts that leading politicians who are visible in the media do not leave public perception to luck and therefore plan for it. The intensity of questioning and the frequency of media contacts, as well as the broad range of issues journalists might want to scrutinize, may tempt public relations staff and politicians alike to cut corners and conveniently satisfy journalists' curiosity without painstakingly ensuring that all answers are aligned with the strategic objectives that should be the guiding rod for any communicator. Eustice is conscious that media relations managers to a considerable degree are reactive only, and in so being lose sight of communications and policy objectives. This may limit their effectiveness and reduce their value for the political party or politician they serve.

Price, in his days with Tony Blair, recognized this challenge and cites the planning grid as the response first introduced by the Blair government and since then kept by two successive prime ministers. The grid is a planning chart used as a tool to organize and orchestrate prime ministerial public appearances and announcements independently from unforeseen events and crisis situations that crop up, threaten to dilute the messages and lead the focus away from the initially agreed objectives. The grid's strength is to visualize the narrative and to coordinate, calibrate and forecast the Westminster calendar of policy decisions and announcements, publicity, events and public resonance as best possible. The grid perhaps reflects actions and decisions that can reasonably be planned, while it is arguably a less useful tool in dealing with external issues that are beyond the control of communicators.

To illustrate how a grid can help to coordinate communications activities, Jones reminds us that the frequent public appearances of the respective party leaders' wives in the course of the 2010 campaign were considered planned activities that were entered in a planning diary. Likewise, themed visits that evolve around one subject area may be nicely and easily planned and noted in a grid, as Hazlewood illustrates with respect to the planning process for the for Wales secretary.

Price points out that strategic planning of media relations and images may happen intuitively. He cites Tony Blair, who allegedly spent considerable time thinking about the right public perception of his party and government. This centrality of image planning is underpinned by the observation that Blair considered issues of perception 'all the time' (Price). To which degree these considerations are enshrined in a written plan is difficult to establish.

Richards claims that on policy and communicative issues cabinet ministers receive written memoranda from their advisers, which are instrumental within departments in guiding ministers' views and helping them to plan ahead. However, there is little evidence from interviewees that communications plans are usually written down. This practice seems to be rare at best, which is not due to the fact that communicative issues are not being considered. Instead, there is a constant fear that written material could be leaked to the media. Jones has been dealing with reputation management for many years but has not yet come across a written plan to detail how a politician is ideally presented and how this should be achieved. He assumes that the Labour pollster Philip Gould may in his day have had a clear-cut plan on how to present Labour and its leader, although even in the case of this prominent Labour adviser it is not known if a written physical plan existed or if the leadership avoided written evidence. Livermore, on the other hand, is adamant that a plan on issues of reputation management existed and was explicitly known among advisers and the politician in question. In his view, the main arguments had been discussed with everyone involved and agreed, and only fear of leaks to the press prevented them from being formally typed up.

Hill concurs with Livermore's observation that planning does exist in the form of a broadly considered and agreed process, but that this may not require a written document. He argues that advisers to a politician need to be imbued with the direction that policies and communications should take. This alignment in views would facilitate brainstorming in the communications department and assist the development and optimization of planning. In other words, planning processes that are well integrated into the communicators' mindsets and activities are seen as as essential for effective communications as a written plan would be. Hill's remarks read as if in his view the effectiveness of communications tools to achieve desired objectives depended in part on the staff's awareness of and support for the plan. Price concurs by saying that the alignment of political decisions and the integration of policy statements in the Blair governments required communicators who were thoroughly familiar with the policy and communications plan. From this perspective planning has been pivotal in the management of day-to-day communications. However, Price cautions and clarifies that even a comprehensive and systematic approach to planning would need to make allowance for some events, which at short notice would be accommodated in the general narrative of a politician or party.

Davies gives the figure of 80 per cent to quantify the share of unplanned, reactive media relations, compared to a mere 20 per cent planned communications activity. To illustrate this in an example, Davies talks about appointments that he scheduled regularly with editors for them to have an opportunity to talk to Justice Secretary Jack Straw in an attempt to present the minister in a specific, more rounded way. These meetings were also an opportunity for discussing and advocating forthcoming policy initiatives. However, many of these prearranged, informal meetings were cancelled, as more urgent commitments had to be dealt with, which had not been envisaged. Richards concludes that communicative work at cabinet level gives only limited opportunities to plan ahead and stick to an agreed plan: 'Most of it is reactive.' Kelly in this context talks about the humility that communicators need to show as they recognize that their communications objectives cannot usually be achieved directly.

Beyond 10 Downing Street – at cabinet level – ministers may to different degrees engage in forward planning of policy announcements and public appearances. Waring disclosed that apart from the ministerial diary she has her own tally of talks Vince Cable has had with specific journalists. This is how she tries to keep track of which media has been missing out for a while and who needs to be contacted and talked to next. The success of these planning tools hinges on a number of variables. Apparently, the politician's personality and readiness to espouse a formal planning structure appears to be not insignificant in this. Davies and colleagues sought to align Straw's public appearances with stakeholder interests, but this careful planning was not always adhered to by the minister. Davies mentions that Jack Straw at times unexpectedly agreed to public meetings and stakeholder engagements in spite of other commitments and in the face of the advice he may have received from his communications staff.

Davies emphasizes another limiting factor in the planning process, which is related to what he refers to as 'official engagements'. While official engagements are counted among events that can very well be organized with a long-term perspective, their presence in the diary on occasion seems to be owing to objectives that are unrelated to communications goals. It would appear that only to a limited extent is the diary in the control of communicators, who try to use it as an instrument to address a politician's reputational objectives. Other parts of the civil service insist that a substantial share of ministerial time is taken up for commitments related to a different set of publics.

Another limitation to planning at a ministerial level is to do Downing Street interference. Davies experienced how some policy initiatives were claimed by the prime minister. While this does not limit the planning process itself, it curbs the areas and issues of which any politician at cabinet level is in command. Davies also cautions against assuming that newly appointed cabinet ministers are free to direct and steer policies in their department as they think best. Decisions that had been taken by previous ministers of the same party may be less easily altered than initiatives that come up for consideration for the first time. In other words, policy planning is much less comprehensive and often limited by variables outside a cabinet minister's control.

Eustice considers the need for planning in opposition. He refers to communications management operations for David Cameron as leader of the Conservatives prior to 2010. In those days, a weekly meeting of communicators discussed and agreed policies and turned them into a grid that detailed which message would be sent out, how and when. This strategic plan was passed on to media relations staff and speech writers, who were in charge of implementing the plan on a day-to-day basis, overseeing activities and offering technical support. This regular update of communications briefs and instructions suggests the relevance of planning within the opposition's media department, which was expected to work within the planning framework.

A final point of note emerged in the course of interviews. One may want to keep in mind that actions taken or statements made by a politician may be random or ill advised, even though expertise and a planned course of action had been available. At times, interviews and encounters with stakeholders may be planned and aligned with the policy and communications objectives to which politicians had previously agreed. Yet when the situation comes up, they may choose not to adhere to the intended advice. This resistance to planning may be owing to a politician's personality or a poor briefing beforehand, which perhaps lacked clarity or comprehensiveness. While this may be a criticism of internal communications, it is not evidence of a lack of planning.

Recognition of strategic options

How a politician's intended reputation can be constructed is a question related to the selection of an appropriate strategy. The evidence collected suggests that, regardless of strategic considerations raised by communicators, politicians themselves have not always been keen to espouse long-term, strategic reputation planning. In the view of Price, neither Gordon Brown nor

John Major ever had a vision for their premierships, which translated into a strategic deficit in their communications. As both heads of government found it hard to explain the purpose of their respective political visions, it was an uphill struggle for communicators to generate a narrative as a means to prepare, explain and justify policy decisions.

Price argues that the need to think ahead is not always understood by incumbents. In Price's view, Blair considered long-term projects and implications, while his successor, Brown, was too much preoccupied with short-term tactical ramifications. This constrast illustrates how in part a commitment to strategy in communications hinges on an individual's personality or professional background. In part, however, strategy may also be dependent on the kind of issues that emerge on the agenda, which in turn condition the very approach politicians and communicators choose in response (Price). Price observed that government is more likely to integrate big issues such as budget and foreign affairs statements into a communicative strategy. A range of other themes would compete for time to be widely discussed and options of response could not be fully weighed. Price cites the hours following the death of Diana, the Princess of Wales, as a case in point. In this instance polling data and focus group research that would otherwise be necessary to create a balanced response were not forthcoming on the spur of a moment (Price). This reflects another of Price's observations, which questions whether if a strategic underpinning is conceivable at all for at least a number of instantaneous decisions and scenarios. In his view, therefore, politics is, as he puts it, 'an imprecise science'. It is probably more than just a well-informed speculation to surmise that this applies not just to the substance of policy decisions, but also to the communications both of policies and policy makers.

Davies specifically details the case of former Cabinet Minister Jack Straw, who would never get round to planning ahead his communications engagements and statements for more than two weeks. Even the content of columns he wrote as minister was more often than not written under the impulse of the moment and therefore did not constitute part of a grand design or strategy of perception management. The selection process for a theme was anything but strategic, as Davies relates how Straw described his own working style: 'I'd better write my column. What shall I write about? Oh, that's been annoying me. Yeah, I'll write that.'

Jack Straw is said to have agreed to or turned down requests for interviews almost instinctively (Davies). Davies goes on to describe Straw as a person who, rather uncharacteristically for a leading politician, would grant interviews even if he dreaded the questioning and was uncomfortable with a particular subject area. His decisions in relation to what at some distance amounts to a somewhat erratic and not particularly strategic relationship with the media were grounded in his understanding that responsiveness to public questioning was part of what the democratic process required of him. On the other hand there seems to have been what Davies calls a systematic quality control in the sense that Straw and his media staff would not agree to appear on shows and would turn down interview requests if the format, the style and content were not commensurate with Straw's role as a senior cabinet member. The BBC 5 Live programme, for example, would be shunned systematically (Davies).

Likewise, other politicians try to stay clear of any type of public appearance that places them in an awkward or disadvantageous position. They are conscious of their attributes and skills and how any kind of public engagement plays to their perceived qualities. Patricia Hewitt personifies this approach that is not tactical or responsive, but instead well considered and planned. Richards confirms that Hewitt was known to be – as he puts it – 'a very cerebral and academic woman', who sought to strengthen this public perception by making set-piece public appearances that gave her an opportunity to play to her strengths and present big ideas to a sophisticated audience.

Neather explains how Alastair Darling's approach to media relations was carefully considered and guided by a long-term strategy. Essentially, he tried to avoid media contact as best he could during his time as a cabinet member. In the meantime, he cultivated a persona of competence and efficiency both as work and pensions secretary and transport secretary. This low media profile effectively helped to disassociate the minister to some degree from negative stories that might otherwise have caught up with him. Consistent and time-bound attempts to shun public attention count as a communications strategy in its own right, of which PR staff are apparently aware. Darling's successor at the Treasury, George Osborne, has stringently pursued the same communications strategy since moving into No. 11, trying to avoid public statements, press meetings and the like (Neather).

Communicators seek not to be tempted by media requests to diverge from longer-term strategic messages (Waring). Waring is very much aware that a constant concern with day-to-day story handling distracts from the narrative that in the long run is expected to contribute to a politician's reputation. She therefore considers the need to adopt marketers' strategic view, which is more committed to reputational objectives that reach far beyond the lifetime of tomorrow's headline. Kelly talks of zigzagging when he tries to define the relationship between reactive tactics and planned strategy in government communications: 'You zigzag between the typical day-to-day events and your strategic message.' He and others warn that communicators who try to stick slavishly to strategic outlines will lose the connection with relevant publics (Kelly, Hazlewood). Waring, too, concedes that, even though she plans with a long-term perspective in mind, much of her communications work is event driven.

McBride makes the point that the politician's seniority and position in the party or government is taken into consideration when drawing up a strategy to guide style and content of media relations. He explains that the leading politicians such as the prime minister, the chancellor and their respective shadow portfolios in opposition are being covered by news media to a degree that risky media gimmicks or outrageous statements are not needed to catch headlines. However, a strategy of aggressiveness and exaggerating statements may be needed for less prominent political figures to secure public attention (McBride).

McBride reflects on the different approaches to media relations and their respective effects on a politician's reputation. He doubts if the mere attempt to grab headlines and media attention feed into the build-up of a specific public perception. To the contrary, he appears to argue that the objective to secure media coverage requires behaviour and statements that may go counter to the values and features on which one would like to base one's reputation in the long run, and thus harm the foundations of the public persona. Eustice agrees with this diagnosis and points out that some politicians are tempted by daily media headlines. This does not echo the long-term nature of the political process and arguably does little to contribute to the evolution of perceptions and, ultimately, reputation.

It appears that in many cases the advice given and the approach taken in media relations transcends the narrow tactical view and takes strategic features on board. Kelly suggests that, at different stages in the lifetime of a government, different approaches are taken to media relations. He concedes that at least initially the Blair government was eager to act in a way that would shape the subsequent day's headlines, while at a later stage Blair's communications were pursuing objectives that were committed to less generating news. In order to ensure that government communications were not only coordinated, but also served an overarching goal, Blair decided to set up a strategic communications unit at 10 Downing Street, which his successors kept in place as they recognized the need to organize communications tactics strategically (Price).

McBride sees the politicians' communicators as the resource for strategic advice. We may infer from this that the decisions which politicians take in their public relations may be contingent on the quality and kind of advice they receive. Eustice makes an interesting distinction between communicators who are trained in journalism and those of have a background in marketing. It is argued that journalists tend to take a more tactical view of communications. They are also more inclined to have their actions guided by what is needed to satisfy journalists' requests. By contrast, marketing staff have a tendency to plan ahead and align their actions to corporate and communications objectives. Two cases in point are the former tabloid journalists and erstwhile directors of government communications Alastair Campbell and Andy Coulson, both of whom were by intuition reactive, and only after a while came round to projecting strategic messages (Eustice). By contrast, Peter Mandelson is seen as the stereotypical strategic communicator who, in the view of Kettle, in the 1980s was the first adviser in the Labour Party to speak of communications strategy. In the view of Eustice, a successful political communicator would have to give up being a journalist and assume a marketer's mindset.

It has been argued that the objectives which strategic advice is meant to help to achieve are at times not fully known and agreed among politicians and their respective advisers. To illustrate this, McBride cites the case of Alan Johnson. While he may not have been sufficiently ambitious to covet the prime ministerial job, his advisers allegedly worked towards this target. This case illustrates that the internal communications between politician and advisers may not always be fully functional. In this case it may be difficult for the politician and his team to work jointly towards aligned communications objectives as the strategic advice will be blurred at best, and ineffective at worst. McBride clarifies that good strategic advice is contingent on a staff's ability and willingness to place the politician's personality and interests at the centre of considerations and above their respective personal ambitions.

While Jones emphasizes that government politicians are taking a long-term and systematic view of public perceptions and their respective positioning in the political spectrum, he implicitly agrees that the quality of advice is not necessarily grounded in research or guided towards serving a politician's best interests. Michael Portillo's image as a hard-line Thatcherite hopeful throughout the early and mid-1990s draws attention to Jones's point. Portillo's media adviser apparently sought to manoeuvre him into an ideological right-wing position with which allegedly he was not happy (Jones).

Richards stresses a closely related point. Advice tends to be more intuitive than research led, which makes claims to a strategic underpinning appear shaky. Richards, for instance, suggests that government advisers ground their suggestions in their personal experiences with and backgrounds in particular sections of society. Likewise, Kelly from Northern Ireland would vindicate the quality of his advice to the prime minister in connection with the Good Friday Agreement in 1998 with his personal roots in the Province (Kelly). He advocated that based on his intuitive appreciation of the public opinion in the Province and the conversations he overheard among supporters of local rugby matches, government policy on Northern Ireland had to be adapted and decommissioning needed to be emphasized.

Eustice, a former media adviser to Cameron, places strategic communications planning in a broader context and explains how research and a good understanding of the politician's personality and aims, as well as the immediate political environment, are indispensable in the forming of a strategic plan. Eustice implies that it is in the nature of communications strategy to recognize and address the discrepancy between what people think about an individual and the person's actual qualities. To illustrate this, Eustice highlights how in his view the public perception of Michael Howard as having 'something of the dark' about him would not match the decent and kind personality Howard allegedly displayed with his staff. Eustice contrasts this analysis with his experience as part of Cameron's communications team. They had to deal with a politician whose actual personality and perceived character were not as far apart as in the case of Howard. This insight would help to understand which messages were to be communicated and build a strategy.

In other words, the person who needed to be presented on the one hand and the audience's existing perceptions on the other are the variables that guide the selection of appropriate communications activities. Only one of these variables appears to have been considered when, following the 1997 election, William Hague succeeded as leader of the Conservative Party. While advisers focused on what they understood to be public expectations, they largely neglected a thorough analysis of Hague's actual strengths and qualities to the detriment of their subsequent strategic approach. Wood agrees that relevant publics expected the Conservatives to present themselves as a reformed, modern and outward-looking party. The new leader and his wife were expected to espouse these qualities and their media advisers skewed their public engagements in a way that would demonstrate this. Hence, Hague was, for instance, seen visiting the Notting Hill Carnival in the expectation that this unconventional setting might reflect on his own brand. This strategy reputedly failed since the second relevant variable was being ignored in this design: Hague's personality did not match the intended image. This tangible mismatch led to the adoption of a strategy that had detrimental effects on the public perception (Wood).

By contrast, New Labour demonstrated how policies and communications were blended in a unified strategic approach to reform the perception of the party. Hill reminds us that this strategic design only became feasible once it gained backing among key groups in the party. Eventually, this strategy was sustained and followed up by members and officials once it had become evident that it was a recipe to re-establish Labour's electoral fortunes. It is probably critical to point out that in Hill's view, reputation is linked to behaviour in general and political decisions in particular. Strategic communications would generate and add to the narrative that helps explain and justify decisions. Eustice agrees and suggests that a strategic perspective requires presentational aspects to be considered in combination with the policies, since from an audience's perspective behaviour and messages are by necessity associated. In his answers he deals with Cameron's efforts to take the Conservative Party out of its 'comfort zone' (Eustice) by advocating both new policies that were aligned with new messages. Blair in his days and Cameron years later recognized that a change in communications was insufficient as long as the product brand of their respective parties stayed the same (Greer). Since change in the party was instigated in both cases by the leader, implications for their respective personal reputation are conceivable (Greer).

Davies reminds us that at a smaller scale a politician's personal behaviour is translated into messages as well. He identified honesty and his insistence not to over-promise as features that defined Jack Straw's values, which were expected to add to his public persona. Davies reminds us how poorly devised or over-ambitious policies may immediately lead to problematic media relations, which have a tangible knock-on effect on the politician's reputation. He mentions pledges made by Gordon Brown as prime minister to reduce incidents of violent crime by banning the carrying of knives and to introduce a mandatory sentence for all who still did. While the Department of Justice and the judiciary thought these arrangements were impracticable and would not work, Brown went ahead in announcing them, only to see this policy backfire shortly afterwards when the independent judiciary refused to pass the mandatory sentences to which the government had pledged itself.

In this context Kelly warns us of the risks incurred as a result of inconsistent policy pledges and over-ambitious promises. He raised the point in response to a question about adapting messages to match them to expectations held by specific audiences. In his view, the head of communications has to ensure consistency or take up the point with the politician in charge. According to Kelly's opinion, mixed and contradicting messages are picked up by audiences and what initially may perhaps just have been a routine policy statement may develop into a crisis situation if it emerged that the policy and pledge are poorly aligned.

Considerations of timing

There appears to be a view of time as a resource in strategic communications. The need to transcend day-to-day tactical considerations and plan for a longer period of time is stressed by Thorogood. Waring even defines success in reputation management as being contingent on good timing. In her view, to do or say the right thing at the right moment is critical to constructing reputation. Timing is pivotal as the environment changes. In other words, public opinion is volatile and, for a politician to resonate with the public, an accurate understanding of expectations linked to a good sense of timing are, in Waring's view, instrumental in shaping public perceptions. Waring illustrates her view by detailing the timeline of Business Secretary Vince Cable's public statements about an economic downturn. Apparently, Cable had predicted the slump in the economy years before it actually occurred. He also identified the housing bubble as a key factor that at some point would trigger economic turmoil. Since at the time the housing market was profitable, the media were not eager to pick up on Cable's warning, which at the time was anything but popular among investors. This only changed when the market crashed and the media went in search of causes, culprits and answers. It then became obvious that Cable's foresight testified to his competence as an economist and suggested that he might have the qualities one would wish to see represented in government. In brief, not only the content of policy statements and decisions is relevant; timing them for when it is most likely that they will find broad approval is a strategic function that, arguably not just in the case of Vince Cable, can make a difference to the public perception of a politician.

From the government's perspective time is a factor that decides if actions and communications are tactical or, alternatively, planned and forward looking. With time available, government can fine-tune policies and present them in a way that key publics may consider acceptable (Macrory). Environment Secretary Caroline Spelman's bill to privatize the forests, which eventually had to be withdrawn amid widespread opposition, arguably might have stood a better chance of winning hearts and minds had it – with a more generous time budget – been more thoroughly prepared and alliances been built beforehand (Macrory).

Livermore takes this train of thought even further. While for Macrory time is instrumental in implementing policies, Livermore considers both policies and timing as tools in the communicator's weaponry. He insists that politicians may usually have limited flexibility with the kind of political objectives they pursue, yet the timing should still be flexible and allow the communicator to organize the sequence and emphasis of political initiatives with a view to achieving the highest effect on key publics.

Stevenson more specifically points out that a number of senior government politicians can make better use of the time factor as the role of their departmental brief allows them to control actions and communications. By contrast, politicians in opposition are said to find it harder to set and time the agenda, and instead end up reacting to policy decisions and announcements, the timing of which was set by government (Livermore). Waring cautions against this conclusion by arguing that, while previous governments did have control over the timing of policy initiatives, in the era of the spending review and considerable budgetary austerity, the departmental privilege to launch costly political initiative is diminished.

Linking policies and reputation

What to policy advisers seems a reasonable decision, from a communicator's perspective may appear detrimental to a politician's reputation (Price). Stevenson acknowledges that communication shapes both the public's perceptions of politicians as well as opinions about the very policies being pursued. The line between presentation and policy becomes even more blurred by the fact that special advisers to minister are tasked with dealing both with policies and media relations (Richards).

Thorogood reminds us that the whole range of communications activities is planned with policies in mind. She claims that media relations in particular are pivotal in preparing stakeholders for policies that may subsequently be introduced. The intention is to send out messages that help publics understand and view sympathetically specific policy announcements and decisions (Thorogood).

Livermore considers the implications of these considerations and reflects on the relationship between policy and reputation. In his view, reputation in politics is the driving force. Once the intended reputation is agreed, communications strategies and policies are drawn up in support. In the course of the interview Livermore clarifies his position by arguing that the sequence and timing of policies as well as their presentation are instrumental in moulding reputation.

The close link between public relations activities on the one hand and policy issues on the other is illustrated by Eustice, who explains how Cameron's identity and intended public persona were being defined immediately after his election as Conservative Party leader in 2005. From then on, policy initiatives and statements were being aligned with what Eustice calls Cameron's 'character type issues'. This was deemed necessary in order to bring structure and direction into the media relations, the effectiveness of which hinged on consistency.

Such a close link between political decisions and the public persona may also have damaging effects, as McBride points out by reminding us of Prime Minister Brown's decision not to call an election shortly after he took over from Tony Blair. In the words of McBride, Brown subsequently was accused of 'being a bottler'. He details how a politician who over years had acquired a reputation for being single minded and even 'stubborn' was now described as being indecisive (McBride). Jones concurs and explains that the politically motivated decision not to call an election revealed that Brown did not have 'the killer instinct'.

Politicians who newly emerge on the political radar and whom both the media and the electorate seek to understand and categorize need to associate themselves with events or policies. Stacey believes that, for a politician who only recently became visible on the public stage, a joke, a particularly good speech, a youthful and dynamic appearance or similar features would 'distil a lot of things and kind of set somebody's reputation' (Stacey). To illustrate this he mentions Cameron's visit to the Arctic, which helped to portray his green credentials.

Rather than doing an analysis of media stunts, it is perhaps more interesting to see if policies are drawn up with the explicit intention of designing a politician's public profile and ultimately establishing a politician's reputation. Price takes up this question by pointing out that some politicians manage to combine their notion of what is the right policy for their country with an understanding of what can further their own public persona. He argues that, in political communications, politicians need to make use of big decisions and harness their symbolic value to feed into their reputation. Price cites, for instance, Tony Blair's reaction to the death of Princess Diana, or decisions taken in response to terrorist threats. Price seems to be thinking of politicians who interpret events and decisions in a way that vindicates or praises their respective behaviour.

Politicians in some instances seem to reinvent themselves, which specifically requires a reconsideration and repositioning of their policies and political objectives. Iain Duncan Smith seems to be a case in point, which Macrory mentions. In his view, this radical shift in political emphasis and personal political agenda was a long-term engagement that could not have been advised or orchestrated by communications staff. He argues that in the case of Duncan Smith it is a function of his genuine interest in and passion for welfare reform of which he became more aware once his stint at the helm of the party was over. Wood insists Duncan Smith was aware that policy change as the most effective approach to image change. Here the difficulty in pinpointing the motivation behind policy decisions becomes clear, particularly as

Duncan Smith's interest in social welfare reform was allegedly not a deliberate attempt to redesign his reputation.

Stacey contrasts this case with the challenge faced by Labour leader and hopeful for the next general election Ed Miliband, who spent the first months as leader trying to rid himself of the pejorative categorization 'Red Ed', which the media came up with to describe his policies. His advisers seemed to recognize early on that a left-wing opposition leader might not be electable. Henceforth, Miliband refused to endorse public service union strikes against government cutbacks and turned down invitations to speak at their demonstrations. Indeed, his public statements about the protests were judged to be critical rather than encouraging (Stacey). Stacey is adamant that this behaviour and the policy statements were closely tied into strategic efforts to reposition Miliband as a mainstream politician who is seen as a potential national leader rather than a union protester. Richards made a similar observation. He found that initially Ed Miliband was portrayed as indecisive, which required him to take stances on policy issues that appeared bold, courageous and direct. The choice of his leadership team afforded him an opportunity to appear single minded, which is the kind of message that would impress itself on the minds of people and in the long run alter his public persona (Richards).

Jones expands on this point by stressing that policy issues tend to be ignored if it is difficult to communicate them. He lists the renewal of the energy infrastructure by building new power stations, as well as problems with benefit fraud and the extension of Heathrow Airport, as examples of issues that the Labour government was unwilling to tackle, since communicators were not sure how to connect them to public sentiments. From this, one may want to extrapolate that individual politicians make a careful choice as to with which policies they like to be personally associated, while bearing in mind that this selection might have an impact on their public persona. Jones and Greer summarize that politicians tend to bear in mind that a policy they advocate needs to be marketable and saleable.

The ability of ministers to select, advocate and shape policies that match or boost their reputation is limited by variables they cannot control. I mentioned the impact of unpredictable events elsewhere in this chapter. In this context it is worth mentioning the government's own agenda directed by the prime minister, who tasks cabinet members with policies they are expected to implement regardless of consequences to their public persona. Richards reminds us of Caroline Spelman, who as a minister in Cameron's cabinet was tasked with introducing a policy that envisaged the sale of forests. She encountered heavy opposition and was forced to withdraw her bill, which she might never have wanted to support and see associated with her name in the first place (Richards). In a similar case, Patricia Hewitt did a disservice to her public persona when years earlier Prime Minister Blair tasked her with reforming the National Health Service (NHS), which earned her strong protests from nurses (Richards).

Richards points out that ministerial freedom to act is limited not only by prime ministerial interference, but also by the party manifesto and at times by a coalition agreement: 'So they are often projecting an image that is not really of their own making.' Admittedly, prominent politicians with a high public profile who represent a coalition party other than the prime minister's may enjoy more freedom to manoeuvre and to some degree pursue their own agenda (Waring).

Davies made a similar point with regard to the focus of British foreign policy during the final Blair years. Since the prime minister claimed responsibility for the Iraq policy, the foreign secretary needed to find niches in which to assert his own effectiveness. Davies recalled that Straw decided to focus his attention on Iran instead, and helped to defuse a conflict between Pakistan and India. Also Britain's efforts to push Turkey towards European Union (EU) membership is a policy that, in the view of Davies, 'probably wouldn't have happened' without Straw's contribution. These initiatives may have helped to mould the public perception of Straw.

Richards raises the point that, in the absence of appropriate actions and policies as a tool to differentiate and position a politician's public persona, conflicts – real and fabricated – may be used to communicate messages. He mentions Tony Blair in particular, who deliberately picked fights in the media with members of his own party in an effort to position himself. Richards appears to suggest that it is important to select adversaries carefully. This would be a way of distinguishing oneself from either the right or the left of one's own movement. Arguably, it is easier for former advisers to concede that policies or controversies may only have been pursued as a means to build up a politician's reputation. This cautioning one should perhaps bear in mind when reading the claim made by Vince Cable's current media adviser that policies in government are predominantly advocated in pursuit of a principle or for the good of the country, and not in an effort to build an image (Waring).

When decisions and policies are drawn up that impact on a politician's reputation, it would be interesting to know if communicators have a say and are involved. Since decisions appear to have repercussions that affect public perceptions, it is worth asking if communicators therefore consider policy design as part of their brief. It appears that the divide between policy and presentational issues can apparently be bridged through close collaboration. As a result of close internal collaboration, Stevenson suggests that a disconnect between decision makers at a higher hierarchical level and communicators lower down in the organizational chart did not exist in the years of the Labour government. When Cameron took over office the collaboration between decision makers and communicators apparently continued: for Eustice, the link between the two is a must, as communications managers make judgements and recommendations about the timing of policies. This in reverse implies that they may suggest whether certain policies should stay on or off the agenda for strategic communicative reasons. For instance, it was agreed that Cameron as leader of the opposition would continue to talk about immigration. The rationale for this was the notion that, if immigration resurfaced in the national debate, Cameron could claim that he had been taking this issue seriously long before it reappeared in the popular media (Eustice).

Both Jones and Hill detail that for Tony Blair communicators pointed out the media relations implications of policy options and tried to make predictions as to how the media would be most likely to react. However, Hill makes it plain that after these considerations it would be upon the politician to decide the policy. Hill is aware of the fine line between getting involved in the policy making and the media advising, and defines this line as follows:

> I know what my job is, and my job is to support what you are trying to achieve, but it is also to advise very firmly in terms of developing your success in this field and your reputation. If you do it, you do it like this, if you do it now you will cause more harm than good. So do it later and do it like this are certainly things that you can be involved in. But, but, but saying that, I'm sorry you can't ... that policy is wrong, I think you should introduce that policy, that goes ... that's a step farther, a step too far, that, and you don't really do that.

The Conservative Party director of communications is credited by Macrory with a similarly powerful role. He is said to influence which politician is to represent the party on a specific news programme. The rationale for this selection is grounded in the agenda that directors of communications wish to promote and the issues they wish to take off the media agenda by refusing to provide broadcasters with senior members who are likely to offer a statement about these very subjects (Macrory). To what degree special media advisers consider it their responsibility to stop or to alter a policy that may have a detrimental effect on the minister's reputation is hard to define. Davies confirms:

> Yes, I am sure that went on a lot, absolutely [...] They would definitely, try and keep their minister away from something that they felt was going to look bad for them publicly, media wise, parliamentary wise, whatever, absolutely. I mean without a shadow of a doubt.

One may take this speculation somewhat further, as Jones does, and imagine how communicators have been involved in the most central decisions that a political party has to take: the selection of the party leader. Jones, however, does not provide any more evidence to back up this speculation. His notion of the communicator's role in the process leading to the selection of a party leader is based on anecdotal evidence, gathered throughout his career in political journalism.

6 Managing news

Comparing communicative styles

Communicative style varies from politician to politician. Abilities and techniques of communication hinge on personality traits and training. Also the willingness to consider communications as a management function that requires objectives, strategy and planning is not universally espoused by politicians. Yet Eustice makes the point that today leading politicians cannot afford to ignore communications advice: 'They would not last very long in politics.' He is arguing that the breed of politician who would happily concentrate on the politics of the job and leave the presentational matters to others has become inconceivable. Jones has observed during recent years how politicians have recognized the necessity of honing their skills as celebrity performers. It seems to be evident to Jones that the media solicit celebrity status from individuals in exchange for publicity. Jones calls Cameron's readiness to open up his private sphere to journalists as well as his decision to allow the media to share in his family life unprecedented and evidence that he 'plays the media very, very well'. Redfern adds that Tony Blair should be credited with blending content, forcefulness and personality in his personal communications.

Jones acknowledges that the level of interest in and concern with personal presentation varies between politicians and reminds us that some are more prepared to engage with media opportunities than others. The success of personal presentation of candidates and incumbents in the view of Jones depends in part at least on the politician's desire to engage in it. Arguably, the technical knowhow and strategic advice available to party leaders is understood to be solid due to the financial resources earmarked for the purpose. Moreover, experts are readily available, since working for party headquarters comes with professional prestige.

Having said this, there appear to be tangible differences in the quality of personal communications. Some leading politicians seem to outperform others, regardless of the strategic management support at their disposal. Jones mentions how, due to a candidate's or incumbent's personality, both tactical and strategic efforts in perception management may fail. William Hague's image as a 'freak' (Jones), as well as perceptions of Gordon Brown as 'mad' (Jones), were characteristics that throughout their respective leadership tenures would never go away regardless of considerable efforts by media advisers, who, for instance, encouraged Brown to be seen with a girlfriend in public in order to appear as normal and human (Jones).

Tony Blair, by contrast, is said to have had a natural talent for taking media advice and dealing with both the media and audiences more comfortably. Jones reminds us of Blair's visit to Moscow in the 1990s where by invitation of the British embassy he travelled on the metro and naturally posed to photographers as a man on his way to work. This scene not only made it to the front pages of the papers but also reiterated the image of Blair as a normal citizen – a tag highly coveted by leading politicians, who are constantly afraid of being portrayed as aloof (Jones).

Beattie specifies that an individual's lack of presentational talent may cut across efforts to manage images strategically. He acknowledges that the impact of communications advisers on the quality of a leading politician's public perception may be tangible. However, he cautions anyone to think that expertise and staff resources are the communicative panacea for a struggling politician. Instead, Beattie argues that an otherwise gifted contender can be helped to improve their performance in public, while someone who lacks looks and confidence with audiences is bound to fail no matter what kind of support is available. He mentions the Labour leader Ed Miliband to illustrate his point. In Jones's view, Miliband is 'the most uncomfortable person with the media'. Jones believes Ed Miliband does not understand the media and how it operates. Richards adds a different example to the argument by pointing out that Gordon Brown had never been popular with the electorate, and as time went on he even repelled people. His communicative skills and his ability to take on and use communications advice are perhaps best characterized by a joking remark attributed to Lord Mandelson, who was frustrated with Gordon Brown's inept presentational style. Mandelson allegedly claimed Brown would not even manage to keep his tie straight (Richards).

Livermore believes that, in part, Brown's poor personal communications were related to his decision-making style. He is known to take a considerable amount of time to make up his mind. As chancellor he may have had this time to reflect, but in the prime minister's office external and internal events had to be faced and responded to at a high frequency, which put Brown on to the back foot and placed him in a position that never allowed him to regain the initiative. This frustration with Brown was shared by other advisers. When it became evident that Brown could not deliver as a public performer, many decided that they had better leave Downing Street (Redfern).

Jones suggests that Brown's lack of presentational talent may have been matched by his unwillingness to take on board communications advice (Jones, Redfern). In fact, as Jones points out, even intense efforts by his media handlers and strategic advisers eventually could not manage to hide Brown's personality as a man who to those close to him appeared to be 'mad' and 'politically obsessive'. Likewise, Neil Kinnock as Labour leader in the 1980s and early 1990s was known for his emotional outbursts. Reporters would be waiting for this temper, and draw it into the centre of their coverage regardless of the messages media advisers tried to push onto the agenda and the style they recommended Kinnock should adopt (Jones). While Kinnock found himself framed as a man lacking self-control, Iain Duncan Smith, who was unable to collaborate with journalists, found himself described in the media as 'peculiar' – a judgement that was similarly damaging to his image (Jones).

Neather illustrates a specific difference in communication styles by comparing Gordon Brown's and Tony Blair's respective approaches to public speaking. He outlines how both Blair's ability to structure a speech as well as his talent in delivering it outclassed Gordon Brown, who limited himself at party conferences largely to delivering a laundry list of achievements and future aspirations. While speech writers appear to have polished specific parts in Brown's oratory, his statements still tended to be confused and confusing, and contained a somewhat random collection of past and future policy initiatives. Neither ability nor training allowed Brown to put the draft of a speech to good use and thrill his audience.

By contrast, Kettle describes meetings with Tony Blair as fascinating as he would give journalists the beguiling sensation he was about to share 'the run of his mind' (Kettle). He describes Blair's personal communication as almost subliminal. The way he portrayed himself as normal and reasonable and used language and gestures to communicate differentiated him markedly from Gordon Brown, who, in the view of Kettle, was deemed a thoroughly ineffective communicator.

In discussions with his staff, Gordon Brown would not openly admit to his rhetorical shortcomings and instead would blame his deficient style on his long stint as chancellor, which he thought forced him over the years to adopt a rather twisted way of setting out his ideas (McBride). Kettle argues that the reason for his poor communication skills can at least in part be explained by his use of an old-fashioned terminology and syntax that Kettle calls 'private language', which meant one thing to Brown and his closest staff and something else to the country. If Kettle's analysis is right, this would make us wonder if and to what degree the communications strategy that seeks to align audiences, objectives style and content can be upset and rendered irrelevant by a politician's ineptitude.

The former Conservative leader Iain Duncan Smith is a case in point: his 2003 party conference speech was deemed of the poorest quality, not for reasons of content but for how it was delivered. Neather stresses that the quality in political speech making is defined only in part by the actual content, but also by the confidence of delivery. At least on the latter account Duncan Smith failed comprehensively. Neather reminds us that, if a speech does not convey the factual or psychological message intended, strategic considerations may be thrown into disarray and objectives not achieved. This problem may have been exacerbated by Duncan Smith's unwillingness to accept and implement media relations advice (Jones).

The role of expertise and resources to ensure high-quality communications remains contentious. If the availability of expert support and resources – quality advice and help with the preparation of public appearances – cannot substantially improve the presentational performance of a politician who by nature tends to feel uncomfortable with the media and struggles as a public performer, we may also conclude that a lack of support and resources may not necessarily preclude a media- and audience-savvy contender from making a mark and gaining the support of audiences. This assumption is made by Stevenson, who refers to John Prescott, the former Labour deputy leader and an individual who for many years commanded considerable public support, even though he had little or no interest in systematic media advice or intense media training.

Apart from polling data, intuition and gut feeling are believed to help politicians find the right tone to address diverse audiences. On this account, too, some politicians have an edge over others. Reactions to the death of Diana, Princess of Wales, were cited to show how political leaders' ability to sense and reflect public opinion made a difference to the quality of their personal presentation and their public persona (Price). Both Blair and Hague had to appear and express their condolences, the wording of which was due to time pressures on this occasion not being grounded in focus group feedback, drawn up and calibrated by the party leaders themselves. While Blair received much acclaim for the words he found, Hague's remarks are far less memorable. Even though he had prepared under the same circumstances, he had 'got it wrong' (Price).

Journalists, communicators and the shaping of narratives

On the following pages I will be asking who actually drafts the storyline that encapsulates politicians' images and answers fundamental questions about their personality, ambitions, policies and abilities – in short, who shapes the narrative of a candidate or incumbent. Hill characterizes a narrative as essential in all political or corporate communications as it helps to establish a message and stick to it consistently over the course of time. The narrative is meant to be 'a clear set of values and ideas and aims […] against which everything is measured' (Hill). It is used as a benchmark and a means to organize messages, public engagements and events in a way that echoes the values encapsulated in the narrative. In other words, the narrative is the storyline that has been defined through the strategy and, while it may at times not match easily, any event or message should be presented or interpreted to fit and support it.

Hill acknowledges that the day-to-day political communications need to be aligned with a long-term perspective. If this is not achieved, audiences may not comprehend the rationale for a candidate's or party's actions, nor do they see how what is being done is consistent with overall objectives. Hill expects communicators 'to convert an event into something which either helps the narrative or doesn't hinder it'. Some events and actions are not only interpreted but explicitly planned and orchestrated to play into the larger narrative. Kelly finds a reduction of EU expenses and Blair's diplomatic activity leading to it in line with and supportive of the narrative of Blair as an internationally recognized champion of British interests.

For Hill, the narrative takes a much more pivotal role and goes beyond the guiding of the day-to-day media relations. It is a focus point to which all communications staff and the politician are committed. This would probably facilitate internal communications as a narrative offers shared ground to participants in strategy discussions, and allows for reflections about content and style of policy and presentational issues. To build this narrative as a tool to shape reputation and to ensure its consistency is seen as the communications adviser's core responsibility (Hill).

In the view of Hill the narrative is apparently set by the politician in collaboration with advisers who spend considerable time thinking through this part of the strategy. He also acknowledges that Prime Minister Blair occasionally would get involved in this discussion to ensure that strategy and narrative were effective. McBride differs in his analysis about the genesis of the narrative. He argues that in reality the narrative emerges and appears to be a negotiated process, driven both by journalists and politicians and their communications staff. McBride recognizes that Prime Minister Brown's decision not to call a general election early on in his premiership, despite signs of pondering the option, was widely interpreted as indecisiveness. He goes on to point out that communicators tried to control the situation and rationalize Brown's behaviour at the time. On the other hand, journalists and their audiences found it hard to believe any of the defensive messages churned out by the Brown team. Communications advisers' assurance that Brown had not been tempted by favourable polls and never really intended to call an election only rekindled the suspicion that he had essentially been dithering and subsequently tried to blame others for decisions he should or should not have taken (McBride). In the context of this research project it is perhaps most interesting to remember how McBride portrays this incident as a defining moment for Brown's narrative, which fed into a reputation that was to stay and might only ever have been remoulded with great difficulty.

It appears that the public's interpretation of a politician's aims, records, actions, successes and failures contributes to what McBride terms a narrative. In other words, it is the interpretation that makes sense of what a politician stands for. Clearly, each side of the political divide would like to control this process, as Eustice implies when he recapitulates the 2005 election campaign. At the time he was spinning a narrative that suggested that Labour's prime minister would make pledges on which he would never deliver, while the Conservative challenger was credibly promising action. Disregarding the factual evidence for this claim, Eustice's attempt was understandable: a narrative, if controlled by the candidate and accepted by the public, can be a defining theme no matter how distant from reality.

Not mentioned by Eustice, but implied by McBride is the media's role in shaping a politician's narrative, which Beattie insists is in turn heavily influenced by the print media and much less by television, which in the UK is committed to party political neutrality. The notion of what politicians stand for and what can be expected of them, in Beattie's view, takes time to shape. Stacey cites as a case in point the initial label stuck to the then new Labour leader Ed Miliband, who by a number of right-wing and centre-right papers was dubbed 'Red Ed' for his alleged political leanings. This label, in the view of Stacey, might have haunted him for years to come, had Miliband not immediately tried to challenge it by repositioning his stance on domestic policies, which allowed him to retake control and counter the leftist tendencies that he was believed to represent. Arguably, the 'Red Ed' label was later replaced by the image of a dithering Miliband who found it hard to take firm and clear decisions. Stacey seemed to suggest that this insinuation, if unchecked, could over time turn into the narrative that clings to the Labour leader.

With regard to the media's perception of a politician, Beattie talks about 'accumulation of coverage', which is judgemental, at times thoroughly critical, and amounts to a build-up of opinion and sentiment. If unchecked, the notion that emerges of specific politicians may be thoroughly derogative and have them end up as the object of sketch writers or the butt of jokes in TV programme such as *Have I Got News for You* (Richards). *The Guardian*, for instance, presented Cameron's head in a male contraceptive to illustrate a critical narrative that appeared to take shape in the print media.

This case, however, reminds us that narratives can change over time, which Jones illustrates in more detail. He touches upon the implicit collaboration between the opposition and the media in maintaining or changing the government's and Cameron's narrative, which at the time of interviewing in February 2011 was grounded in support for the coalition, its economic policy and the prime minister. Jones points out that the media may well want to change the interpretation of one or all three of these claims. This change in attitudes towards the prime minister might be facilitated if the leading opposition party gained credibility on economic issues: in Jones's view this was critical if Labour wanted to make voters forget how its own narrative in the preceding months had been tainted by the economic downturn and attacks by the conservative media that linked Labour to overspending and financial deregulation, which allegedly had been a cause of the economic trouble into which the country had slid. Jones cautions that it is hard or impossible to predict if and when the narrative of Cameron's government or the opposition party might change.

News reporting and its consequences for the public persona

Personality, personalization and an individual's public persona appear to be features to which journalists direct attention in political news reporting. To put this into perspective, Neather suggests that the focus on individuals and their respective reputation is by no means a new phenomenon. At the same time, political communicators have intensified their efforts to manage images just as the news outlets have reached unprecedented levels of competitiveness with the advent of 24-hour TV news, increasing numbers of broadcasters and the incremental growth of internet news services. These structural developments are thought to have led to the practice of reputation management for individual politicians on 'a much more comprehensive and continuous basis' (Neather) than before. Jones identified the same phenomenon and describes politicians' opportunities to present themselves to mass audiences as a function of relentless competition within a growing media.

This relevance of projecting a politician's public persona in the media subsequently leads to more careful media relations (Stevenson). Clearly, the reason why politicians would want to gauge and predict how the media treats an issue is understood to result from journalists' presumptive roles as gatekeepers who present politicians and their policies to key stakeholders. McBride takes up this point and looks at a scenario that illustrates the media's power to develop a public persona. The case he refers to quite dramatically highlights how Prime Minister Brown in a number of media exposures was expected to play by the media's rules. With regard to media coverage, there seems to be considerable power residing with the journalist who dictates issues of content and style, even though this may not allow politicians to emphasize their strengths, features and core messages, which might otherwise have helped to expose their personality more authentically.

The incident mentioned by McBride also evidences how media may over-interpret statements in a way that is outside the communicators' control. The case proffered was Brown's reluctant expression on a radio show of his cautious preference for a music group he barely knew, given to a presenter whose questioning he was displeased with but found impossible to evade. Newswires took Brown's quote out of context, and overstated it to add effect: 'Gordon Brown says he wakes up every morning to the Arctic Monkeys', the news presenter is quoted by McBride as having said.

Politicians regularly seem to be concerned that the media's rationale leads at times to the misinterpretation and distortion of policy content to a point where their initial intentions are no longer recognizable. George Eustice reminds us of headlines that suggested that the Conservative leader David Cameron was soft on crime when he tried to explain the situation of young offenders who suffered from a lack of support in society and limited opportunities in life. The media soon notoriously dubbed his stance as the 'hug a hoodie' policy (Eustice). In Eustice's view, Cameron's intentions had been to encourage society to take responsibility for their children and thus to prevent them from turning into criminals.

The level of interest demonstrated among journalists is also beyond the communicators' control. Still, this lack of control over news reporting may not always be detrimental, as Katie Waring points out with regard to

Business Secretary Vince Cable. His professional record as an economics expert who prior to the recession had pointed to flaws in the economy attracted the media's interest only once the financial downturn had hit. At this point journalists were keen to present a witness in support of their reporting to testify to the government's poor economic judgement. Yet the same issues raised to warn of likely troubles ahead had hardly made inroads into mainstream news reporting in the period leading up to 2008. In other words, Cable's ongoing media relations were not nearly as successful in positioning him as a publicly visible economics expert, as was a change of emphasis in news reporting. In this case a shifting media agenda worked in Cable's favour.

McBride goes on to argue that the framework and rules of engagement in media appearances have been established by journalists, and both communicators and politicians at times are talked into accepting arrangements for collaboration that are not necessarily in their favour. Often the politician is expected to accept the style and emphasis of a broadcast: 'Um, but you almost were saying to him [the politician] you have to do that, that's part of doing this' (McBride).

Hill argues that a communicator's leverage in dealing with journalists hinges in part on the public perception of politicians and their media advisers. He sees his profession defamed and explicitly refers to news stories that framed political communicators as practitioners of the 'dark arts' and 'fiendish spinners ... who were sprinkling dust on stories so that they could change themes'. In the view of Hill, the irony is that the practice of reputation management hinges instead much more on the media that are willing to listen and engage with arguments. He contends that particularly towards the end of the Blair period the media had decided that they were unwilling to take up and consider No. 10's messages. Hill believed that journalists discouraged the public from listening to the government's and its communicators' explanations any more. In brief, once the public standing of politicians and communicators is undermined, their leverage with journalists loses the power to achieve objectives.

From the communicator's perspective the situation is not helped by the media's fickleness when interpreting the politician's reputation. This shiftiness in part explains changes in a politician's public perception. It also encapsulates Eustice's portrayal of news reporting. In his view, journalists' reporting follows a cycle. While initially they may be happy to support an aspiring candidate editorially, at some point they have to reverse direction and attack the same person. The rationale for this alteration in loyalty may be rooted in the media audience's longing for entertainment.

Part of this entertainment in political news reporting seems to be writing up rising celebrities and dragging them down again in the expectation that the audience might enjoy the spectacle (Eustice). What Eustice is saying here amounts to a claim that news reporting is perhaps the strongest factor in the shaping of reputation. He talks of downward and upward spirals of news reporting, but what he is probably trying to say has more to do with framing a public persona rather than reporting per se. The power of news reporting in the process of moulding the public persona is nicely captured in a detail that Eustice mentions only in passing. He claims that even the views of members of the parliamentary party of their own government are guided by judgements generated through the news media. Perhaps we may not agree with Eustice's view of arbitrary news cycles, which cause an entire government to receive negative headlines when perhaps only a cabinet minister's actual political performance is less than impeccable. However, what we might want to take seriously – as it draws on Eustice's longstanding experience as a PR manager – is his acknowledgement that news reporters' framing of a politician's public persona is grounded in a rationale beyond the communicator's control.

Jones fully concurs with this analysis. He reminds us that in 1997 journalists agreed to advocate change for reasons that were not necessarily linked to the quality of government performance but instead to the rationale of media production: 'Well, we'd have a new government, we'd have new ministers, everything would be thrown up and down, it would be great for the media'. Jones goes on to argue that in the run-up to and in between general elections the media hold a distinct agenda of their own, which leads to politicians and their policies being framed regardless of their strategies in political communications management. Jones echoes Eustice's sentiment of the media's tendency to write a politician up and down as it suits them. He admits frankly that 'we love to build somebody up and, you know, when the pack turns, when the dogs turn, you know, we go after them'.

Apparently, the media's tendency to turn against a politician at some point can be found in the cases of Margaret Thatcher, Tony Blair and, more recently, Gordon Brown. While Jones is describing the phenomenon, his analysis falls short of explaining how and under what circumstances the media starts attacking a politician's reputation. While they provide abundant evidence to support and clarify the point, none of my interviewees could confidently identify the trigger of or the indicator for a fundamental change in the narrative.

The pivotal role that news reporting appears to take in the shaping of reputation is indirectly confirmed by Price, who mentions in our interview how the Blair government at least initially judged its success by the amount of 'good headlines and applause' it received. One reason as to why this crude system of public opinion measurement was in place is arguably found in the media's actual power to shape reputation. An alternative explanation as to why communicators allow their judgement to be guided this heavily by news headlines may be related to the professional background of leading communicators, who are often firmly rooted in journalism and whose mindset was generated in the process of this experience. This could explain why Alastair Campbell might have been reluctant to recognize that generating headlines may not be the only criterion of success in political communications (Price).

While admittedly the media are undergoing rapid changes, in the period leading up to and covered by my interviews, the opinion makers may arguably still have been largely newspapers and television news programmes. Jones insists that the personalization is not just reflective of TV's style of reporting, but, instead, the emphasis on personality may well be in the nature of British newspaper tradition. This news culture attributes to editors of print publications a central role in opinion forming that is being picked up by other media. It is important to keep this balance of media power in mind when considering what may trigger a swing in media coverage to the detriment of a politician. In the view of Jones, the print media are pivotal in providing interpretation and thus lead the opinion-shaping process. Yet he concedes that the framing of specific events such as the leadership debates is complemented and sometimes led by television coverage and increasingly influenced by social networking activities (Jones).

Both Price and Eustice recommend not to 'let the media do whatever they want' and allow the politician to 'take all the criticism' (Price). This statement not only implies that the media have their own agenda, which is critical in creating a narrative about government and politicians, but more importantly, it also suggests that communicators consider media relations an instrument that potentially allows them to rein in and alter the media's agenda to some extent and to take ownership of reputation management processes. Jones considers this competitive relationship between communicators and the media as an incentive for and explanation of the professionalization of media relations.

Events and their consequences for reputation management

Tom Kelly shares what is perhaps the most powerful illustration of how events upset planned communications management. On 11 September 2001 Prime Minister Blair visited Brighton to deliver a speech to the Trade Union Congress about the need for reform in public services. With this selection of topic, Blair could be sure to capture his audience's attention. Concurrently, in New York the World Trade Center was hit by two hijacked passenger aircraft. This event instantaneously rendered irrelevant all communications objectives that had been intended and planned for the day. The agenda was upset and Blair's audiences were looking not only for different answers, but for a different theme altogether. The reason why events are a concern to politicians, their communicators and hence this investigation is nicely encapsulated by Richards, who reminds us that reputations are built in a slow step-by-step process, while an adverse event may be all it takes to crack this painstakingly developed public persona.

Anything unforeseen threatens to derail the planned communications process. Events stand for what strategic communicators appreciate least: they are hard to control and difficult to plan for. Andrew Neather therefore credits what he refers to as 'spin' – or the interpretation of events – with only a limited effect on the communications outcome. Katie Waring, the head of communications to the business secretary, estimates that 95 per cent of her daily routine is determined by unexpected events, and a meagre 5 per cent has been planned beforehand. In her view, the 24-hour news cycle and global news reporting have led to the agenda being driven by events. George Eustice adds that in opposition, too, communicators predominantly spend their time doing what he refers to as 'fire fighting'. Unsolicited issues with which he would have to deal range from problematic remarks by backbench MPs to allegations of fraud against councillors.

Neather acknowledges, therefore, that both politicians and communicators find events awkward to address and therefore try to minimize both their occurrence and impact. To this effect, cabinet ministers and particularly the prime minister's office maintain a grid tool, which allows forward planning and integration of events and policies as much as they are foreseeable, to suit the politician's agenda. This is an attempt to anticipate events, to frame them in support of one's respective agenda, and to align their interpretation with planned speeches, budget forecasts or policy announcements. What this grid is derailed by time and again are adverse events, which are difficult or impossible to integrate into the politician's narrative, such as, for instance, the announcement of new job redundancies. Beattie adds talk of sex scandals and question marks over the leader's calibre to this list of unforeseen incidents that can easily overshadow all planned messages (Beattie, Macrory).

Livermore differentiates the degree to which politicians need to deal with unpredictable incidents. In his view, the chancellor – as indeed other cabinet ministers – is less affected by adverse events that emerge in day-to-day politics than is the prime minister. This is because a chancellor is not directly associated with any specific policy area to which one would expect him to respond publicly. At the same time, he is not endowed with an overarching responsibility such as the prime minister, who would be associated with and publicly quizzed about any incident that turns into a major public debate. Livermore makes it quite clear that the prime minister is ultimately not free to select at will the themes he engages with and to stage manage all his appearances. His diary therefore is arguably more driven by events than that of the chancellor. This leads to a multitude of variables to be considered during a prime minister's day that constitute a risk in their own right. Specific unforeseen events may cause prime ministers to seem responsive rather than active, apologetic rather than confident, which can affect their reputation tangibly. The government of David Cameron was apparently aware of this risk, and so policy tasks and issue management were systematically devolved to the individual departments to save the prime minister from involvement with concerns with which he might not want to be associated. Kelly remained suspicious of this modus operandi, and found that the approach had failed within the first 12 months of Cameron's government.

An alternative way to conceptualize events is to think of them in terms of a self-inflicted scandal. Richards mentions particularly John Prescott, whose idiosyncratic behaviour engulfed his career with issues that were neither planned nor intended. Richards mentions the episode that saw Prescott punch a voter and reminds us of reports that detailed the former deputy prime minister's affair with his secretary. Apparently, none of these incidents has ruptured his career, even though other politicians might arguably have resigned over lesser offences. In other words, events may in part be self-inflicted, while the consequences for the individual politician involved may be unpredictable.

Events may also be engendered by deficient planning. Neather illustrates this category of events by relating an incident dating back to his stint as the prime minister's speech writer. At the time he had drawn up a speech about education, the thrust of which would resonate negatively with the Treasury, to which Neather had passed the draft shortly before it was due to be delivered. In turn, the recipient at the Treasury Department seemed to have leaked the text to the media, which immediately started framing the intended messages critically before they had even been raised in public by the prime minister. In other words, adverse incidents may be generated by individuals within the same office, party or government, and likewise are beyond the communicator's full control.

Greer concurs and reminds us that politicians may unwittingly invite scathing media coverage when they blatantly fail to forecast developments or act slowly in response to a predictable scenario. Greer contends that politicians may occasionally have the information to anticipate events and still fail to engage in considered responses. To illustrate this, Greer refers to the failure of public bodies to prepare for and deal with heavy snowfall in winter, which has led to resignations in the Scottish government.

At times, responses to adverse developments do not receive the required long-term, comprehensive research and planning. A mere lack of attention to detail in day-to-day media relations repeatedly generates critical comments and images, which, in the view of Stacey, accumulate and feed adversely into a politician's reputation. He cites a picture taken of the former Liberal Democrat leader Sir Menzies Campbell as he was staring at a toilet, or David Miliband who was photographed when munching a banana. Stacey argues that a streak of these and similar minor anecdotal blunders and embarrassments over time inadvertently shape a politician's public persona.

Those politicians who try to predict events and anticipate responses, in the view of Jason Beattie, may come prepared and thus stand a chance of interpreting them in their favour (Beattie). Davies even talks of opportunities when politicians succeed in framing incidents in line with public expectations and sentiments. More specifically, he points out that 'you sometimes can't do anything about the event but you can do something about how you handle it'. How events should be handled is reflected upon by Davies, who suggests that the electorate expects politicians to demonstrate clarity and confidence in difficult situations. To illustrate this, he relates a widely reported case of a murderer who was being hunted by the police. Prime Minister Cameron at the time commented that crime was part of life and, while he promised that the police had tried their best to get hold of the culprits, he cautioned that one could not guarantee that similar cases would not occur in future. In Davies's view, this was a skilful and wise response. A guarantee to rule out these crimes once and for all would probably be ill advised, as this pledge in all likelihood could not be kept. In the view of Davies, therefore, events appear to be an opportunity for politicians to demonstrate how they deal with unpredictable, difficult challenges. If the handling of a challenge is applauded by the public, the incident may even pay into the politician's reputation.

McBride recounts a similar strategy applied during the foot and mouth epidemic in cows, when Prime Minister Brown gave his impromptu media statements in the poorly lit corridors in Downing Street with evident lack of attention to his hair and attire. On ending his statement, he abruptly turned away from the journalists to return to work, while the cameras were still running. These appearances carried the message of the committed, hands-on and hard-working politician who was dedicated only to his country's good, and patently paid little or no attention to sophisticated presentational concerns. While the foot and mouth epidemic certainly was an undesired and unplanned adversity that brought inconvenience to many and material loss to a good number of families in farming communities, Gordon Brown used this situation to portray himself as the no-nonsense manager type who gets things done.

Likewise, Brown's decision at the height of the epidemic to drive down from his Scottish constituency to London at 3 am in order to be in time to chair a morning meeting of his crisis management team was a skilful ploy. He used the emergency situation to create a feeling of urgency. This gave him an opportunity to respond in a way that conjured up images of an ever-present crisis manager – an association that eventually helped to build his reputation. However, it should be added that what appeared to be a strategic approach to dealing with the situation had arguably not been developed by communicators. Instead, it was a decision that Brown at the time thought necessary for the sake of handling the crisis – not the ensuing media perception (McBride). This detail does not diminish its communicative value but cautions against the conclusion that this scenario was managed exclusively with Brown's public persona in mind. This case may even draw into question the special adviser's function and ability to offer and pursue strategic communications advice. McBride on this occasion at least was happy to follow the prime minister's lead.

Contingency planning and protecting perceptions

While there appears to be agreement that events can potentially make or break a politician's career and certainly impact heavily on public perception, there is astonishingly little attention placed on long-term contingency planning (Greer). The reason for this lack of planning may be to do with the breadth of items for which a politician or government department needs to prepare (Neather).

The Home Office, for example, is responsible for a variety of issues, ranging from prison to courts and asylum seekers, and is therefore perhaps not entirely typical of other government departments that deal with a more limited portfolio. Neather claims that adverse events 'essentially come out of nowhere' (Neather), and estimates that the Home Office might have to include a hundred different potential incident scenarios in a contingency plan.

It is pointed out that government departments such as the Home Office do have memos and statements ready in response to eventualities, which illustrate what measures the department is taking and has taken in the past to deal with the situation. However, in Neather's view, this does not amount to a comprehensive and in any way effective contingency planning activity, as the consequences of policy flaws, technical mistakes or private scandals are hard to contain regardless of memos anticipating them. Neather concludes, therefore: 'I don't think you can plan for it.' His acknowledgement that a concurrent catastrophe elsewhere in the world might deflect media attention from domestic adverse events may be a valuable strategic consideration. A competing news story as a means of diversion appears to be what communicators hope for in response to a contingency situation on their own turf. In other words, this suggests that communicators may place their hopes in a coincidence if contingency planning is not forthcoming (Neather).

McBride illustrates how little forward planning exists in anticipation of a contingency situation when media pressure mounts and a guideline on what to say, where and how to respond may be of help. He contends that, while a communications crisis is being dealt with, public expectations and reactions should ideally be gauged in order to calibrate responses and decide on next steps. This systematic and measured approach that could lead to an adaptation of strategy and action and may thus be instrumental in saving reputation is not planned for in government communications. Instead, when media pressure is at an apex, communicators hurriedly research options, decide on strategy and respond simultaneously. Arguably, the team responsible for this response is made up of the same limited number of people upon whom the day-to-day protection of reputation hinges, regardless of the intensity of public pressure and media interest.

McBride indirectly also clarifies that the usual time constraints arguably do not always allow for staff members to have their minds on the ultimate and long-term communications objectives and potential obstacles likely to be encountered on the way to achieving them. We may therefore be sceptical and question if ever or under what circumstances communicators are sufficiently committed to planning for and the consideration of contingencies.

While long-term contingency planning seems to gain little attention, at a more short-term, technical level, an attempt is being made to control and avoid crisis situations. Interestingly, politicians both in government and opposition at times engage in detailed management of their day-to-day media relations to ensure that style and content are on message and cannot be misconstrued. To achieve this, technical tools are used. Apart from the provision of technical support, politicians are trained to demonstrate a considerable level of self-discipline to stay on message. While none of this amounts to long-term or even medium-term forward planning, it does account for the reduction in adverse incidents and political gaffes. Hill stresses the relevance of this point by reminding us how a lack of attention to detail in presentation and rhetoric may upset media relations.

Another reason why attention to the details of content and presentation is perhaps accepted to be the only viable recipe for contingency planning is given by Eustice. He refers to policy gaffes that occurred during Cameron's first 12 months in office, and particularly points out plans to privatize forests and school sports funding. Eustice claims that the prime minister's eagerness to get decisions taken was the cause for these contingency situations, which caused the government embarrassment and forced it to withdraw policies. Eustice mentions that these issues may initially not 'have had the attention of the top team, but were burning away and suddenly exploded, that people hadn't quite predicted' (Eustice). Successful contingency management and crisis avoidance may therefore be functions of detailed planning, even though this model does not allow us to judge whether an initiative's success is perhaps at least as dependent on the quality of the policy itself. In other words, incidents with a tangibly negative effect on reputation may be managed, attenuated or even avoided if carefully and sensibly handled by communicators. Frameworks to predict risks and adverse issues in the long run may be desirable, but do not seem to be widely in use or considered practicable in political communications management.

Managing a politician's communications

If we assume that reputation management requires third-party media endorsement, an observation made by McBride appears relevant. He points out that Gordon Brown at least initially did maintain solid relationships with editors. Tony Blair could solicit support and endorsement from individual columnists even towards the end of his premiership when the media had become critical of him and his policies (McBride). This emphasis on close working relationships with the media is probably justified, as both editors and columnists are pivotal figures for anyone who seeks to control images.

McBride raises an interesting point by asking whether a distinction needs to be made between politicians who gain popular support and those who may not be widely liked among the electorate but who at the same time entertain very good relations with the media. As a case in point, he mentions Tessa Jowell. As cabinet minister she was supported by sympathetic journalists who would even ring 10 Downing Street to make it clear on the eve of a cabinet reshuffle that the media would react adversely to her demotion (McBride).

These cases suggest that a solid relationship with journalists may generate desired media coverage and facilitate dealings with editors and correspondents behind the scenes. The following paragraphs therefore are dedicated to communicators' and journalists' thoughts about skills, qualities and strategies needed and deployed to ensure effective relations between politicians and the media as well as efficient communications management. It is highlighted how attention to detail and technical aspects impact on the quality of strategic communications management.

Once target audiences are identified and their core expectations taken note of, an ideal image considered and a plan drawn up, the success of strategic reputation management hinges on the practicalities of communications activities. Stevenson lists some of what he calls the 'bread and butter' issues of media presentation, which span from appearances on live television and engagements with social networking sites all the way to short messaging tools such as Twitter. This range also includes speechwriting and conventional media relations as well as the practical minutiae of media advice that was offered to Gordon Brown, for instance, to help with photo opportunities that were directed in a way to ensure that his blind eye stayed in the background.

One of the pivotal, yet rather technical, media relations tasks in political communications was the preparation of the TV debates in the weeks leading up to the 2010 elections, as well as the briefing of candidates. It has been argued that one reason for Cameron's disappointing performance in the first debate and Clegg's unexpectedly strong showing was the difference of quality in the candidates' respective briefings, both about likely policy content and the arrangements and rules that had been agreed on for the individual debates (Jones).

While it is probably critical to emphasize media training and coaching for party leaders, the public image of an individual MP, by contrast, is arguably not the crucial concern of the party's communications unit. Macrory interestingly does not downplay the importance of reputation in politicians. However, he insists that, in opposition, perception management is an issue that the individual MPs will have to deal with themselves, and is not seen as part of the party's media staff's brief (Macrory). While the Conservative Party's media office does arrange and manage TV appearances for MPs, Macrory quite explicitly talks about 'using' MPs to respond to media requests. Rather than work on and build up a backbencher's presentational skills and position a politician, media staff at party headquarters merely select MPs who are believed to perform effectively in front of a camera. By contrast, no interview arrangements are made for those individual MPs in whom party headquarters has no confidence.

Davies describes the demands that the party's media department places on popular and media-savvy members in the party leadership, parliamentary party or government. Party headquarters' objective at times was to satisfy media requests. For this purpose they recruited cabinet ministers to agree to a considerable number of interviews and broadcast appearances. Davies was wary of agreeing to these requests, as he feared it would put too much pressure on Secretary Jack Straw. Davies concedes that some of the media management decisions he made or advice he offered was motivated not exclusively by communications objectives and audience expectations, but by the consideration of 'protecting him [the minister] as a human being'. More strategically, Davies also queried particularly if the interviews with less prestigious media and limited audiences were appropriate for one of the most senior cabinet members to accept. The party's media department and Davies as special adviser each pursued what appeared to them respectively as reasonable communications strategies, albeit with different objectives. Even though party spokespersons and special advisers see media as a resource that needs to be addressed professionally, this does not always assure an alignment of strategy and objectives.

Davies talks about his frustration with the discrepancy between Jack Straw's personality and the public perception. The positive qualities that the people who worked closest with him observed at times became submerged in the mediated persona. To counter this, Davies made use of specific media outlets such as *The Guardian* and *The Daily Mail* to instigate coverage that afforded Straw with the opportunity to emphasize publicly characteristics and ideas that echoed his personality more closely.

Likewise, changes in the politician's job description or environment may require a readjustment in communications behaviour. McBride reminds us how Gordon Brown's communications practice during visits in Brussels changed once he was tipped to be the next prime minister. While as chancellor he cared to meet only British correspondents informally in Brussels, he later asked to have press conferences organized for the European media, which had all the formal and official trappings with which a head of government would usually be associated (McBride).

Effective media relations hinge only in part on a well-considered media selection policy. In the past we were reminded on several occasions that attention to technical detail can make or break any otherwise reasonable communications plan. A case in point is what became known as 'bigot-gate' during the last general election campaign, when Gordon Brown was overheard ridiculing a voter in a conversation with his driver on his return journey from a market square gathering. Brown's staff had failed to remove a microphone and transmitter that the broadcaster had previously clipped to the prime minister's jacket to record his public conversation with voters. Greer suggests that Tony Blair would have been equipped with a microphone that his own team had provided. This level of detail may at first glance appear to be only a technical matter, but it is worth remembering that the fallout of this mishap cut into Brown's already shaky reputation.

Attention to technical detail not only appears relevant in preventing presentational hiccups, but is also seen as being critical in any exercise of reputation building (Beattie). As an example, Beattie cites a leading politician who is seen by journalists to walk upstairs alone without any entourage. In his view, this image failed to conjure up the desired associations of relevance and power. Attention to details that if overlooked or deliberately ignored could backfire or cause embarrassing situations is implicitly mentioned by many interviewees. Redfern looks at it in the context of social media, and in particular tweeting. For the online community authenticity is important and it is perhaps for this reason that Redfern is very careful to discern which politicians are writing and answering their tweets personally. If a politician who pretended to keep a personal blog or tweet him- or herself was caught out tasking staff members to generate messages, this would most likely incur criticism from the web community. It is understood that, due to lax approaches to these technical details, reputations took flak (Redfern).

Price argues that, regardless of the intensity of public opposition and media criticism, a politician needs to keep communicating. Allegedly, Bill Clinton gave this advice to Tony Blair (Price). One may interpret this suggestion as recognition that communication often is the only opportunity for a politician to overcome opposition and achieve objectives. A politician's reputation is contingent on their communicators' ability to persevere and keep channels of communication open. Price reminds us that neither Thatcher nor Blair at any point in their often controversial careers gave up communicating and arguing their case. What has changed in terms of media management in the past two decades is identified by Stevenson. He found that, with the onset of the 24-hour news cycle and instant news rebuttal strategies, communicators have more micromanagement to do to fine-tune, add to and direct messages as they make their way through a plethora of media channels (Stevenson). This is believed to be a basic rule of effective political communications (Hill).

Hill takes this notion further when he talks about the concept of 'discipline', which he uses when describing the transmission of information from the party or government to the media, which he thinks need to be controlled – or disciplined – by the communicator. However, he makes it clear that, in government, apparently a considerable number of individuals breach this discipline and engage with their autonomous and at times clandestine media contacts, which results in a constant haemorrhaging of information that eventually minimizes the effectiveness that one could expect if media relations were tightly and centrally managed. Also, a lack of central control in communications is detrimental to consistency and effectiveness, as Eustice reminds us. All messages that diverge from the projected image distract the audience and fail to deliver on objectives. Interestingly, Stacey compares corporate to political communications and concludes that, while media staff in business keep a tighter grip on the distribution of information, similarly rigid control is not known in politics. Instead, it appears to be usual practice for MPs, government members and journalists to keep a 'more matey kind of atmosphere', which allows 'more gossip' to be 'traded back and forth' (Stacey).

However, this does not imply that communicators are willing to wait until the media establish issues, judgements and narratives. Instead, communicators try to identify and guide issues in the expectation that they can control and frame stories and commentary (Jones). Jones insists that the remarkable competition between the media in the UK even heightened the need for politicians to communicate pre-emptively and establish control both of the message and, as mentioned above, sources.

As pointed out before, it is a key quality in practical communications management to envisage events and gauge media stories (Hill). If staff and politicians successfully distinguish between issues that they need to take care of and those that will evaporate without further ado, they stand a chance to communicate effectively (Hill). Hill recognizes a connection between this skill to predict media stories and communicate on the one hand and the ability to manage politics and pursue policies on the other. The latter is difficult to imagine without the former. Perhaps this had been the case for quite some time and only the 24-hour news cycle made the link between the two even more obvious (Hill).

Therefore, the ability to predict media behaviour and anticipate issues, and more specifically questions, that the media are about to raise appears to be an essential tool in a political communicator's tool kit that is critical for the implementation of planned message strategies (Hill). Hill describes how, towards the end of official meetings, Blair's media staff briefed about subsequent media engagements. This exercise helped to anticipate questions and thus eliminate surprises with the media, which at their worst could upset a communications plan and the policy itself (Hill).

These technical arrangements to pre-empt news and predict issues are related to communicators' concern with agenda setting and the framing of news stories. The Conservative opposition in their time tried to vie for the power to set the media agenda and not allow the government to define which issues should be discussed (Eustice). To this purpose, on Mondays or Tuesdays the party leader was scheduled to give a speech that introduced a theme (Eustice). On Thursdays a second, smaller issue was presented in the expectation that the media would take it up. Taking the initiative is pivotal in daily media management and through a selection of issues a politician's personality is being projected (Richards). Richards cautions against the view that this strategy could easily be implemented in day-to-day media management. Instead, he shows awareness that 'most of your time is spent being battered about by external forces and reacting to things or crisis management when things go wrong' (Richards).

Stevenson differentiates further by arguing that, media management and agenda setting become easier for politicians in opposition and more of a challenge to those in government. Livermore concurs and adds that in opposition one is 'not forced to keep responding', and therefore one can escape the news agenda or set an alternative one. It appears that politicians in opposition not only indulge in opportunities to shun awkward media issues, but are also well placed in a position that opens up 'more chances to attack and to deploy your points' against government (Stevenson).

Controlling the news agenda

In the next few paragraphs I intend to establish to what degree and under which circumstances communicators attempt to frame stories that are being picked up and developed in the media. Neather reminds us that Gordon Brown's staff sought to control access to government information as a means to deal with journalists and to steer news reporting. This implies an endeavour to arrange trade-offs and provide information in return for specific coverage and commentary.

Beattie acknowledges that communicators can potentially use major set-piece events – he refers to these as road-stops – and statements of 'extra-ordinary' importance to steer the agenda. Livermore refines the argument and suggests that, in the days after an election victory or the days following and leading up to budget day or the Queen's Speech, the government communicators stood a chance to control items on the news agenda, unless a major unexpected event such as a terrorist attack were to occur. Livermore concludes that, while for governments the power to control the news agenda is limited, in opposition there are even fewer occasions that allow a politician to predict, determine or frame what the media would be picking up and running prominently.

In particular, foreign trips are apparently used to structure media coverage and entice journalists to follow a particular storyline. However, McBride remains less than sanguine, as 'you could never sort of predict what you'd be talking about in a particular week' (McBride). Therefore, foreign trips, according to McBride, offered only precarious opportunities to set the news agenda. This squarely contradicts the view that a trip is a set event which news reporting may have to pay attention to and which potentially can squeeze other events off the news agenda. In contrast, McBride argues that foreign trips felt more like 'wild escapes' (McBride). One reason may have been that stories in the British media were even harder to control while the prime minister was engaged abroad: 'You didn't know what would happen back home while you were on them and it was all about sort of rolling with the punches and being able to react' (McBride).

Stacey reminds us that news reporting in the periods in between the major road-stops mentioned above is difficult to guide, let alone control, which makes coverage potentially more critical for the politician's reputation. However, opportunities for communications management always exist, as Stacey contends in his illustration of Westminster correspondents as largely reactive, allowing themselves to be guided by the debates in the chamber, particular speeches being given and the key stages of the legislative process. The Labour government for years was keen to grasp this opportunity by organizing daily media briefings, which according to Hill would usually only provide context and help journalists to interpret current events. One day out of five was earmarked to emphasize a government story or departmental initiative with a clear eye on the impact this might have on subsequent news reporting.

Stacey argues that the planning grid helped to plan and control the news agenda to some extent. However, he also refers to the Labour government's skilful use of announcements, which might be repeated on subsequent occasions, conscious that audiences seem to forget specific policies that had already been announced. Stacey calls this approach to media relations and agenda management 'absolutely fantastic' (Stacey). He concludes that this kind of government communicators' work is instrumental in managing news reporters' agendas. By writing politicians' speeches and including statements likely to make it into the headlines, communications staff, in his view, can help to steer the debate in the news media. In the same vein, he cautions against thinking that political journalists generate daily coverage on their own initiative. Instead, they rely heavily either on cues generated through media relations activities or unexpected events that may distract from the politician's intended news agenda or even replace it.

It appears that Beattie's and Stacey's experience with government communicators is related to their positions as Westminster correspondents who are physically based on the premises of Parliament and whose brief it is to keep track of day-to-day political business. Their approach to the selection of issues, their interpretation and more generically the shaping of a news agenda are different from the political columnist's routine. Martin Kettle from *The Guardian*, who keeps his distance from day-to-day politics, is a case in point. Kettle clarifies that the variables that make him take up and pursue a political issue are of a different nature and are not the result of current political announcements and press briefings. Instead, he dedicates himself to concerns that are by some standards of consequence to society in a broader context. Often this choice of topic is conditioned by his personal preferences and limited only by the themes his colleagues decide to write about. This does not mean, however, that communicators do not try to stay in touch with columnists and offer themselves as interpreters of policies. Arguably, some of these suggestions are taken up by columnists (Kettle).

Beattie outlines how communicators from the major parties would not only be available for the Westminster-based correspondents, but would also actively seek journalists out and help them to understand and accept their respective party's interpretation of an issue. Jones adds that policy announcements are trailed hours or days before the actual statement. This is an arrangement that was pioneered by successive chancellors ahead of budget day, and is seen by journalists as an attempt to manage the agenda (Jones).

Particularly in the hours following policy announcements or events, communicators are seen to be contacting correspondents with the intention of influencing how a story is being interpreted and commented on. Stacey illustrated how, through the amount of information they dispense and the kind of background they add in one-to-one discussions with journalists, communicators can influence the news reporting. Jones provides as a case in point the recurrent debate about benefit abuse, which is taken up by a range of media outlets. He assumes that the information, the cues and the interpretation are being provided from within political parties. In his view, the rationale for stirring these stories has to do with politicians' and parties' interests in rallying public support. Jones also suspects that Cameron feels comfortable with the immigration debate in the media, which allegedly is spurred with the help of data provided by Conservative communicators. Stacey did not try to challenge the suggestion that in some cases political communicators, in an attempt to influence the news agenda, may even threaten to cut out specific media from the flow of information. Instead, he maintains that his newspaper would not change reporting for the sake of a good relationship with a politician.

When considering the leverage that communicators have with journalists, the decision which journalist is granted an interview and background information is critical (McBride). By placing a story with a carefully selected journalist, a message could be framed, but framing one story does not amount to control of the agenda. Beattie, for instance, talks about the difficulty that both journalists and communicators have with controlling a message once it is published. Statements do migrate from one medium to the next as they are picked up, shared and recycled by journalists. To illustrate this, Beattie cites a remark he made about Ed Miliband in *The Daily Mail*, which on the subsequent day was quoted on Sky News during an interview with the Labour leader. This highlights how the course that information takes is unpredictable and therefore hard for communicators to keep track of, let alone guide or curtail.

When selecting specific media to target, communicators are allegedly still keen to get their message across to newspaper editors rather than journalists from any other media form. This perspective may be contentious, but it seems to be the view shared by Beattie, Kettle and Jones that time and manpower among party communicators is mainly being invested to explain issues to journalists from the print media. Allegedly, this is due to the recognition that stories presented and framed in the print media are later taken up by broadcasters and online publications. Even video material on occasions is leaked to newspapers, as they, through their commentary, act as opinion leaders, while electronic media limits its role in political communications to broadcasting the material. In conclusion, Jones offers a balanced perspective on the media's power to frame news when he concludes that 'the media, you know, are driving the agenda in many ways but equally one has to accept that the strategists had a strategy' (Jones).

7 Managing resources

Past record: opportunity and burden

Politicians in the UK tend to be visible to the public and the media long before they attain more senior positions in cabinet or on the opposition front bench. In a country the size of the UK it is unlikely that a politician would rise in the ranks without drawing the attention of the national media (Neather). This in turn implies that in the course of their careers leading politicians in all parties leave publicly visible traces through statements, actions and policies, which constitute what we may refer to as 'past record'.

A politician's past election campaigns probably add a considerable amount of detail to the narrative that defines the individual. This suggests that, by the time a politician is elected to Parliament or appointed to a cabinet post, they have generated a public persona that is, according to Thorogood, at this point 'very difficult to actually change'. The more familiar publics are with a politician, the more their willingness and ability to rethink images and reshape their perceptions of that individual is limited.

What makes up this baggage that defines the current and future reputation may consist of set policies, personality features, decisions taken and actions that publics may have interpreted one way or another. Price points out that the 'room for manoeuvre was greatly reduced because of the mistake you have made in the past'. Even inaction or silence at some point in the past may be interpreted by audiences and come back to haunt a politician years later. Redfern comes up with a particular case of how inaction may be construed to the detriment of an individual. He talks about David Miliband, who as foreign secretary in the Brown government decided on more than one occasion not to challenge the incumbent party leader. While at the time this inaction may have met with tacit approval, in hindsight, views were being voiced that criticized Miliband for not having stood and thus forgone the opportunity to save the fortunes of the Labour Party by replacing a doomed Gordon Brown. Interestingly, what at the time seemed like thoroughly justifiable and reasonable caution was later framed as evidence for dithering and serves to discredit David Miliband's personality (Redfern).

Yet, at the same time, a past record may be 'incredibly valuable' (Livermore). Livermore refers to Brown as one of the most striking examples to illustrate this point. When he took over the leadership he had a very strong record as the person who handled the country's economy very well over almost a decade. This initially supported his credibility in any statement that the new prime minister made about the state of the economy. Likewise, Vince Cable was actively sought and framed as an opposition expert on the economy when in 2008 the banking crises commenced, as for years he had been on record with predictions of an imminent economic downturn (Waring). Cable's warnings had contributed to a record that on the one hand limited his public persona to that of an economic expert, while on the other hand it established features that in subsequent years appeared to be positive and popular with his key audiences.

Stevenson speaks of the 'human hinterland' that differentiates a politician from a product, which may be introduced to consumers on a blank canvas. He continues to make the point that politicians of a certain age must have accrued a life history that precludes the option to reposition their personality and policies. Thus, over time a narrative emerges that deprives communicators of the opportunity to alter their candidate's or incumbent's public persona. Redfern takes up this point and reminds us of his work for David Miliband, who at the time of the Labour leadership contest had already been well known both within the party and among the electorate. A complete repositioning of the contender was therefore never a possibility. Rather, it was sought 'to nuance it and sort of tease it out and get people more aware of the person' (Redfern). This implied fine-tuning messages with regard to his policies and record as well as his credentials as a good speaker, family person and politician with international standing. While much of this may have been known, it would be necessary in the view of Redfern to emphasize and explain some of these features and thus adjust the public persona.

Price reminds us that the mood in the country may change and a politician's past decisions that may have been applauded at the time could at a later stage be viewed more critically. A way to deal with changing expectations among key publics might be for politicians to adapt their public persona and align it with demands. However, Beattie cautions against the belief that a politician's reputation can be reinvented as a means to restart or redirect a faltering career. He mentions Michael Portillo as an example of a politician who only managed to recreate his public persona once he had left Parliament for good. We may speculate at this point that his reorientation only became credible once he directed himself towards an entirely new career path – in this case a transition from Conservative politician to journalist. This transformation eventually did succeed and resulted in what Beattie calls the 'renaissance and resurrection of Portillo'. However, we need to keep in mind that he succeeded at the price of leaving politics.

Iain Duncan Smith, according to Beattie, has not completely changed the perceptions the public had of him when he was leader of the Conservative

Party. However, unlike Portillo, Duncan Smith decided to stay in politics and pursue social welfare policies within the parliamentary party, which eventually led to his appointment to a cabinet post. To what degree Duncan Smith managed to use his current concern for social welfare as a means to make publics forget about his dismal record as party leader is hard to determine.

Wood insists that, when William Hague was leading the Conservative Party in the late 1990s, his public persona was still marred by the images of the 16-year-old Hague lecturing a Conservative Party conference in the late 1970s. This episode, according to Wood, was still in the public folk memory and framed the perception of Hague as a far-too-clever schoolboy who was not up to the job.

However, there seems to be evidence to suggest that some politicians have quite successfully disassociated themselves from past decisions and behaviour that would have clashed with images they at present consider more desirable. Richards recounts how the radical politics with which Jack Straw was associated in the 1970s do not seem to have been a liability for his career as a cabinet minister with New Labour. Richards calls Straw and individuals with similar track records 'survivors in politics ... who are very fleet of foot and can move quickly and be very tactical and flexible and nothing really sticks to them as they make their progress'. This somewhat metaphorical explanation gives us very little information that helps us to understand how Straw managed to develop his public persona in accordance with evolving expectations and regardless of his past policy stances.

For the purposes of this research, however, it is entirely satisfactory to conclude that past baggage may be but is not always a hindrance, which limits communicators' options to shape reputation – with some notable exceptions. Another politician apart from Straw who overcame a record that would in other cases have terminated a career and certainly precluded easy cohabitation with New Labour is Margaret Beckett, who in the early stages of her career played a critical role in writing the notorious 1983 party manifesto.

The cases of Beckett and Straw illustrate a phenomenon that is perhaps evocative of an observation made by Waring, who reminds us that politicians in opposition and candidates in the early phase of their careers need to take risks in order to be noticed and draw attention to their arguments. This may require them to make statements and voice criticisms they feel awkward about when at a later point they find themselves on the government benches. Waring may have had in mind a number of policy commitments that the Liberal Democrats made during their years in opposition, which once in government they had to go back on due to financial circumstances and the compromises forced upon them in coalition government. Arguably, this phenomenon is a challenge that a number of politicians have had to deal with who have been around for a long time and started out their parliamentary careers in opposition, as did Beckett and Straw.

How past baggage associated with a specific government job burdens the current incumbent is recounted by Hazlewood, who arranged for the secretary to go onto the radio and sing the Welsh national anthem. Admittedly, there was no reason to do so, had it not been to quieten nationalist voices who criticized the minister for having pursued her political career outside the Welsh borders. Her past record suggested that she might not sufficiently identify with Wales. This kind of wariness among the Welsh peaked in 1992, when the then Welsh secretary, the Englishman John Redwood, failed to remember the lyrics of the Welsh national anthem. To ensure that they did not inherit someone else's embarrassing track record by association, Redwood's successors as Welsh secretaries had to be heard singing the anthem.

Reputation management over time

The Conservative Party press office insists that reputation management for individual politicians is not being done and that since his election as party leader David Cameron has not engaged in systematic activities to shape his public persona in order to meet specific expectations. This claim should be acknowledged and put into context. Henry Macrory in the Conservative Party press office is very much aware of the bad press that New Labour earned itself when journalists speculated about Labour communicators' spin doctoring and their attempts to fabricate the images of their party leaders.

Apart from Macrory, all respondents representing the three major parties agreed that politicians' reputations are managed over extended periods of time. This view is shared by Eustice, Cameron's former communications officer, who suggests that reputation can be changed and reinvented in the course of years. Labour's Lord Stevenson clarifies that persuading people to believe a politician is likeable and can be trusted is an ongoing process. This section, therefore, is looking at the timescale communicators have in mind when they deal with shaping a politician's reputation. It does not come as a surprise to the observer that reputational change over years does take place. Clearly, alterations go both ways and Tony Blair's fall from public grace in the course of a decade is a well-publicized example to illustrate this phenomenon.

Neather draws our attention to the initial success of Brown's reputation management. His remarks help us to remember that in some way Brown's team for years must have managed to emphasize some positive personality traits, while keeping others off the media's radar. This is in line with Livermore's assertion that a communications team worked intensively on Brown's public persona over years both while he was chancellor and prime minister: 'We worked incredibly hard on Gordon Brown's reputation.' Neather asserts that even early on Brown was seen as dull, dour and stoic, which by anyone's standards may have been just the attributes with which a chancellor of the Exchequer would want to be associated.

McBride points out that reputation management can be considered in the context of a timeline, with a starting point when a politician and communicator are discussing and agreeing how the politician is best projected to their publics. McBride particularly refers to individuals whose public persona is not yet existent and whose publicly visible traits may yet be shaped. Interestingly, this initial phase is not limited to considerations of media statements and the style of public appearances. Instead, McBride is talking about the emphasis and thrust of policies that are associated with a person's identity. The two – presentational and content related – may be integrated to shape the public persona. McBride categorizes the options that communicators may have in a politician's early career stage. They may decide to position a politician alternatively as straight talker, theorist or what McBride calls 'a safe pair of hands'.

Eustice reminds us that prior to the 2005 party conference David Cameron was largely unknown to the electorate and most observers who were not intimately familiar with the Conservative Party. This was perceived by Cameron's media advisers as both a challenge and an opportunity. Eustice claims that the week of the conference was used to acquaint the public with the presumptive new leader. In an intense media campaign, the recognition level is said to have rocketed from 4 per cent to 80 per cent thanks to images that were being used to present the new Conservative leader (Eustice). This case would suggest that within the briefest imaginable period of time a politician who was hitherto virtually unknown can be given an identifiable public persona.

Eustice contends that in the case of Michael Howard the time available for repositioning and associating him with the key values of the 2005 general election campaign seem not to have been sufficient to make the electorate forget the less endearing statements he was known for during his tenure as home secretary during the 1990s. In his case, past perceptions militated against the new agenda and the single defining event was missing, which for Cameron in 2005 was the party convention that catapulted him out of obscurity into the leadership. Reminiscence of the previous Conservative government was still in people's minds and the intervening period was arguably not long enough for Howard to make them forget (Eustice).

Stacey mentions William Hague as a third case in point to demonstrate how over time reputation can be altered and built up. He calls Hague's tenure as party leader 'a disaster', while he admits that as foreign secretary he has been respected (Stacey). In his view, the period of time available to make over the public persona is crucial. According to Stacey's counting, it took Hague a decade to turn around what at the time may have been considered an image flawed by cheap media stunts. Wood details how over years the way the electorate perceived Hague changed dramatically. He refers to a slapstick comedy on TV, which initially ridiculed Hague as a precocious schoolboy. By contrast, years later a comedy show depicted him as a 'skinhead driving a taxi' (Wood). While at the time neither image appeared intensely desirable, the case demonstrates how 'not by any conscious sort of image making but through adjusting, changing the content of what Hague was about', public perceptions could be shifted. Wood reminds us that over the years Hague's communicators had to deal with the ingrained impressions created by his party conference speech in the late 1970s, which associated him with a schoolboy's bravado – an image that still stuck when years later he took over the party leadership. Wood concedes therefore that Hague at the time of his accession to the leadership may have been seen as 'a child come to do a man's job'.

To communicate reputation or a change of it to publics Eustice reckons what he calls a 'cathartic moment' is needed, 'where public perceptions are directly challenged'. Alternatively, politicians over time can rehabilitate their image if they 'go away for a bit and come back' (Stacey). This analysis chimes with a more general observation made by Redfern, who contends that, while communications for commercial products sometimes require designing and building up a reputation from scratch, a leading politician already has a reputation and communicators' options are limited to changing nuances over time.

This point is illustrated by the history of Oliver Letwin, who acquired a reputation for being gaffe prone as a result of a number of unwise statements and interviews. Eustice insists that the media at some point was poised to look for evidence that confirmed publicly held stereotypes about Letwin. In this case Letwin's advisers agreed not to challenge already entrenched perceptions. Instead, the strategy was to avoid specific situations that might tempt Letwin to make ill-considered responses. In other words, Letwin focused on doing his job and kept a low media profile.

In the long run, a low public profile alone may do little to change public perceptions (McBride). McBride points out that over time reputation does not build up automatically but requires media management. In his view, Ed Miliband's initial problem when ascending to the party leadership was rooted in his neglect of the media and the advice he received. While Miliband's performance and public persona may still change for the better, former Labour leader Kinnock lost much of his charismatic power and persuasiveness as a public speaker because as party leader he allowed himself to become entangled in prescriptive communications advice that sapped his spontaneity and authenticity (Richards).

It appears that changes in the public persona over time are not just inevitable, but also desirable. Hill questions if the intended reputation needs to be adapted over time in order to match the politician's specific job profile or the office to which one aspires. Hill believes that a public persona needs to echo some core qualities that publics would expect politicians in general to possess, while some other traits may have to be developed to reflect a politician's current job profile.

Michael Portillo started out in the 1980s and early 1990s as a provocatively right-wing politician, who in the course of time repositioned himself. This change came about when it appeared that a Thatcherite Conservatism would hinder rather than help the opposition's return to power. Kettle asserts that Portillo is known to be a highly able political brain who perceives his environment politically. This may have helped him to anticipate and emulate changes both within the party and in the electorate. Likewise, a change of office or political role would require a reputational reassessment and potentially a readjustment. To put this crudely, we may, for instance, expect a leader of the opposition to act and react differently from the prime minister, who seeks to communicate with different publics and whose stakeholders expect him to display a specific set of qualities that a politician in a minor party may not have to possess (Hill).

Politicians who have been visible in the public for a long period of time, such as Tony Blair or Gordon Brown, need to adapt the narrative that explains their role in politics and to integrate a changing environment and altered expectations. Price explains how a politician at the beginning of their tenure in office tends to be supported by an alliance of publics who over time incrementally become dissatisfied with issues of content or style, and as a consequence revoke their support. By adapting their narrative, politicians try to ensure that this erosion of support is slowed down or reversed. Price is stressing the point that the management of policies and reputation over time is more effective in holding together the coalition if it is being guided by an awareness of objectives and a strategic approach to achieve them. Livermore agrees and describes the advantages of making reputation management a planned exercise that deserves attention early on in order to have politicians and their advisers concur on an understanding of what the ideal reputation is. He argues that this should be clear at the outset of any term in office as subsequently pressures and distractions mount and time may not always be available for communicators and politicians to fine-tune communications strategy.

In the course of a decade Blair worked his way through a changing narrative (Hill). Towards the end of his tenure his message became a new one yet again, now emphasizing his intention not to leave important work unfinished. According to Hill, Blair even decided to give his narrative a new twist by adding a degree of self-criticism when he admitted that some of the projects he had promised to address should have been tackled quicker than had been the case. Stacey takes up this point and reiterates it from a journalist's perspective. In his view, journalists are keen to find and process different and changing storylines. This would require the images of political parties, governments and individual politicians to progress over time. Stacey puts very bluntly the pressure the media places on individuals to adapt and develop their features and messages. Over the course of months and years 'the public want a change of tune, change of story'. If this fails to materialize, 'it gets boring' (Stacey). At this point the question may be raised of how often politicians can reasonably expect to change their storyline and rearrange public perceptions. Price argues that a makeover may be successfully attempted once or twice but would most likely not prove successful if ventured more often. Blair is the example to which Price refers. People apparently thought differently about him towards the end of his tenure but their views were arguably not improved.

Beattie is looking at this argument from a different perspective and asks if over time the true personality is bound to become more visible to the public. He speculates that over the course of time as politicians may become comfortable and confident in their jobs they are also more easily persuaded to let down their guard, which initially media relations staff have held up to conceal their true nature. At some point keeping up a manufactured public persona allegedly becomes dispensable (Beattie). Another aspect advanced by Beattie relates to actual changes in personality, which also may lead to an altered public perception. Beattie reminds us of the view that politicians in high office undergo changes in their personality as a result of their job and the responsibility, the privileges, pressures and roles that come with it. He makes the point that specifically prime ministers' personalities are known to have shown the pressure of the job as years went by. While this happens inadvertently, it is a tangible phenomenon that may account for changes in the reputation of party leaders and prime ministers. Kettle concurs and asks whether perhaps the changing public perceptions of politicians over time may, after all, not be the function of communications management tactics but the result of a genuine change of personality. To highlight this argument he summarizes how Tony Blair started out as a young and articulate party hopeful who could communicate with the middle classes, and ended up as 'an idiosyncratic, rather defiant, self-righteous and unpopular' prime minister (Kettle).

In all fairness it should be added that personality change and alterations in the public persona are not always for the worse. Kettle clarifies that Duncan Smith may have changed genuinely since he lost the party leadership in 2005. His dedication to social welfare reform might not even be the result of strategic advice but a genuine interest that he has developed for this subject over time, as Kettle, Wood and Macrory confirm.

Professional advice: quality and implementation

In the view of Hill the effectiveness of political communications advice depends to a large degree on whether politicians do recognize its value and understand how to make use of it. The kind of advice and support politicians solicit from communicators can be quite diverse. While some ask for specific guidance with preparing statements and speeches, others might discuss strategy or use the adviser as a sounding board to give feedback following public appearances (Davies). The relevance of good public relations advice is increasingly understood as 'most modern politicians are absolutely up to speed' on image management (Stevenson). It is argued that this recognition is reflected not only in the 'number of people working on this issue', but also by the amount of time dedicated to it (Stevenson).

Hill mentions the former Labour leader John Smith, whose interest in presentational issues was somewhat limited. In a way, communications staff found this attitude almost liberating as due to lack of interest Smith tended not to interfere with their jobs. Tony Blair, by contrast, made time available to advisers to discuss current and upcoming matters and reflect whether approach and tactics to communications were right or needed to be adjusted (Hill). Hill explains that Blair was prepared to discuss media and political issues that his advisers thought needed to be put on the prime minister's agenda. If we contrast Smith and Blair, we find that the role and effectiveness of political communications advice on reputation management hinges to a large degree on the politicians and whether they are willing to engage with this issue and their advisers (Hill).

Tony Blair used to consult a number of external experts and confidants on major policy issues before he made up his mind and took a decision. This limited the influence of his Downing Street communications staff, whose advice remained only one source of many (Hill). Eustice counters the assumption that in the team of advisers surrounding Prime Minister Cameron there are rows going on between rival camps about which policy and style to adopt. In his view, discussions within the core team of six to eight staff are at times 'healthy' and 'very robust', which he portrays as being constructive. Clearly, this view reflects Eustice's experience in Cameron's team and may not be typical of other cases, where internal and external staff perhaps do not agree and collaborate that easily.

Much less open debate existed at the time among the members of Prime Minister Brown's team. McBride speaks of communications staff who in conversations with Brown 'were careful with him'. What made them cautious was his reaction to personal feedback or critical comments on his professional behaviour and his personality. McBride clarifies that Brown would 'get embarrassed about being told'. Perhaps this reluctance to discuss problems openly is the reason why a number of communications tools deployed by Brown were misguided; arguably it was difficult to make it clear to him that 'his speeches were awful' (Richards). Richards imagines that anyone who did voice frank views with him may not have been heeded: 'There were people saying those things but they didn't get anywhere'. This scenario suggests that communications problems arise and cause lasting damage if the organizational culture lacks frank internal communications. Other politicians, by contrast, expected their advisers to be 'brutally honest' and understood this open and frank critique as an asset that vindicated the special adviser's position (Richards). Richards argues that the value of communications expertise offered by special advisers hinges on their ability to be critical and honest about their views.

Kelly is explicit about the need for communications advisers to be frank and straight forward with the politician. He defines this as the core of the advisory role and values it higher than other functions and services:

> I think the one thing I would say is that the personal relationship matters, right. You don't have to be … It's quite often advantageous not to be the leader's best friend. You don't have to be a soul mate. You don't have to have the same political instincts as the leader. You do have to have the

> ability to tell that person the truth and not to be afraid to tell that person the truth because if you pull your punches in saying how things are going to be perceived then the leader is not going to know how to present things in a way … the leader has to think 'I'm going to say this in such and such a way, and I'm being told the reaction is going to be such'. If the leader is under an illusion about what the reaction is going to be, you haven't done your job. So, however uncomfortable it is, however much the leader doesn't want to hear it, you've got to be able to give the message. And at the end of the day, that becomes the truth-teller role, the strategic counsellor role, and I do increasingly think of communications advisers as strategic counsellors rather than just communicators. And that means you have to have the relationship where you can look the person in the eye and say, 'Look, whether we like it or not, this is how it's seen'. So that's what you're … that's the context. You've got to understand that context. That's it.

Hazlewood concurs fully and argues that advisers who regularly tend to agree with the politician are not in a position to give guidance and steer them away from risks and issues.

If advice is taken up or not depends on whether politicians and their communicators build up a relationship of trust (Hill, Waring). For this to happen special advisers need to learn to understand intuitively the personality and values of the politicians for whom they work (Eustice). It is essential for them to be familiar with how the politicians they are employed by react, mimic, speak and respond to adverse events. This insight helps communications staff tune advice to the politician's character. Price concurs and adds that advisers should not set up their communications strategy autonomously but always link it to the politician's inclinations, aspirations and personality.

Davies notes that Jack Straw, for whom he worked, 'basically wants to be as upfront and as open as possible'. This understanding of Straw's personality helped Davies project communications and develop a public relations plan that suited Straw and gave him a chance to appear authentic. In his final years as a cabinet minister he may have been less keen on media opportunities and career advancement than some of his younger colleagues. This was an important feature in his personality that a communications adviser needed to consider (Davies).

Likewise, Davies knew which kind of public appearances would match Straw's personality and hence tried to turn down any engagements that the minister would think were inappropriate. These ranged from interviews about popular music to appearances on comedy shows such as *Have I Got News for You*. None of these options would have done justice to Straw's personality (Davies). Advisers can best manage and consult if they are aware of the basics that shape a politician's communications behaviour and the signposts politicians set out to define what their dos and don'ts are in communications practice. At the same time, Davies tried to take Jack Straw out of his comfort zone and suggested that he overcome his aversion to an interview about his modest upbringing on a council estate. Davies encouraged Straw to share this story with people as it was interesting and promised insights into the politician's values and convictions.

In the view of Eustice, good advisers must not be too much concerned with pushing the politician into the media's attention. He argues that successful and effective media relations are not just about looking good and appearing in *GQ* magazine, but instead the objective should be to identify a politician's personality and present it to audiences. Once advisers succeed in getting access, have their advice heard and considered, the final decision may still be taken by the politician, regardless of the quality or range of advice offered (Waring). Macrory clarifies that the politician 'is his own man' and the ultimate decision is his or hers. David Cameron is said to turn down communications advice if he is not perfectly comfortable with it (Eustice). In part this regards technical issues such as the right pitch of voice when giving a speech. Eustice maintains that Cameron would also reject policy and strategic advice, as he did in the run-up to the Conservative leadership contest in 2005 when it was suggested that he should launch a robust attack on his opponent, David Davies – a piece of advice Cameron thought was wrong and did not match with his personality and values. He therefore chose to ignore it (Eustice). This decisiveness in presentational issues and his willingness to override expertise may be explained by Cameron's professional past when he worked as a communications consultant himself (Stacey). In other words, he held his own views on strategic communications that he integrated into advice he received (Stacey).

Richards believes that the quality of advice is an important variable in predicting whether or not it is taken up and pursued by a politician. Davies maintains that his suggestions were heeded in almost every instance by Jack Straw. That is a remarkable feat, as cabinet ministers find it difficult to imagine that at this advanced point in their careers they should still have to defer to someone else's suggestions and adapt their style and content accordingly (Richards).

Price concurs and discovered that politicians of a single-minded disposition find it difficult to follow advice and instead pursue their own agenda. In his view this was one of the reasons that accounts for Margaret Thatcher's downfall in 1990. This scenario contrasts with politicians whose lack of intuition and emotional intelligence makes them more reliant on communications advisers' support (Price). If the politician finds it difficult to connect with publics and to gauge their interests or envisage their reactions, internal or external advice becomes pivotal (Price).

In this context one should mention that poorly researched and tested policies may also originate from advisers and be at the root of a politician's flawed reputation. Greer vividly illustrates how the Conservatives' former strategic adviser Steve Hilton pressed the vision of a 'Big Society' on his party and only subsequent testing revealed this policy to be extremely unpopular among focus groups. One may want to speculate about the repercussions this or similar cases may have on a politician's willingness to take up external or special advisers' communications advice in the future.

Internal communications and management structures

In Gordon Brown's office at 10 Downing Street McBride encountered a disconnection between the operational and strategic levels. In discussions with the prime minister, policy staff would consider and decide upon issues that were of relevance for media relations. At some point this information was passed on to those staff who on a day-to-day basis were involved with tactical media relations. McBride regards this lack of direct communication between tactical media handlers and the politician problematic. He senses that behind closed doors there was a power game being played about privileged access to the prime minister, which never resulted in improved access for communications staff and a more horizontal structure within the media unit, which might have been beneficial to the communications task.

This struggle for access to the politician and competing advice offered from internal and external experts makes systematic and strategic communications difficult, as McBride explains. He points out that, once in 10 Downing Street, Brown received considerably more advice from a larger range of individuals. As a consequence, for staff members who were in charge of the day-to-day media handling it was not clear what the messages and the communications objectives were meant to be. Also, McBride makes the valuable point that this kind of arrangement reduced the opportunities for media relations officers to influence policy and presentational decisions.

To illustrate this, McBride refers to the Al-Megrahi case, which caused outrage among publics in the UK and the USA as soon as it transpired that a Libyan citizen convicted for his part in the terrorist attack on a US passenger aircraft near the Scottish town of Lockerbie was released from prison and sent home to his native Libya. McBride is concerned that in this case decisions were taken in line with what foreign affairs staff thought appropriate and with no apparent reflection on what implications this move would have from a public relations perspective. It is not clear, therefore, if the internal communications always ensured that the party leader or minister would be given a public relations perspective, particularly if this view ran counter to current policy objectives or civil service recommendations. Likewise, McBride questions whether Tony Blair was told by his pollsters how unpopular his pledge to support the war that the Americans fought in Iraq had become.

McBride is suggesting that staff numbers and training as well as the dimension of a government department may all constitute variables upon which the quality of internal and ultimately external communications hinge. He points out that at the Treasury media advice on relevant policy issues was being sought and discussed. By contrast, in the larger and more complex prime minister's office, decisions – as here in the Megrahi case – were prepared and taken while leaving communications managers completely in the dark. McBride acknowledges that in the Chancellor's office, under the stewardship of Brown, decisions may have been taken that ran counter to media advice. However, this would usually have happened after media and image implications had been considered.

Eustice made the same observation. He is concerned that, due to the considerable number of staff and both internal and external expertise, it might be difficult for politicians in government to arrive at a decision. Wood points out that already in opposition advisers are competing with each other to have their respective and conflicting policy agendas espoused by the leader. This problem of competing advice as well as flawed coordination seems to aggravate in line with increased structural complexity when in government. Responsibilities are not as clearly allocated as they may be in a smaller team and the delegation of tasks may lead to errors being made. While, in opposition, a handful of relevant advisers would easily come together via a conference call and decide what needed to be done, the same level of swiftness is missing in government (Eustice).

Due to time constraints and competing engagements, communications advisers arguably find it difficult to approach and talk to the prime minister and decisions therefore may get delayed in the tussle for access. There is competition for the prime minister's time, a limited resource, when government business demands extended slots in the diary. Contact time with Gordon Brown was often used up by civil servants whose concern was much less with media and presentational issues (McBride). McBride mentions foreign policy commitments, international phone calls and liaising with international heads of government as well as increased prominence in the UK, which made Brown the most popular visiting speaker on a wide range of political, economic and cultural bodies. Stevenson calls the job of prime minister extremely demanding as it requires the presence and commitment of the individual 24 hours a day, seven days a week. He suspects that the civil service could organize it better, but, even if it did, the nation's international commitments and the need to stay in touch with heads of governments and events in different time zones give the incumbent little respite (Stevenson). Kelly warns of this gruelling schedule and insists that leaders in politics need thinking time to reflect on what their role is and what publics and the media expect.

McBride believes that this intensity did not allow Brown or his media advisers to discuss and agree on what was important and what activity he should focus his resources on. It was apparently not reflected comprehensively which commitment would aid his public perception and resonate with the media and the electorate. As Brown was only sporadically available for his communications staff, advisers had to be familiar with his views to a degree that allowed them to second guess which stance he might have taken on specific questions and which response he might approve of (Stevenson).

If issues were left undecided and decisions open at No. 10 for too long, the communicator could take the initiative and force the hierarchies to come out in favour or against (Kelly). Both in the mornings and afternoons at set times the media expected to be briefed by a Downing Street spokesperson. Kelly used this timing as leverage to ask for clear directions. He made it known that on some issues a delay in deciding or declaring would result in a loss of credibility.

Admittedly, this exercise in exerting pressure on the deciders may not have been an option for a number of lower-ranked media advisers who are in charge of the day-to-day handling of communications. They were made to wait for up to two days at times until they got a decision from the prime minister on statements or media engagements. McBride believes this is too long, and did not allow him to operate effectively. Stevenson details how communications advisers tried to make up for this lack of direct deliberations with Brown by arranging to meet among themselves from time to time to discuss if the presentation of Brown was as desired, or could be changed and fine-tuned.

While this may be a fair description of a challenge faced by the communications staff of the prime minister, in ministerial departments, by contrast, special advisers for communications have direct and virtually unlimited access to their minister's policy meetings. Richards recalls how in hour-long discussions about health care reform the minister responsible, Alan Milburn, granted continued access to his media advisers. In Richards's view, this is necessary in order to consider the media ramifications as the policy emerges. Alternatively, the advisers would have to limit their role to fire fighting afterwards.

Greer gives a pertinent example that illustrates why all communications experts I have talked to judge the quality of political communications by the degree to which advisers have access to the politician for whom they work:

> I have a very good example, um, an individual, um at CCHQ [Conservative Campaign Headquarters] when, um, when Andy Coulson was brought on and Steve Hilton obviously was the big brains. So they had this big meeting one day with … a lot of the staff was there. So you've got, right at the top, you've got, you know, Andy Coulson, Steve Hilton and then all these other staff who weren't anywhere near that senior. And they were talking about this new idea that Steve really wanted to push, which was about, you know, equal pay for men and women and how it was important to ensure that this was enshrined in the workplace and promoted and so on. And of course everyone was really on board with this idea, absolutely, we should do it, bring it on, a really good idea. And Andy Coulson hadn't said anything at this point in the meeting and he stopped them and he said, 'Well can you guarantee me that we live this at CCHQ?' And the room fell silent because they couldn't and that was a classic example of where you have policy was being discussed and a policy formation in a sense and then you had the communications guy who was then going, 'Well it might be a great idea but if we go with this

> now and someone comes back at us and says, "Well look at CCHQ there's inequality and pay there," you're going to be in trouble'. So I think that was a good example of how the comms built.

Greer concludes that politicians who did not grant their communications advisers this kind of access would be 'very, very, very silly', though he makes it clear that the communicators' participation may not have to extend to shaping policies as was the case in this scenario: it would be sufficient to involve them in the discussions on presentational questions early on. By contrast, Kelly questions whether the communicator's role as minder of presentational concerns is sufficient. He recommends that the communicator should be involved from an incipient stage in the 'production line' (Kelly).

Hill and Kelly agree about the importance for communicators of direct access to politicians. This view is based on their experience with Blair, whose daily 8 am meetings they used to attend along with the head of strategy in order to plan the day ahead. These meetings covered policy as well as presentational issues. They also included a clarification of emphasis to identify which stories would need attention in the course of the day and which might not (Price, Kelly, Hill). Kelly understood his role in the prime minister's meetings to be the 'voice of common sense' who would listen to discussions and occasionally remind the participants of his concerns.

Access in Hill's view had to be organized efficiently for two reasons. First of all, it was critical for the communicator to know what the politician intended and had on his mind. This would help to focus communications and achieve objectives. However, he also reminds us of a second crucial reason as to why close and ongoing contact between adviser and politician was essential for the success of political communications management. Journalists would try to test if the communicator was in the loop and privy to what the politician was doing. If this was the case, the communicators would be taken seriously and their word carried weight (Hill). Professional gravitas would be undermined once the media doubted if the spokesperson was well briefed. The consequence of this would be a loss of trust and interest in the spokesperson. Related to this is Davies's notion of the ministerial spokesperson as the 'hub' of information and point of contact for all attempts to get in touch and arrange interviews with the minister. He considers it important that communications decisions are centralized within the department and that the ministers refer requests for interviews back to their respective spokesperson to ensure coherent answers and allow them to use their position of ministerial gatekeeper as a bargaining tool in their dealings with the media.

A variable that complicated efficient communications processes within the departmental context was interference from Downing Street. The prime minister's communications team to different degrees tried to direct and streamline departmental communications activities. Blair and his head of communications, Alastair Campbell, apparently insisted on all statements in government departments being orchestrated centrally. This was meant to ensure that all messages 'fit into the big picture' of government strategy (Price). Price reminds us of Blair's and Campbell's heavy-handed methods used to make all departments toe the line and adhere to centrally stipulated messages. Price claims that some ministers were sacked over time if they repeatedly failed to recognize and adhere to shared communications objectives. Price points out that these arrangements were in place in order to coordinate the government's image and demonstrate support for the prime minister. A similar centralization of government communications has been observed in the Labour Party, which Kettle finds has become post-ideological and less democratic. This might suggest that internal organizational structures are not grounded in democratic principles but may be chosen for managerial reasons. This is a price that communicators apparently were ready to pay in order to make the party's image more manageable and the annual conference more controllable (Kettle).

Scrutinizing the communicators and their expertise

'Understanding the strategy, helping with the language, understanding how to develop the stories, but also […] having people there who are particularly good at presentation.' This is how Hill describes a communications manager's brief. At this point I seek to explore if this view is agreed, what skills might be required and what educational and professional background communicators should ideally possess in order to make an effective contribution to political reputation management. Hill suggests implicitly that a manager might not possess the whole range of skills and that therefore communications teams try to bring complementary essential skills to bear.

Eustice insists that in political communications one finds two types of manager. On the one hand there are communicators with a background in journalism. In his view, they are keen on collaborating with the mass media and generally try to help journalists find the information they need in order to get their stories produced. This contrasts with what Eustice calls campaigners, who take a more strategic and message-oriented perspective. Their objective is to communicate a message, which may or may not match the news agenda on which journalists are working.

In the light of Eustice's remarks, it does not come as a surprise if the journalist Beattie insists that communicators with a background in journalism are more to his liking, 'because they understand what we want and how it works'. Beattie likens the journalists' job to 'trading in stories' and it was therefore critical to collaborate with a political communicator who is familiar with how news stories are selected and written. Stacey concurs and prefers to work with journalists employed in a party press office 'because they get the idea of a story and they know what you want as a journalist'. By contrast, 'the marketing people want to sell you a product' (Stacey). Stacey goes on to outline what the interests of a news reporter are in politics: *exclusive* and *new* are the attributes journalists are looking for, while marketing strategists appear to be led by neither of these considerations and instead fabricate messages about policies and candidates that transport specific images and are rife with spin.

Davies acknowledges that journalists are predominantly interested in a good story that sells, and that the intuition of what constitutes a good story is probably the strength of communications managers who used to work in journalism. As a former journalist himself, Davies's concept of communications management is somewhat skewed towards media relations, as is the picture he generates of the communicator's responsibilities. As special adviser to the justice secretary and in response to queries raised by reporters, he needed to assure the liberal media that Jack Straw was no authoritarian, while the conservative media had to be told that whoever deserved to go to prison would be sent there and that the institution of prison would not be turned into a carefree 'holiday camp' (Davies).

More specifically, communicators with experience in local media, it may be argued, bring particular value to bear as advisers to a politician. Apart from the understanding of journalists and their way of dealing with stories, former local reporters may be endowed with a sense of how people in local communities think about politics. This helps to develop public relations activities and gauge the public mindset. Davies goes on to argue that perhaps media relations advisers who joined their respective parties straight after graduating from university (he mentions Oxbridge and indeed about half the special advisers in the last and current governments graduated from these two universities) might not have had that same experience needed to appreciate expectations raised in their respective local constituencies.

A politician's connection with tabloid journalists is, in the view of Jones, instrumental in reconciling politicians to the populist cause. He illustrates this view by citing campaigns for 'our boys in Iraq' or advocacy 'to expose benefit scroungers'. This grounding in what the public is concerned with appears to be an asset just as is the knowledge of what drives journalists. Jones adds to this another desideratum: a particular robustness in their dealings with the public and journalists in particular is a critical requirement for leading managers in political communications. He recalls a quote from an interview with *The Daily Telegraph*'s commentator Bill Deeds, who allegedly said 'every British Prime Minister needs a thug sitting beside them who understands the British media'. Redfern, too, judges the services of what he calls 'an attack dog' essential in a politician's media team and blames the lack of success in David Miliband's bid for the leadership in part on his failure to recruit a 'vicious' operator who would 'pull no punches' (Redfern). Wood also sees a need for someone trained in 'hand-to-hand fighting' who can survive 'the day-to-day battles that need to be fought'.

Hill reflects on the advantages and disadvantages of having former journalists on the communications staff's payroll. He is suspicious of their inclination to disseminate information, as one would expect from a journalist. In his view, this runs counter to a communications manager's job description, which is skewed to control information. Yet he recognizes a journalist's ability to sense how the media deals with stories and to anticipate the subsequent day's headlines or potential problems that are waiting in the wings. These skills make journalists an asset in any communications team (Hill, Jones, Hazlewood). This view is countered by Waring, who warns that communicators with a journalist's mindset are tempted to get bogged down by day-to-day media handling and lose sight of the long-term objectives. To stay focused on the long-term goals would in her view be the brief for staff with what she calls the 'marketing frame of mind' who are not constantly following leads to secure front page headlines (Waring).

In contrast, Neather is sceptical of marketing approaches in government communications. His experience in Downing Street's strategic communications unit did a lot to question his belief that marketing and brand experts have an impact on the perception of policies and public service. In his view, popular support for public services and policies does not hinge on the ability of marketing communications to generate a brand. Instead, he finds the marketing planning and implementing process cumbersome and time consuming. He explicitly refers to the NHS, which in his view gained popularity and increased satisfaction levels as a concomitant of the extra money that the Labour government spent on it. Neather considers the contribution made by marketing communications strategy negligible.

Neather thinks that marketers in politics work on the false assumption that the messages they devise will be picked up and communicated by the media just as they had intended. In his view, this disregards the journalists' role as gatekeepers who select the chunks of information they consider relevant and may choose to ignore in part or entirely the marketer's message.

Stacey expects political communicators to sense which statements stand a chance of making it into the news headlines. In his view, this is a critical skill for anyone who does not want to be wrong footed by public feedback. He cites as an example Ed Balls's pledge to cut value added tax (VAT) once Labour is returned to office. Stacey was surprised when he learned that the Labour leadership had not anticipated at the time that this announcement would make it to the top of the news agenda. Clearly, the strategy and resources available for media relations in the aftermath of a headline-catching statement need to be calibrated, which is not likely to happen if the kind and intensity of public reaction takes the party leadership by surprise, as happened in this case (Stacey).

To be able to anticipate media reactions and comments, Macrory spends half of his working time talking to journalists. This, in his view, is evidence of the pivotal role that media relations experts play in political communications. To him, therefore, it appears obvious why political parties should entrust their communications operations to individuals who have extensive professional experience in journalism and 'understand the media very well', as did David Cameron's former spokesperson Andy Coulson (Macrory). Coulson, just like Macrory, had a background as a news reporter.

In the discussion about journalists' and marketers' contribution to political communications, Wood takes a balanced view. He agrees that journalists have a somewhat short-term perspective and tend to be concentrating more on creating tomorrow's headline. On the other hand, he sees a weakness in the marketing approach and cautions that long-term strategic plans drawn up by marketers are more often than not of little or no interest to journalists. He therefore believes that good communications teams need a balance of both sets of knowledge and skills.

Richards suggests that the Conservatives view communications in a broader sense than Labour. Since Thatcher, the party has relied on individuals with a broad marketing communications perspective and has made use of a range of communications tools. In contrast, Labour's communications efforts were more grounded in the media relations expertise accrued from former journalists (Richards). In Richards's view, this limited the communications armoury and emphasized newspaper coverage out of proportion, which evidences Labour's failure to recognize 'the broader marketing and communications challenges' (Richards).

Macrory takes the discussion beyond the dichotomy of a marketing versus journalism orientation. He reminds us that, regardless of individuals' respective professional backgrounds, the quality of communications experts and the level of their specialization have increased due to financial resources at the civil service's disposal. While Wood agrees that government departments have considerable numbers of communications staff on hand, he is critical of civil servants with a communications brief. Usually civil servants limit their remit to the 'transmission of factual data', while the political communications are left to special advisers (Wood).

By contrast, opposition parties' core worry is limited financial resources. Wood clarifies that he used to pay in the range of £21,000–£22,000 a year for a press officer, and concedes that this kind of money would only allow the recruitment of beginners on the job, which led to a number of complaints by members of the shadow cabinet who were unhappy with the performance of their respective communications officers.

Price adds a new argument to the discussion with regard to the recruitment of skilled communications staff. Depending on a politician's perceived career chances, the kind and quality of advisory staff may vary. Jones explains this as a bandwagon effect, which favours opposition parties that are expected to take over power in the subsequent general election. He details that, for many journalists, this is a calculated decision to join a party that is tipped to gain a majority and swap a job at the news desk for a career in Westminster. 'If it is possible that you are going to win or it is likely you are going to win and then you get a lot of support and a lot of feet, arms and legs on the ground', Redfern points out, and reminds us of the Labour Party conference in 1997, which attracted a number of 'beautiful women and […] very good-looking boys' whom he did not recollect having seen at party conferences during Labour's long years in opposition. Hill acknowledges that the quality of staff may be more of an issue towards the end of a politician's tenure. Governments and individuals who are tipped to be on their way out may lose out on good staff who are trying to use their networks and expertise in political communications to find work in the private sector. This trend he observed towards the end of Blair's premiership, when it appeared that chances for staff to stay on under Gordon Brown were slim. Both Blair and Brown appear to have had their best communications advisers at the beginning of their respective terms in office (Livermore). However, Livermore is not sure if this can be fully accounted for by the bandwagon effect discussed above.

Resources as a quality factor in reputation management

Compared to the size of communications departments in large corporations, the manpower in government communications offices appears modest. Stacey points out that cabinet ministers are usually supported by one special adviser in charge of media relations who collaborates with the respective departmental communications unit made up of 10–15 civil servants. Downing Street does not have a much larger number of media relations staff at their disposal. Apart from the civil servants, two party political special advisers are in charge of Prime Minister Cameron's media relations and the amount of support available to the deputy prime minister is largely similar. 'A very impoverished system', Richards calls the communications resources available to cabinet ministers and the prime minister. He compares the arrangements with communications staff numbers at a politician's disposal in the USA, and finds that two ministerial political appointees to deal with media, policy and speech writing are meagre at best. In terms of this research project, Richards's conclusion is significant. He considers the staff numbers against a backdrop of an excessive workload and concludes that staff arrangements as they are leave communicators little chance to pursue proactive communications strategies. Similarly explicit on this point is Hazlewood, who asserts that with a larger staff there are 'always things you could do more'. Due to a lack of experienced personnel, work pressure is mounting on advisers, who at the same time need to comment on policy issues, react to media questions and public criticism, which leaves little chance to dedicate a few hours to 'looking ahead' (Redfern).

Waring's experience in the Department of Trade and Industry is similar. She wonders if a department that is overseeing a budget of £16 billion should perhaps be allocated more than two political advisers.

The complexity and demands of political communications management are such that the number of staff appears to make a difference to the effectiveness of messages. Macrory gives an outline of the functions that are needed to help prepare and support the media relations for a prime ministerial key note speech. In brief, organizational matters and the need to build public alliances in advance of delivery and in support of the message both require staff with expertise.

Some of the personnel involved are civil servants in press offices that are at the government's disposal. However, in Waring's view the comparatively large numbers of civil servants in the departmental communications unit do not pull their weight, react slowly and try to go into hiding when the news coverage turns critical. She thinks that the reason for this is related to the civil service status. Its members do not usually share the current minister's political agenda and tend not to consider it their brief to engage in controversial or party political advocatory media relations. This apparently minimizes the effectiveness of departmental communications. It also puts into perspective Wood's claim that government departments each have in the range of 50 to 100 civil servants dedicated to PR – a figure Wood contrasts with the number of press officers that the oppositional Conservative Party in the 2001 campaign could afford to enlist: In total 40 or 50 permanent media relations staff, including researchers.

A vivid case to relate staff numbers to the quality of communications involves an article that David Miliband, in his days as foreign secretary, wrote for *The Guardian* about the future of the Labour Party. In this text he failed to mention the then leader Gordon Brown among the group of individuals whom he thought would be important for the party's future. This caused a massive stir in the media and coverage to a degree that Miliband and his media adviser could not handle. The media fallout was critical and reactions from within the Labour Party negative. This example suggests that, due to a lack of qualified communications personnel, the media discourse can get out of hand, with repercussions on the reputation of those involved (Redfern).

Greer agrees that human resources available to communications management are critical, and adds in this context the role of financial resources. In the run-up to the 2010 general election the Conservatives may have had the most generous funding, yet this advantage was partially offset by Labour's experienced staff who had many years of government communications experience to draw on.

In this context it is worth discussing whether the quality of communications hinges more on the qualification of staff or staff numbers. Beattie believes that the failure by Miliband's adviser to handle the media stir following the publication of his article in *The Guardian* was not related to a lack of staff, even though he acknowledges that cabinet ministers can only draw on a single special adviser in charge of the media. He directs our attention to former Health Secretary Andrew Lansley and argues that much of the flak that Lansley was taking for his policies on health care reform was caused by the lacklustre approach of his media advisers and not by an apparent shortage of media handlers on Lansley's ministerial payroll.

Price questions, therefore, if extra numbers in communications staff are the recipe needed to secure a politician's successful communications. He sees at the root of poor communications not a lack of personnel, but instead a failure to conceptualize communications strategically and an inability to define objectives.

8 Debunking the strategy myth

Quite tactical after all

Findings and discussion

The initial assumption of this study about the centrality of reputation in political communications practice was corroborated by respondents who broadly recognized its power to make and break politicians' careers. Insofar as journalists tend to personalize their news reporting, they are on common ground with communicators, who are keen to present images of politicians in an effort to manage and protect their respective public persona. Macrory is the exception in this phalanx of agreement as he strenuously tries to talk down his party's concern with personal reputation management. This almost amounts to David Cameron's personal narrative and the Conservatives' identity that lays claim to substance in stark contrast to their Labour predecessors whom they seek to taint as the masters of spin. Macrory's perspective appears less credible when compared to other responses and against the backdrop of current research about political communications practice in the Conservative Party. We may therefore find our initial assumption confirmed and infer that throughout the political communications industry a politician's reputation is credited with attention and is at the focus of managerial activity.

In this context it is somewhat astonishing to find evidence to suggest that communications managers in this country may never commission opinion research to gauge external perceptions of a senior politician's public persona. Personalized data about public perceptions appear to be collected systematically for the prime minister and party leaders only, although it appears that on occasion chancellors, too, have comparable research commissioned. Some political leaders allow their reflections about popular opinion and public perceptions to be informed by mere intuition, which some interviewees think to be a critical – if insufficient – tool to guide a leading politician's public relations activities. While party leaders and prime ministers may for reasons of personal preference on occasion be inclined to rely on a hunch rather than corroborated data, politicians at cabinet rank and below do not have the luxury of choice. Lacking the resources needed for polling, they base their judgements on anecdotal evidence or broadly accessible secondary data instead.

Richards insists that in the course of his career as special adviser to several cabinet ministers he has never had the resources to commission a piece of opinion research. There is full agreement among interviewees that financial limitations would not allow cabinet ministers to commission polls, and one might even suspect that Chancellor Gordon Brown only became alert to the need for researching publics once data commissioned by 10 Downing Street indicated that his popularity was much less pronounced than had been expected. Even though this is contradicted by Spencer Livermore, who talks of data about Brown's personality being collected and analysed throughout his incumbency in No. 11, starting in 1997, this would only affirm that, if need be, the chancellor's office does stand out among ministries in as much as funding for opinion research was available.

In this context I particularly noted a remark made by Henry Macrory about David Cameron, whom he claims was recognized while still a back-bench MP as a potential future leader in possession of the traits and credentials deemed necessary to win a general election. As the Conservative Party claims it does not conduct opinion research to identify personal image issues, one may only speculate if the first and in this case perhaps decisive impression of leadership credentials are originating from a hunch.

This scenario would be somewhat dramatic and leads us to wonder whether Macrory's sensation about Cameron's qualities is an echo of the feelings nurtured by those party members who decided Cameron's eventual nomination. In other words, the pivotal decision in personal reputation management – the selection of the leader – is arguably not a researched response to popular demand and expectations, but instead may hinge on subjective feelings that contenders stir among party officials and MPs early on in their careers. This would marginalize strategic public relations advice and adversely impact on the relevance of a subsequent communications strategy.

This approach questions textbook concepts of political communications management. Political communications literature does give the impression that opinion surveys are not only needed and universally available, but also widely practised. In contrast, my observation emphasizes the centrality of personal judgement as well as anecdoe that elude any strategic research-based approaches in political PR. My findings also cast a light on how limitations in resources may upset intentions to conduct research-based strategic communications management plans. More broadly, this evidence questions notions of professionalization that have conditioned the academic discourse about political communications management in recent decades.

If due to a lack of systematic data a communicative approach hinges on anecdotal evidence, it is probably fair to say that subsequent communications techniques will likewise have to be designed with only a sketchy understanding of audiences and their respective expectations. By implication, the availability of opinion research about public perceptions may have improved the communicators' efficiency and effectiveness to operate. Those who dispose of data about the consequences of potential political decisions for personal public perception would be in a position not just to consult on presentational concerns, but to help draw up policies that bring about the public feedback intended.

This connection between communications and performance is illustrated in frameworks of strategic communications management, which suggest that effective reputation management hinges on both action and presentation. It would therefore be a temptation for any communicator who is intent on managing a politician's public persona to have a say in the design and implementation of policies and not only in their subsequent communications. Interviewees from the major political parties draw a fine line between research as a tool to guide communications campaigns and research as a means to define policy objectives. In light of this distinction, they insist that the latter does not echo their practice. Even though unanimously professed by communicators, it is hard to go by this assertion as arguably a party communicator may not be keen to admit that their respective leader allows pollsters and PR managers to dictate the party manifesto. It is difficult to establish if advisers do not want to give the impression that unelected officials shaped government or party policies or, alternatively, they actually were not in the room when decisions were discussed and taken. Equally, one might surmise that communicators for reasons of professional pride and in an attempt to manipulate the historical record do not like to admit how they were sidelined in crucial moments by decision takers or intra-departmental rivals. As it is, the question of whether communicators' expertise is drawn upon to inform the political agenda in an expectation that policies subsequently resonate with important stakeholders is beyond the brief of this investigation and would need to be picked up and verified in further research projects.

Given the dearth of research and systematic data analysis, it is perhaps not surprising that among communicators there is little understanding of the features that render a public persona ideal and how to align with messages that engage with specific publics. Although there is the generic presumption that publics expect different qualities from politicians in different situations. My interviewees recognized that politicians and their publics needed to connect, which in the academic discourse about best practice in PR is considered a critical prerequisite. Evidence that communicators and politicians make good use of their hunches when positioning a leader and steering public perceptions is provided by Kettle. Among the more telling examples Kettle refers to is a politician's age, which he believes to generate images that advisers seek to control. In response, communicators and politicians take age into account when framing narratives in an effort to establish associations of experience and youthfulness. Kettle names the Liberal Democrat leader Nick Clegg, who may have benefited from the seniority of his second in command, Vince Cable. Likewise, the youthful opposition leader Cameron recruited the seasoned veteran Conservative Kenneth Clarke into the shadow cabinet, and one may want to speculate how, to what degree and why this might have reflected on his own reputation.

We can tentatively conclude that judgements on a candidate's popular support, advice on policies that are hoped to generate public backing and reflections on the electoral popularity of decisions are largely not based on research and instead echo advisers' and politicians' intuition. Where one would have expected research-led action, personal anecdotal experience gathered in a constituency is at times the only factual evidence communications advisers can muster in support of policy advice and reputational recommendations.

Perhaps in contrast with our initial assumption, the researched definition of an ideal image for a political leader is of less relevance for practical reasons. Communicators agree that the ideal public persona cannot be fabricated in part because politician's respective space to manoeuvre and position themselves publicly is limited. It is recognized that the public persona has to be closely linked to a politician's actual identity. Discrepancies are picked up by journalists and frustrate the electorate.

Attempts to make over a politician's public persona and model individuals on putatively more appealing competitors seem to fail invariably. Gordon Brown and Michael Portillo were mentioned in this context, and in neither case did ambitious designs materialize. Instead, they were being detected and derided as lacking in authenticity and subsequently scorned by the electorate. Communicators therefore reiterate that authenticity seems to be a core prerequisite for anyone who sets out to practise reputation management. Instead of remodelling a politician's public persona from scratch, communicators can at best highlight strengths and minimize visible weaknesses. This in effect is more about tinkering with technical details than strategically modelling a candidate to chime with public expectations. Instead of pursuing a grand design, communicators are limited to tactical media relations. These restrictions to manoeuvre raise the question as to whether and to what degree reputation management can be a process led by objectives. However, even if reasons of personal authenticity were not an issue and the respective persona could be repositioned at will, communicators could not make good use of this freedom since – as we have seen – due to a lack of personalized research, the understanding of what a distinct audience would expect a politician to be like hinges at best on anecdotal evidence.

However, at a more technical level, there were some open remarks about the communicative actions deployed to position politicians and control their public perception. With the intention of positioning a public persona, political views are developed and voiced to impact on perception. In keeping with Boorstin's (1992) concept of pseudo-events, politicians engage in controversies to highlight their respective stance and distinguish themselves from their competitors. These stage-managed conflicts for the benefit of the audience are often internally discussed with advisers, agreed upon and aligned with the politician's identity and intended public persona.

These tactical stratagems confirm communicators' commitment to planning and a certain amount of strategic perspective that transcends day-to-day media relations. Indeed, staff in No. 10's communications unit claim that strategic plans with respect to the prime minister's public persona are being collectively discussed. They concede, however, that this hardly ever happens in writing for fear of leaks. Therefore, it is all but impossible for a wider circle of political communications staff to base their operations on a written plan or written objectives and strategic instructions, as these papers – where they exist – are not circulated. This raises questions about the relevance of plans whose purpose it could have been to align actions and synchronize messages. If strategic outlines of how to manage and control a politician's reputation are kept under lock and key, even to those whose work they should guide and support, the question as to whether or not they do exist at all becomes irrelevant.

If we were to assume that a written plan to guide personal reputation management strategies existed and was known and adhered to by the communications team, serious doubts remain as to the practicability of such a roadmap in a volatile environment. It is acknowledged that a plethora of events emerges and cannot be predicted and addressed ahead of time. While not a communications strategy in its own right, the planning grid that is kept in the prime minister's office is an attempt to coordinate public appearances and align messages. Some cabinet ministers use similar devices, while others value spontaneity and do not like their weeks and months ahead to be subjected to rigorous planning. Apart from unpredictable external events, it appears to be politicians themselves who militate against a more planned approach that takes reputational designs and communicative goals into account. It has been noted that politicians in their actions and statements value their unbound flexibility to a degree that does not allow a more strategic and coordinated approach to personal reputation management.

Thus, the existence of a long-term, planned strategy or the absence of it depends in part on the politician, whose PR actions may by nature be poorly thought out and somewhat intuitive. The strategic element also seems to hinge on the individual's position and seniority: when media attention is needed to increase name recognition, tomorrow's headline appears to become more relevant than long-term strategic considerations. How politicians are presented may also reflect their advisory staff's professional ambitions and vested interests, which are deemed to impact significantly on what communication style is adopted. The approach chosen is also related to a practitioner's professional background: former journalists-turned-communications managers are found to be more responsive and accommodating to news media's needs and arguably allow themselves to be guided by what reporters like to know. By contrast, marketers tend to stick to a plan, even though this may not correspond with the stories that journalists are seeking to generate.

The intention to generate and follow through a communications plan would require an ability to time issues, which among communicators is understood to be a core tool in the management of the political news agenda. Timing is seen as a means to match public expectations with political actions. Timing and selection of policies are instrumental in setting the news agenda in a way that allows politicians to be associated with objectives and values that help shape their public persona. It is by no means clear where a communicator's influence ends and whether or not it encompasses the timing only or expands into the policy-making process. As already mentioned above, interviewees seemed to agree that the communicator advises on implications of political decisions but does not design policies. There is also consensus that timing tends to favour government politicians who find it easier to select policies and issues and determine when and how they are tabled, pursued and promoted publicly. By contrast, politicians in opposition are at the receiving end of someone else's timing and thus may struggle to respond.

Once the timing of policies and public appearances is agreed, the effective implementation of a personal communications plan is dependent on the politician's presentational prowess. In other words, the feasibility of strategic communications hinges on the politician's talent to communicate. Good advice and media management staff may not be able to compensate for a politician who is either unable or unwilling to act on advice and relate to the media. In some sense this is a notion of personality which is reminiscent of charisma, and Livermore recognizes a similarity between the two concepts. He believes that how a politician engages with the public can be managed only to a degree. To excel beyond this point, the individual needs to be imbued with communicative talent. Jones, too, conceptualizes good communications as a function of personality and intuition, and Kettle quite explicitly describes Blair as a communicator who relies not only on presentational skill, but also his charismatic power.

It is this communicative ability that in part informs the narrative by which a politician's public persona is defined. A narrative is seen by communicators and journalists as the function of a politician's behaviour and communications that is moulded over time by journalists, politicians and their communicators who seek to control it. It appears that the perceived need to generate a politician's narrative serves communicators as a communications objective in its own right that informs a strategy, which in turn aligns a politician's messages and actions. These objectives and strategies appear not to be the result of planning. Instead, these are in Mintzberg's (1987) sense emergent strategies that result from ongoing competing attempts by journalists and communicators to frame a politician's behaviour, values, experiences and aspirations.

The notion that a politician's narrative is shaped in both a collaborative and competitive effort by communicators and journalists blends in with the proposition that political reporting is a strongly personalized activity in which journalists take a commanding role in the framing of a public persona. What transpired in interviews is that journalists do follow their own agenda and exert their power in writing politicians up and down as they please. These findings confirm a phenomenon that features prominently in political communications writing, but tends to be marginalized in political marketing literature. This omission is arguably related to marketers' focus on the manageability of communications programmes and their tendency to pay little attention to and make little effort to accommodate the news media. Subsequently, political marketers' concepts do not appreciate the centrality of journalism and the autonomy of journalists to pursue their respective agenda. The rationale of news reporting tends to be grounded in a need for highly personalized coverage of politics and a tendency both to boost and to undermine a politician's career in an effort to generate news that appeals to audiences. Communicators, by contrast, struggle to influence the narrative, particularly if their own role as spin doctors is being drawn into disrepute and viewed with suspicion by a hostile public. We may therefore conclude that, in their relationship with journalists, politicians have only limited means to respond if they find that they are being presented, interpreted or criticized inappropriately in the news media. The interpretative frame is developed by journalists to a considerable degree.

Another factor that cuts across any attempts to plan for communications objectives are both external and internal events that politicians need to reckon with. Findings blend with existing literature that conceptualizes events either as unpredictable occurrences or alternatively brought about by poor planning and insufficient attention to detail. Politicians may try to use incidents in order to present themselves as effective crisis managers, which in turn may even strengthen their reputation. If the adverse incident cannot be averted, at least it can be framed.

While skills in crisis communications appear to be in high demand, the resolve to predict and plan for events appears not to be particularly strong in government departments and political parties. Contingency planning is not comprehensively developed among government communicators or individual politicians' staff. The range of issues is broad and work pressure is described to be so gruelling that communicators insist there is no time to plan ahead. Not even among the chancellor's communicators did I find evidence for a strategically minded unit that is specifically tasked to analyse environments, identify potential issues and address them before they cause damage to the chancellor's reputation. While departments do prepare answers for specific situations, what they generate appears not to be a comprehensive plan. Instead of scanning the environment and predicting upcoming developments, detailed technical day-to-day media relations are trusted to avoid gaffes.

While it is conceded that in media relations the view ahead is lacking, at a more technical and immediate level media management efforts are intensive to avoid adverse images and to safeguard media support. Interviewees agree that attention to detail at a technical level is critical lest communications intentions become derailed by negative coverage about personal gaffes and mistakes of political judgement. Nevertheless, the news agenda remains difficult to control.

While they are trying to keep mishaps off the agenda, communicators seek to instrumentalize major events such as the Queen's Speech to direct and focus media and public interest. However, the debate as to whether government trips abroad and state visitors in the UK concentrate media attention and drive undesirable stories off the agenda is contested. Communicators try to pressure messages onto journalists and the lobby correspondents, in particular, appear to be happy to accept information and use it as a cue for their story. By contrast, political commentators whose columns are intended to shape public opinion appear to be less willing to accept catchwords churned out by public relations departments. Commentators seek to arrive at their judgements autonomously, and thus would not want to be seen to be spun by any vested interest.

On balance, it appears that a claim partially to drive the agenda-setting process can be made not only by journalists but also by government. By contrast, opposition communicators appear to have less bargaining power in terms of exclusive information. A threat, therefore, to cut journalists out of the information loop serves as comparatively weak leverage, and as a bargaining tool it may not help to achieve communications objectives, unless the source of the information channel has access to government or senior party circles and thus becomes indispensable for the media.

The evidence may reiterate two insights: first, depending on their respective brief and task, journalists are by degrees approachable for communicators who seek to guide the agenda. Second, the level of interaction varies between party political communicators on the one hand and journalists on the other. In the view of Beattie and Kettle, this may be due to the journalist's party political orientation or the ideological preferences with which a specific media organization is aligned. This political leaning decides in part if a journalist is targeted by communicators of one party or the other in the first place. Furthermore, the intensity of media relations activities and the comprehensiveness of networking between communicators and journalists may be defined by the quality and the amount of resources at the disposal of the media relations team. As discussed in the communications management literature and corroborated in my data, the availability of resources appears to be a tangible limiting factor throughout the strategic communications process, which may undermine the opportunities to identify and achieve objectives.

Concepts of reputation suggest that communicators' scope of action and options to position and reposition a politician are limited not just by the availability of resources and unpredictable external events, but also by the politician's past record. It is agreed among interviewees that previous experiences with a politician condition the current public persona. The implications work both ways: previously shown expertise may now strengthen a politician's authority, while past failures and questionable actions (or inaction) may undermine it. It is because of this potential baggage that the reinvention or overhaul of a public persona is at times of questionable success. For it to succeed, Michael Portillo had to leave politics altogether and Iain Duncan Smith still struggles to persuade observers that he is a changed person since his unhappy stint as party leader.

However, this does not signify that the challenges to reputation management over time are insurmountable. The cases of Portillo, Blair and Duncan

Smith testify to this. Some New Labour politicians even changed their ideological position from the radical left to the pragmatic centre, without alienating relevant publics. However, high-profile public personae are difficult to alter and it has been argued that a 'cathartic moment' or alternatively a long-term absence from media attention would be needed for a remodelled public persona to be reintroduced into the public sphere. While it is not clarified whether altered reputation over time is due to actual changes in a politician's personality or the result of media advice, there appears to be agreement that the narrative of a politician needs to be refreshed once in a while, if only to provide journalists with new storylines. This requires communicators to engage in considerations that transcend day-to-day tactical media relations and to rethink – if not rewrite – a politician's reputational profile.

A makeover of a politician's public persona requires a reliable working relationship between communicator and politician. This implies the question of why and under what circumstances advice is taken up and acted on. On occasion, advice is followed up, while at other times it is overlooked. In brief, the power of advisers to cut through with their suggestions varies. However, if politicians trust their communications staff and the advice given, the chances are that the communicator exerts decisive influence. By implication, a flawed personal relationship or a working relationship that is not imbued with reciprocal trust would constitute a barrier for the exchange of both technical and strategic support.

The findings squarely concur with the thrust of the literature discussed, which suggested that mutual trust facilitates the exchange of information and that, at a more technical level, access to the politician is critical for the communicator to operate and advise effectively. To anticipate – if not influence – policies early on in the process and to be seen by journalists as the legitimate source of information and gatekeeper, close and regular involvement of advisers would appear indispensable. If this access is not granted, communicators risk their pivotal role and leverage with journalists. As a consequence, communicators may lose their ability to operate as a sounding board for policies and strategic adviser to the politician.

Demands from the civil service, public engagements, foreign leaders and international politics all exert pressure on a leading politician, who requires sophisticated management to organize access and workload. This essentially managerial discourse is not pursued in political communications literature, even though it directly impacts on the working relationship between politicians and their communicators.

Aside from access, communicators' effectiveness to achieve objectives may hinge on their professional background as well as their training. On the basis of the evidence reviewed, we may even surmise that the selection of communications objectives, strategies and tactics varies in accordance with a communicator's respective professional credentials. The approach taken may emphasize planning and be grounded in research. Alternatively, a communicator's activities may be conditioned by short-term, fickle media interests.

Interviewees agreed that the former behaviour tends to be found among marketing professionals, while communicators with a record in journalism lean towards short-term responsiveness. The journalists would add that marketing experts at times devise messages in line with their objectives, which are of little relevance to a mass-media audience. In contrast, communicators with a journalism background are said to understand better how media stories emerge, which makes them more savvy in predicting headlines and anticipating reactions. In response, marketing-led communicators point out that their colleagues from journalism are striving to satisfy journalists' information needs, which may be irrelevant to or may even run counter to the politician's reputation objectives.

It may not come as a surprise that regardless of training and professional background, that the ability of communicators to affect processes and outcomes is also a question of staff numbers. Both in political parties and government departments this is an issue that interviewees thought worth emphasizing. Literature about the subject tends to describe how professional communications could be designed and implemented, while it is largely oblivious to the resources in terms of money and staff that party and ministerial departments need to have at their disposal to pursue their objectives and strategies. Quality and intensity of communications activities are said to suffer as a result of a shortage of qualified personnel. Departmental civil servants tasked with communications narrowly define their role as disseminators of information, which is of limited use in the reputation-building exercise. Still, communications resources available in government are more generous than in opposition parties.

Throughout this discourse it has transpired that reality is somewhat more complex than reflected in any model that portrays political communications as a more or less straightforward planned process. This level of complexity would have to be taken account of in a framework which appreciates the variables that condition a politician's personal reputation management practice.

Theoretical and managerial implications: a new perspective in political communications management

The findings of this research were intended to appreciate the correlations between specific variables and the likelihood of a politician's reputation being planned and directed strategically. Likewise variables have been identified that allow us to predict if activities in which communicators engage can be expected to be predominantly tactical and reactive in nature.

The practitioner interviews covered broad areas of communications practice. This is in the nature of an explorative study that was planned as an iterative process, the course of which was adjusted as themes and patterns emerged. As may have been expected, perhaps, the answer to the research question is neither mono-dimensional nor is it conditioned by a single and decisive causality. We may conclude that personal reputation management is at best only partially planned and strategic. I am reluctant to interpret my data more forthrightly as it provides only a limited snapshot of a phenomenon and relies heavily on information furnished by the very practitioners whose work practice I investigated.

I surveyed, identified, compared and linked phenomena and established correlations between activities, considered implications and drew conclusions, which may feed into emergent theory. This methodological design generated insights, which allow me at this point to present my conclusions in the form of an incipient theoretical model that may be used to make predictions about presumed strategic activities in the context of personal reputation management in politics.

In the following paragraphs I intend to categorize the variables that allow us to forecast if and to what degree processes are likely to become more strategic or, alternatively, more tactical. A prediction hinges on the features of each specific case: external and internal circumstances, intentions, resources available, professional background and a number of other variables I have picked up and corroborated in the course of the interviews I conducted with communicators and journalists. These themes were identified, structured and presented in Chapters 5, 6 and 7, and have been discussed and critiqued in the first section of this chapter against the backdrop of current academic discourse in communications management research.

I concentrated attention on phenomena and correlations that emerged in the course of data collection. Themes that stand out insofar as they contradict or diverge from current academic discourse have been discussed earlier on in this chapter and will not be specifically flagged up at this point. I shall not take the reader through the entire range of individual variables we already established and discussed earlier in this text. Instead, I have organized the most prevalent variables into categories, which I expect can be used as an analytical framework and applied as predictive tools to analyse communications behaviour. This constitutes a model that could help with the analysis of specific politicians and their respective communications behaviour, to understand if and to what degree the management of their personal reputation is likely to be strategic and planned. The categories of variables are:

- The *personal relationship* between the politician on the one hand and the communicator or the communications team on the other is a condition both for close collaboration and also for communicative and political input and access. This relationship hinges on mutual trust and understanding. A good personal relationship does not guarantee that advice is strategic, or even ensure that strategic advice is accepted, but a poor personal relationship makes the exchange of any kind of advice appear unlikely.
- *Financial means* are needed to research, plan, implement, measure and readjust. While the availability of money may not guarantee access, trained personnel, expert advice and professional implementation, it is understood that the lack of financial resources is the reason why research

may not be conducted. Insofar as this results in a failure to understand audiences, a politician cannot be effectively positioned and presented. Randomness and guesswork are the consequence, at the expense of focus and strategic perspective.

- *Training and professional background* are intended to mean the communications staff's skills and training, which inform the distinct approaches taken by politicians and their communicators to plan and implement political communications activities. To alter or safeguard a public persona, technical and strategic skills are needed. Training in marketing will make communicators understand the value, range and implications of strategies available. Arguably, this approach does not make persuasive communication any more effective per se, but it suggests that the operators appreciate how planning and strategic decision taking may contribute to increasing effectiveness and efficiency. By the same token, if due to a different professional background a communicator were oblivious to the value of planning and disregarded the reflection of strategic objectives, this might have repercussions on how communications activities are conducted.
- *Time* is recognized as a variable that conditions opportunities to alter public perception. This includes an awareness of how a politician's past record can serve as leverage to generate a public persona but at the same time may limit the range of messages and images that can be credibly presented. Bearing this in mind, a strategic approach would require communications management to be conceptualized as an ongoing, long-term process rather than as a one-off, technical intervention.
- *Management* comprises a cluster of activities and approaches that can be equated with the quality of media management and techniques to set and control the news agenda. Accurate media management is pivotal in generating and shaping the narrative that evolves and determines a politician's public persona. The effectiveness of communications management is linked to the efficiency of internal organization and structures to facilitate the communications between politicians and their media experts. These internal processes allow communications expertise to impact both on the creation of messages, but also potentially on the generating, timing and implementation of policies.

What also appears to have been corroborated in this study is the conditioning power of what writers in communications refer to as 'noise', and which for practical reasons in the empirical part of this study I conceptualized as actions and developments outside the communications manager's control that impact on the reputation management process: by degrees, a dynamic political setting and volatile media environment militate against a politician's or a political party's efforts for strategic and planned reputation management. This lack of stability tends to engender short-term, reactive and tactical patterns of behaviour. Conversely, the more stable relations are with key stakeholders – such as the media, voters and opponents – the more likely it is for strategic and long-term communications objectives to be drafted and systematically followed up on.

The visualization in Figure 8.1 relates the main variables that have been identified in this study to their effects on the practice of reputation management. While the categories of variables listed in the column on the left are all positively correlated with the presence of a strategic approach, the occurrence of an unpredictable action beyond the communicator's control (indicated in the right-hand column) correlates negatively – depending on frequency and intensity. When applied to a specific politician in the context of a given scenario, this model may help us to predict the kind (strategic or tactical) of personal reputation management that is likely to be practised. Boiled down to its critical essence, this predictive tool could translate as follows:

> Personal reputation management in politics is most likely to be strategic and planned, as opposed to tactical and reactive, if the following applies: appropriately trained communicators who enjoy a relationship of trust with their respective politicians are equipped with sufficient financial means to engage in efficient and professional communications management processes over a period of time long enough to allow public perceptions to evolve.

Limitations

It should go without saying that these conclusions are valid with reservation. The profession of political communications practitioners is heterogeneous and the fluctuation of personnel is considerable. The interviews reflect what individuals thought, knew, remembered or predicted at that time.

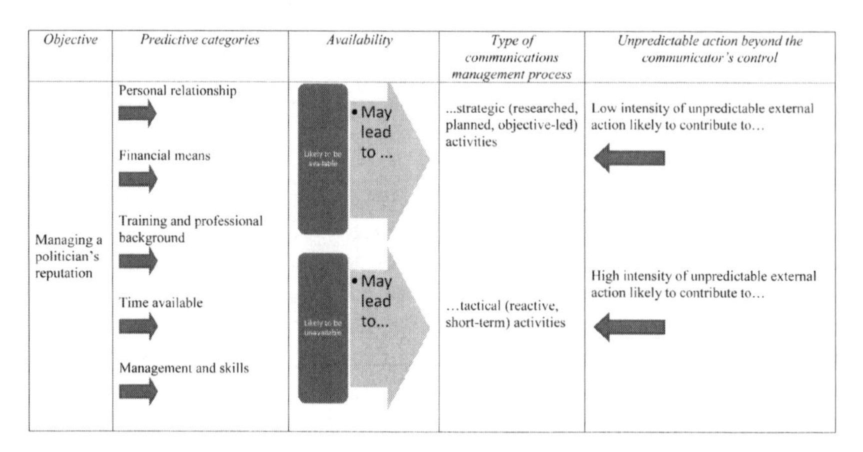

Figure 8.1 Predictive model of personal reputation management in politics

I realize that what interviewees professed to be unbiased and frank views on the issues raised deserve to be treated with caution. While some of them are currently business and may therefore have loyalties towards colleagues and clients, others may be retired and still retain reservations about exploring and revealing past procedures, decisions and events. I therefore tried to talk to a considerable range of experts from different political parties, distinct professional backgrounds and perspectives, while remaining sensitive to the quality of the data available.

Jacquie L'Etang (2008) specifically reminds researchers that public relations practitioners' business is to frame messages or even to manipulate their audiences. It is therefore problematic for scholars to engage in a research interview with the very people whose job description it is to generate a reality that is aligned with their respective purposes. My experience in this study would corroborate this suspicion. Respondents did have a vested interest and it is probably fair to say that each of them was very much aware of how they positioned themselves. Interviewees who are currently in the job took great care not to be quoted with critical comments on the politician for whom they worked at the time, while little surprisingly former advisers were portraying their respective party and colleagues more charitably than their opponents. Journalists I interviewed tended to claim responsibility for the agenda-setting process, against communicators who sought to reclaim it. Current heads of PR agencies attempted to talk up their past contribution to a politician's success, while experts who still work for cabinet ministers were happy to talk down their input and praise their respective bosses for their natural communicative prowess.

The selection of interviewees was designed to balance these interests and interpretations, to aggregate and integrate them, look for patterns they all had in common and identify which ones deserved to be fed into my conclusions. Rather than asking specific questions, I allowed for and even prompted broad discussions that encouraged respondents to talk about cases, politicians and events, or to give factual information about their personal record. I clarified to my interviewees that I did not necessarily expect them to come up with cases in which they had been personally involved, as I thought for some it might be easier to speak openly about a scenario in which they had no vested interest. Some phenomena we talked about, such as the relevance of mutual trust and direct access to a politician, the role of resources and the centrality of personal talent in political communications, could be discussed without reference to an interviewee's previous job and personal professional record. This arguably allowed for a more open exchange of views.

The focus of this book was limited to the relationship between politicians and communicators on the one hand and traditional print and broadcast journalists on the other. When I first thought about this project in 2005, internet communications were already hotly debated, but the notion of the citizen journalist and social websites as sources of political commentary was of somewhat limited relevance. As this changed over time, I had to clarify the focus of my study and deliberately limited my research to the interaction between conventional print and broadcast journalism on the one hand and politicians on the other. This helped to limit the number of variables that define media management, which through a consideration of user-generated content and social media would have grown in complexity. However, for a study that were to be planned now and conducted in coming years, a broadening of the focus would need to be considered to grant online media the role it has attained as a source of commentary and information in the public discourse that reverberates into the offline media coverage as well.

Conclusion

The findings in this study diverge considerably from assumptions about political communications management expressed in academic writing across the disciplines of marketing, PR and political communications, the emphasis of which is broadly on researched and planned campaign processes in the run-up to election day. By contrast, my findings illustrate that the long-term build-up of a political contender's reputation usually is far from systematic and certainly not grounded in comprehensive research. A dynamic environment that is conditioned by organized interests, parliamentary adversaries and political news reporting does not allow for advanced planning and requires flexible frameworks to be altered and adapted on a daily if not an hourly basis.

Generating image as well as the building and management of reputation have been confirmed as core activities in which political communicators are expected to engage. In the first part of this book I presented literature that conceptualized political marketing and PR as frameworks that helped politicians and their staff to guide their strategic communications management. It has been suggested that research is the starting point and prerequisite in which any communications objectives should be grounded, which in turn define and inform both communications strategy and day-to-day communications tactics. The ultimate goal is to help shape and implement ideal images and generate reputation for a party and its politicians.

More specifically, this study looked into how communications managers orchestrate the reputation of politicians. It attempted to explore if and to what degree communications practice reflects our understanding of strategic planned reputation management processes as portrayed in marketing, PR and political communications literature.

The situation I encountered through the interviews is defined by a tangible lack of financial means and staff who often are not familiar with notions of strategic planning or doubt its effectiveness. Little evidence was found of a thorough discussion of what the ideal candidate or incumbent should be like. Instead, tactical moves and short-term victories appear to take up the time and attention of communicators. If energy is used up by the daily political slogging match and protagonists find no respite to focus activities on a long-term reputational perspective, the blame for this short-termism may be passed on to journalists, whose resolute agenda setting forces communicators on the defensive.

While comprehensive planning is largely absent or deficient, the outcome of communications management activities at times appears to hinge on a politician's talent in media relations and natural communicative prowess – a variable for which it is difficult to plan. A lack of intuition when dealing with the media does not bode well for political protagonists. What is worse, shaky communicative skills are difficult to compensate for even if financial means and expertise were abundant and readily available to the politician. No less relevant and therefore well within the remit of communications strategists is the politician's personality, which has the potential to make or break processes of systematic communications management. Politicians who are unwilling or unable to take or act upon their communicator's advice put an end to or severely hamper planned communications activities.

My observations come as a surprise insofar as they do not square with the emphasis I found in the current academic discourse about political communications practice. In political science, PR and marketing communications, the omnipresence of strategic management processes in politics is taken for granted. While I do not intend to question or challenge this claim, I contend that with regard to an individual politician's reputation management, evidence suggests that the perceptible public persona is perhaps more the result of haphazard action than the current literature suggests. The reason for the apparent misconception in current literature is arguably a lack of empirical research into personal reputation management that could highlight how communicators work to shape a politician's reputation. This gap in knowledge has been addressed in this book, the purpose of which was to collect and analyse data, reflect on our understanding of current political communications management practice, and define if and to what degree reputation management of individual politicians is a strategic and planned operation.

The data reviewed suggest that the practice of political communications is multifaceted and grounded both in managerial issues and functional interpersonal communications. Personal relationships, concepts of trust between politicians and their staff, shared values and a mutual understanding are conditional in securing communications experts' access to the politician, whose acceptance of and support for systematic media management advice is critical if communications are to be managed strategically. It is partly this interpersonal theme that is marginalized in current political communications research. Only thorough empirical analysis of political communications management allows us to identify and define how individual talents and preferences, personal backgrounds, trust and mutual understanding shape political communications practice.

In particular, public relations research in the UK has largely forsaken the opportunity to engage with political communications management. Instead, research in this discipline is predominantly concerned with the corporate setting. When reviewing current literature, it became apparent that political public relations is an incipient subject. The theoretical concepts of PR have yet to be comprehensively applied in the ambit of political communications and, more specifically, reputation management. This does come as a surprise, as PR claims to be the very discipline that deals with the build-up and the management of reputation. This book may help to pioneer the application of a public relations perspective in a political setting. Related to this work are questions raised by personality PR, which so far in this discipline is overshadowed by research that focuses on corporate PR. Moreover, it appears that research in personality PR during the past decade has not extended to empirical investigations of political communications management either.

The discipline that dedicates itself most decisively to the analysis of communications processes in politics is marketing. However, writers in marketing avail themselves of models that fail to do justice to the dynamic and adversarial environment in which political communicators operate. Academic political marketing writing is grounded in management models and planned processes, but not always fully acquainted with how political protagonists struggle to gain and keep the initiative in a slogging match with journalists and political opponents. It is these very dynamics that explain why it is little plausible to think a politician's reputation may be the result of planned processes. The 24-hour news cycle, the intensity of media coverage and the seventy of competition between and within political parties arguably add a degree of volatility and surprise to the political debate, which needs to be integrated into existing models of communications management.

Current models of political marketing management tend to focus on a final date to which campaigns are geared. In marketing this may equate to a product's launch date, which writers on political marketing translate into election day. By the same token, the time period political marketing communications plans are designed for stretches over a few weeks or months, which reflect the period of an election campaign. In contrast, PR would understand reputation building as an ongoing process in the course of which information is added and moulded over an unlimited period of time that transcends election cycles. An individual's past record and actions add to the current reputation as a benefit or a burden. Against this backdrop, the safeguarding of reputation is conceptualized as an ongoing concern that requires recurrent readjustment and is better visualized in a loop than in a timeline as marketers suggest.

In a nutshell, the problem identified in discussions about personal reputation in politics is that the approaches taken by distinct disciplines are too limited and therefore fail to do justice to the distinct conditions under which political communicators operate. While marketing models tend not to take the volatility of media relations into account, public relations literature has traditionally – and until very recently – neglected the political context. Therefore, my findings add to existing models by exposing them to empirical evidence of communications management practice. Arguably, the most fundamental discrepancy between existing frameworks of communications practice and my findings relates to the absence of research in reputation management. For this reason there has been only limited awareness that most senior politicians do not have the financial means at their disposal which would allow them to conduct opinion polls, let alone systematically gather data to gauge attitudes towards their respective public persona. Without this research data there is no guiding rod for communicators to design strategies and appropriate techniques. Without research one can only speculate about public expectations and make random assumptions about features that define an ideal reputation. Therefore, any attempt to design strategy and tactics becomes arbitrary guesswork.

When reviewing these empirical findings against the backdrop of current literature on political public relations (Chapter 2), the following theoretical implication imposes itself: in politics the concept of *strategic PR* is viable under certain circumstances only. These are encountered when specific resources are available, which I described earlier in this chapter and defined more specifically in the categories that feature in Figure 8.1. Even if communications managers can count on the resources I deemed critical for a planned approach led by objectives, a strategic pathway still might not be pursued and practised fully, unless the volatility and dynamism that characterize the environment in a political scenario are attenuated. We may therefore, as a result of my empirical findings, want to distinguish in future PR research between a predominantly *tactical variant of political PR* on the one hand and a *resource-based political PR* on the other. Only the latter possesses the potential to be strategic in the sense outlined in Chapter 3, as this variant draws on resources that help PR managers to operate. Hence the current academic debate on whether political PR tends to be persuasive or dialogic in nature may become secondary to a more immediate need to clarify if the communications operators and politicians with which they are associated are in a position to pursue a communications practice that is informed by research-based objectives. Thus, any informed subsequent debate on political PR in general, and personality PR in a political setting more specifically, will need to distinguish whether the resources variant or the tactical variant of political PR are to be considered. In other words, theory building and theory testing cannot be conducted in political communications management unless the two PR variants are acknowledged and their differences recognized.

Thus, the central theoretical inference we may draw from my findings is the understanding that political PR as a unified concept does not exist. Indeed, any attempt to illustrate the practice in a single, comprehensive definition may not do justice to the discipline. Instead, insights gained from analysing empirical data result in a profile that mirrors variations of a strategic and a tactical approach – depending on the resources available and the level of external volatility. Variants of political PR as defined in line with the categories introduced in Figure 8.1 may be of consequence to practitioners' professional profiles and thus directly affect communications management practice. Of similar importance, the notion of two variants in political PR also requires a redefinition of theoretical discourse: agenda setting, symmetrical and asymmetrical communications and, not least, notions about the power exerted by spin represent but a few concepts whose application in political PR may need reconsideration. In other words, theoretical and empirical research that assists in explaining and interpreting communications activities in politics may arrive at conclusions that are contingent on the PR variant – resource based or tactical – which the researcher chooses to explore. This places the onus on the academic to clarify and justify which PR variant – or variation thereof – is investigated. In brief: the illustration of a political PR manager's modus operandi hinges on which of the two variants the case under investigation is leaning towards. A similar distinction is not entirely new in PR, and scholarly texts do juxtapose practitioner roles as technicians and managers. However, these terms are reflective of an undisputed differentiation in job specifications that is linked to hierarchy levels and seniority in an organization, with managers in charge of strategy and technicians responsible for operating tools and implementing ideas. The distinction I am proposing to make in political PR is pointing at a phenomenon that is more covert, not accounted for by levels of hierarchy, not generally admitted by practitioners and overlooked by academic writers. While both resource-based, strategic political PR and tactical political PR are found side by side across the industry, the two variants I identified fundamentally help to differentiate between the two practices and therefore allow predictions of communications outcomes. Therefore, if academic writers strive to increase their understanding both of reality and managerial practice and provide explanations for the phenomena they encounter, the concepts of resource-based political PR and tactical political PR may prove to be a useful interpretative model.

This study's empirical focus was limited to the UK. Yet, it is reasonable to ask if and to what degree the findings cast a light on political reputation management in other party systems. As my work addressed two closely related, yet distinct objectives, the answer to this question likewise twofold.

On the one hand, I came up with a predictive model whose categories derive from insight into the practice of reputation management. This model is applicable to diverse political settings and institutional arrangements. What will obviously change is the categories' empirical content, which is to reflect the respective political environment and culture in which the model is used.

On the other hand, there are the empirical data generated in a series of interviews in the course of this study, which led me to infer that reputation management practice in the UK is not in line with mainstream theoretical perspectives of strategic communications management. Clearly, this is a conclusion that cannot and should not be generalized across political, institutional and cultural boundaries. A range of factors impinge on communications practice and may thus significantly alter findings: the financial resources available to communicators in the USA, for instance, would pay for more comprehensive research into audiences. Arguably, it could also attract a broader range of highly qualified staff. Those two factors alone may impact on input and outcome both of agenda-setting and issue-management processes. In Germany, to provide just one more example, where elected political party officials traditionally have a stronger say on policy and strategy issues than in either the UK or the USA, the room for external political advisers to manoeuvre and position the politician is potentially more limited. In brief, variables that permit, foster or hinder strategic planning are bound to be different from what one encounters in the UK. These distinctions between party systems, political cultures and institutional arrangements constitute variables that future research will need to take into account when replicating or expanding this study. Some of these points are taken up in the following discussion on suggested further research.

Further research

In terms of approaches, professionalism and quality, considerable differences in political communications management activities have become evident. Data presented in this book should allow us to speculate that these distinctions are mainly, but perhaps not exclusively, owing to the different level of resources available to the prime minister, the chancellor, other cabinet ministers and members of the opposition. The design and methodology of this study do not permit to contrast of communications practice engaged in by individual members of government with that pursued in opposition. A further study would need to look into these cases separately, juxtapose practice in government and opposition, and explore correlations more systematically.

It transpired in the course of this study that resources are at the heart of effective communications. It may therefore be worth quantifying the impact of finances and staff numbers on the quality of personal reputation management. As the availability of resources may vary between different political systems, a comparative study would be required to look into funding levels and relate them to communications management practice. Such an investigation may contrast phenomena of communications practice on the one hand and financial as well as personnel resources provided by the state and through private donors on the other. Thus, my supposition that funding and staffing have direct repercussions on communications management quality and the strategic approach taken could be either confirmed or falsified. In other words, a comparative quantitative study would be an opportunity to apply and test the model of personal reputation management that I introduced above.

A point I did not touch upon in this study is the party political and ideological backdrop that ties politicians to certain convictions, a collective record and shared narrative, which in turn may limit their scope of action and affect the positioning of their public persona. A prominent and visible role for the political party may be a constraint on individual politicians' choice of messages and the range of policies they can be expected to pursue. Yet political cultures vary from country to country, and a political party's function as an ideological sounding board for candidates and incumbents is developed to different degrees depending on a political system's traditions and conventions. It would arguably be a limiting factor for a politician's public persona if policies, timing and messages were less conditioned by managerial processes or presentational concerns, and instead be more tightly handled by party officials. One might wonder how much freedom this leaves to the expert communicator to design images and work on a politician's public perception if ideological concerns dictated by the party had to be heeded.

When in the US presidential election campaign the concept of a war room as an operative centre outside the traditional party structure was pioneered, and copied by the German Social Democrats in their 1998 general election, questions were raised as to who took strategic and managerial decisions in an election campaign. These examples suggest that the balance of power between elected party officials and outside experts is not stable, but dynamic and subject to variations from election to election, and country to country.

It would therefore be worth applying the model of personal reputation management in a comparison between different countries as an opportunity to explore how changes at the macro level of political culture impact on the micro level of political and communications management.

Since the variables I have developed and used in my model of personal reputation management are the result of an exploration, they are tentative and subject to debate. The qualitative and quantitative studies suggested above would help corroborate and develop this tentative framework by adding new categories, prioritizing the existing ones, and removing those whose relevance might not be confirmed.

Bibliography

Abels, H. (2004) *Einführung in die Soziologie*. Wiesbaden, VS Verlag.

Aberbach, D. (1996) *Charisma in Politics, Religion and the Media – Private Trauma, Public Ideals*. New York, Macmillan.

Abrams, M. (1963) 'Public Opinion Polls and Political Parties.' *Public Opinion Quarterly*, 27(1), 9–18.

Ake, C. (1966) 'Charismatic Legitimation and Political Integration.' *Comparative Studies in Society and History*, 14, 1–13.

Alessandri, W.S. (2001) 'Modelling Corporate Identity: A Concept Explication and Theoretical Explanation.' *Corporate Communications*, 6(4), 173–82.

Althaus, M. (1998) *Wahlkampf als Beruf. Die Professionalisierung der political consultants in den USA*. Frankfurt am Main, Peter Lang Verlag.

Arnold, S., Fuhrmeister, C. and Schiller, D. (1998) 'Hüllen und Masken der Politik.' In: Arnold, S., Fuhrmeister, C. and Schiller, D. (eds) *Politische Inszenierung im 20. Jahrhundert: Zur Sinnlichkeit der Macht*. Wien, Böhlau, 7–25.

Austin, E.W. and Pinkleton, B.E. (2006) *Strategic Public Relations Management*. Mahwah, NJ, Erlbaum.

Bagdikian, B. (1984) 'Journalist Meets Propagandist.' In: Graber, D. (ed.) *Media Power in Politics*. Washington, DC, CQ Press, 331–37.

Bagehot (2007) 'Taste the Sausage.' *The Economist*, 24 November, 44, www.economist.com/node/10171786 (accessed 31 July 2014).

Baines, P. (2005) 'Marketing the Political Message: American Influences on British Practices.' *Journal of Political Marketing*, 4 (2/3), 135–62.

Baines, P.R. and Egan, J. (2001) 'Marketing and Political Campaigning: Mutually Exclusive or Exclusively Mutual.' *Qualitative Market Research: An International Journal*, 4(4), 25–34.

Baines, P.R., Harris, P. and Lewis, P.B. (2002) 'The Political Marketing Planning Process: Improving Image and Message in Strategic Target Areas.' *Market Intelligence Planning*, 20(1), 6–14.

Baines, P.R. and Worcester, R.M. (2002) 'Researching Political Markets: Market Oriented or Populist?' *International Journal of Market Research*, 42(3), 339–56.

——(2006) 'Voter Research and Market Positioning: Triangulating and its Implications for Policy.' In: Davies, P. and Newman, B. (eds) *Winning Elections with Political Marketing*. Philadelphia, PA, Haworth.

Balmas, M. and Sheafer, T. (2010) 'Candidate Image in Election Campaigns: Attribute Agenda Setting, Affective Priming and Voting Intentions.' *International Journal of Public Opinion Research*, 22(2), 204–29.

Barber, J.D. (1980) *The Use of Politics: Electing Presidents in the Media Age*. New York, Norton.

Barkham, P., Burkeman, O., Meek, J. and Vulliamy, E. (2005) 'Stage-managed Rings of Confidence.' *The Guardian*. 5 May, www.guardian.co.uk/politics/2005/may/05/uk.media1 (accessed 20 February 2012).

Bartle, J. (2002) 'Market Analogies: The Marketing of Labour and the Origins of New Labour.' In: O'Shaughnessy, N. and Henneberg, S. (eds) *The Idea of Political Marketing*. Westport, CT, Praeger Publishers, 39–65.

Bass, B.M. (1988) 'Evolving Perspectives on Charismatic Leadership.' In: Conger, J.A. and Kanungo, R.N. (eds) *Charismatic Leadership: The Elusive Factor in Organizational Effectiveness*. San Francisco, CA, Jossey-Bass Publishers, 40–77.

Bauer, H.H., Huber, F. and Herrmann, A. (1996) 'Political Marketing: An Information – Economic Analysis.' *European Journal of Marketing*, 30(10/11), 152–65.

Baumeister, R.F. (1989) 'Motives and Costs of Self-presentation in Organizations.' In: Giacalone, R.A. and Rosenfeld, P. (eds) *Impression Management in the Organisation*. London, Routledge, 57–71.

Beckett, A. (2006) *Hi kids, I'm Dave Cameron. Keep it real*, www.guardian.co.uk/politics/2006/jan/12/conservatives.davidcameron (accessed 5 February 2012).

Bendix, R. (1998) *Max Weber: An Intellectual Portrait*. London, Routledge.

Bennett, G.A. and George, A.L. (2005) *Case Studies and Theory Development in the Social Sciences*. Cambridge, MA, MIT Press.

Bennett, W.L. (1992) *The Governing Crisis: Media, Money and Marketing in American Elections*. New York, St Martin's Press.

Bentele, G. (1998) 'Politische Öffentlichkeitsarbeit.' In: Sarcinelli, U. (ed.) *Politikvermittlung und Demokratie in der Mediengesellschaft. Beitraege zur politischen Kommunikationskultur*. Opladen, Westdeutscher Verlag.

Bentele, G. and Fähnrich, B. (2010) 'Personalisierung als sozialer Mechanismus in Medien und gesellschaftlichen Organisationen.' In: Eisenegger, M. and Wehmeier, S. (eds) *Personalisierung der Organisationskommunikation*. Wiesbaden, Verlag für Sozialwissenschaften, 51–76.

Bentele, G. and Seeling, S. (1996) 'Öffentliches Vertrauen als Faktor politischer Öffentichkeit und politischer Public Relations. Zur Bedeutung von Diskrepanzen als Ursache von Vertrauensverlust.' In: Jarren, O., Schatz, H. and Wessler, H. (eds) *Medien und politischer Prozess*. Opladen, Westdeutscher Verlag, 155–84.

Bernays, E. (1955) *The Engineering of Consent*. Norman, University of Oklahoma Press.

——(1985) 'Operatives and Lobbyists vs. PR Professionals.' *Public Relations Quarterly*, 30, 27–30.

Black, S. (1962) *Practical Public Relations*. London, Sir Isaac Pitman & Sons.

Blick, A. (2004) *People who Live in the Dark*. London, Politicos.

Blissland, J. (1990) 'Accountability Gap: Evaluation Practices Show Improvement.' *Public Relations Review*, 16(2), 25–32.

Blumenthal, S. (1982) *The Permanent Campaign*. New York, Simon and Schuster.

Blumer, H. (1966) 'The Mass, the Public and Public Opinion.' In: Berelson, B. and Janowitz, M. (eds) *Reader in Public Opinion and Communication*. New York, Free Press, 43–50.

Blumler, J.G. and Gurevitch, M. (1995) *The Crisis of Public Communication*. Hove, Psychology Press.

Blumler, J. and Kavanagh, D. (1999) 'The Third Age in Political Communication: Influences and Features.' *Political Communication*, 16(1), 209–30.

Boorstin, D.J. (1992) *The Image: A Guide to Pseudo-events in America*. New York, Vintage Books.

Botan, C. (2006) 'Grand Strategy. Strategy and Tactics in Public Relations.' In: Botan, C. and Hazelton V. (eds) *Public Relations Theory*. New York, Erlbaum, 223–47.

Branigan, T. (2006) 'Primary Colours.' *The Guardian*. 19 April, politics.guardian.co.uk/media/story/0,1756396,00.html (accessed 19 April 2006).

Brettschneider, F. (2002) *Spitzenkandidaten und Wahlerfolg: Personalisierung – Kompetenz – Parteien. Ein internationaler Vergleich*. Wiesbaden, VS-Verlag.

Brewer, P. and Sigelman, L. (2002) 'Political Scientists as Color Commentators: Framing and Expert Commentary in Media Campaign Coverage.' *Harvard International Journal of Press Politics*, 7(1), 23–35.

Brissenden, J.G. and Moloney, K. (2005) 'Political PR in the 2005 UK General Election: Winning and Losing, With a Little Help from Spin.' *Journal of Marketing Management*, 21, 1005–20.

Brogan, D.W. (1935) *Abraham Lincoln*. London, Duckworth.

Bromley, D. (1993) *Reputation, Image and Impression Management*, Chichester, John Wiley & Sons.

——(2001) 'Relationships between Personal and Corporate Reputation.' *European Journal of Marketing*, 35(3/4), 316–34.

Broom, G.M. (2009) *Effective Public Relations*. New Jersey, Pearson Education.

Brown, T.J., Dacin, P.A., Pratt, M.G. and Whetten, D.A. (2006) 'Identity, Intended Image, Constructed Image, and Reputation: An Interdisciplinary Framework and Suggested Terminology.' *Journal of the Academy of Marketing Science*, 34(2), 99–106.

Bryman, A. (1993) *Charisma and Leadership in Organizations*. London, Sage Publications.

Bucy, E.P. (2000) 'Emotional and Evaluative Consequences of Inappropriate Leader Displays.' *Communication Research*, 27(2), 194–226.

Budge, I. (2007) *The New British Politics*. Harlow, Longman.

Burton, B. (2007) *Inside Spin*. Crows Nest, Allen & Unwin.

Busby, R. (2009) *Marketing the Populist Politician*. Basingstoke, Palgrave.

Butler, D. and Kavanagh, D. (2002) *The British General Election of 2001*. Basingstoke, Palgrave.

Butler, P. and Collins, N. (1996) 'Political Marketing: Structure and Process.' *European Journal of Marketing*, 2(1), 19–34.

Cameron, G.T., Wilcox, D.L., Reber, B.H. and Shin, J.H. (2008) *Public Relations Today: Managing Competition and Conflict*. Boston, Pearson Education.

Campbell, A. (2011) *The Alastair Campbell Diaries. Power and the People*. New York, Hutchinson.

Carroll, C. and McCombs, M. (2003) 'Agenda-setting Effects of Business News on the Public's Images and Opinions about Major Corporations.' *Corporate Reputation Review*, 6(1), 36–46.

Castells, M. (2009) *Communication Power*. New York, Oxford University Press.

Clark, R.W. (1988) *Lenin – The Man Behind the Mask*. London, Faber.

Clarke, P. and Evans, S. (1983) *Covering Campaigns: Journalism in Congressional Elections*. Stanford, Stanford University Press.

Clemente, M.N. (2002) *The Marketing Glossary*. New York, Clemente Books.

Coffey, A. (1999) *The Ethnographic Self*. London, Sage.

Cohen, N. (2001) 'Not Spinning but Drowning.' *New Statesman*, 19 February, 16–19.

Committee on Standards in Public Life (2003) *Defining the Boundaries within the Executive. Ministers, Special Advisers and Permanent Civil Service. Ninth Report.* London, www.public-standards.gov.uk/OurWork/Other_Reports_and_Research.html (accessed 26 October 2006).

Conboy, M. (2011) *Journalism in Britain. A Historical Introduction.* London, Sage.

Conger, J.A. and Kanungo, R.N. (1987) 'Toward a Behavioural Theory of Charismatic Leadership in Organizational Settings.' *Academy of Management Review*, 12(4), 637–47.

Cook, G. (2011) 'The Labour Party's Road to 2010.' In: Wring, D., Mortimore, R. and Atkinson, S. (eds) *Political Communication in Britain.* London, Palgrave.

Cook, T.E. (1989) *Making Laws and Making News: Media Strategies in the US House of Representatives.* Washington, DC, Brookings Institution.

——(1996) 'Afterword: Political Values and Production Values.' *Political Communication*, 13(4), 469–81.

——(1998) *Governing with the News. The News Media as a Political Institution.* Chicago, University of Chicago Press.

Coombs, W.T. (2000) 'Advantages of a Relational Perspective.' In: Ledingham, J. and Bruning, S. (eds) *Public Relations as Relationship Management.* London, Lawrence Erlbaum.

Cooper, A. (2002) 'The Conservative Campaign.' In: Bartle, J., Atkinson, S. and Mortimore, R. (eds) *Political Communications: The General Election Campaign of 2001.* London, Frank Cass, 98–108.

Cornelissen, J. (2008) *Corporate Communication. A Guide to Theory and Practice.* London, Sage.

Curtin, P.A. (1999) 'Reevaluating Public Relations Information Subsidies: Market Driven Journalism and Agenda Building Theory and Practice.' *Journal of Public Relations Research*, 11(1), 53–90.

Cutlip, S.M. and Center, A.H. (1978) *Effective Public Relations.* Englewood Cliffs, NJ, Prentice Hall.

Cutlip, S.M., Center, A.H. and Broom, G.M. (2000) *Effective Public Relations.* Upper Saddle River, NJ, Prentice Hall International.

Davies, N. (2008) *Flat Earth News.* New York, Chatto and Windus.

Davis, A. (2003) 'Public Relations and News Sources.' In: Cottle, S. (ed.) *News, Public Relations and Power.* London, Sage, 27–44.

de Landtsheer, C. (2004) *Politiek impressiemanagement in Vlaanderen en Nederland* [Political Impression Management in Flanders and The Netherlands]. Leuven, Belgium, Acco.

de Landtsheer, C., de Vries, P. and Vertessen, D. (2008) 'Political Impression Management: How Metaphors, Sound Bites, Appearance Effectiveness, and Personality Traits Can Win Elections.' *Journal of Political Marketing*, 7(3), 217–38.

Deaver, M. (1987) *Behind the Scenes.* New York, William Morrow and Company.

Delli Carpini, M.X. (1994) 'Critical Symbiosis: Three Themes on President-Press-Relations.' *Media Studies Journal*, 8(2), 185–97.

Deng, S. and Dart, J. (1994) 'Measuring Market Orientation: A Multi-factor, Multi-item Approach.' *Journal of Marketing Management*, 10(8), 725–42.

Denver, D., Carman, C. and Johns, R. (2012) *Elections and Voters in Britain.* Basingstoke, Palgrave.

Diamantopoulos, A. and Hart, S. (1991) 'Market Orientation and Company Performance: Preliminary Evidence from UK Manufacturing Industry. Proceedings of the

Winter Educators' Conference of the American Marketing Association.' In: Mackenzie, S. and Childers, T. (eds) *Marketing Theory and Applications*, 2, 187–88.

Dowling, G. (1986) 'Managing your Corporate Images.' *Industrial Marketing Management*, 15(2), 109–15.

——(2008) 'Creating Better Corporate Reputations. An Australian Perspective.' In: Melewar, T.C. (ed.) *Facets of Corporate Identity. Communication and Reputation*. London, Routledge, 178–96.

Dozier, D.M. (1985) 'Planning and Evaluation in PR Practice.' *Public Relations Review*, 11(2), 17–24.

Dozier, D.M., Grunig, L.A. and Grunig, J.E. (1995) *Manager's Guide to Excellence in Public Relations and Communication Management*. Mahwah, NJ, Lawrence Erlbaum.

du Plessis, E. (2008) *The Advertised Mind. Groundbreaking Insights into how our Brains Respond to Advertising*. London, Kogan Page.

Eagly, A.R., Ashmore, M., Makhijani, M. and Longo, L. (1991) 'What is Beautiful is Good, but … A Meta-analytic Review of Research on the Physical Attractiveness Stereotype.' *Psychological Bulletin*, 110(1), 109–28.

Edelman, M. (1964) *The Symbolic Uses of Politics*. Urbana, University of Illinois Press.

Edelmann, R.J. (1987) *The Psychology of Embarrassment*. New York, John Wiley and Sons.

Ehling, W.P., White, J. and Grunig, J.E. (1992) 'Public Relations and Marketing Practices.' In: Grunig, J.E. (ed.) *Excellence in Public Relations and Communication Management*. Hillsdale, Erlbaum, 357–93.

Eilders, C. (1997) *Nachrichtenfaktoren und Rezeption. Eine empirische Analyse zur Auswahl und Verarbeitung politischer Information*. Opladen, Westdeutscher Verlag.

Eisenegger, M. (2010) 'Eine Phänomenologie der Personalisierung.' In: Eisenegger, M. and Wehmeier, S. (eds) *Personaliseriung der Organisationskommunikation*. Wiesbaden, Verlag für Sozialwissenschaften, 11–26.

Eisenegger, M. and Konieczny-Wössner, E. (2009) 'Regularitäten personalisierter Reputationskonstitution in der medienvermittelten Kommunikation.' In: Eisenegger, M. and Wehmeier, S. (eds) *Personalisierung der Organisationskommunikation*. Wiesbaden, Verlag für Sozialwissenschaften, 117–32.

Eisinger, R. (2000) 'Gauging Public Opinion in the Hoover White House: Understanding the Roots of Presidential Polling.' *Presidential Studies Quarterly*, 30(4), 643–61.

Entman, R.M. (2004) *Projections of Power. Framing News, Public Opinion, and US Foreign Policy*. Chicago, University of Chicago Press.

Ericson, R.V., Baranek, P.M. and Chan, J.B.L. (1989) *Negotiating Control: A Study of New Sources*. Milton Keynes, Open University Press.

Erikson, E.H. (1964) *Insight and Responsibility*. New York, Norton.

——(1969) *Gandhi's Truth*. New York, Norton.

Esser, F. (2000) 'Spin doctoring als Regierungs-PR. Strategisches Skandal-, Themen- und Imagemanagement der Clinton-Administration.' In: Kamps, K. (ed.) *Trans-Atlantik – Trans-Portabel? Die Amerikanisierungsthese in der politischen Kommunikation*. Wiesbaden, Westdeutscher Verlag, 129–58.

Esser, F. and d'Angelo, P. (2006) 'Framing the Press and Publicity Process in the US, British and German General Elections Campaigns: A Comparative Study of Metacoverage.' *International Journal of Press/Politics*, 11(3), 44–66.

Esser, F., Reinemann, C. and Fan, D. (2000) 'Spin Doctoring in British and German Election Campaigns. How the Press is being Confronted with a New Quality of Political PR.' *European Journal of Communication*, 2/2000, 209–39.

——(2001) 'Spin Doctors in the United States, Great Britain, and Germany: Metacommunication about Media Manipulation.' *The Harvard International Journal of Press/Politics*, 6(16), 16–45.

Farrell, D. and Webb, P. (2002) 'Political Parties as Campaign Organisations.' In: Dalton, R.J. and Watenberg, M.P. (eds) *Parties without Partisans. Political Change in Advanced Industrial Democracies.* Oxford, Oxford University Press, 102–28.

Farrell, D.M. and Wortmann, M. (1987) 'Party Strategies in the Electoral Market: Political Marketing in West-Germany, Britain and Ireland.' *European Journal of Political Research*, 15(3), 297–318.

Faulstich, W. (1992) 'Image als Problemfeld – Systematische Bedeutungsdimensionen, historische Entwicklung.' In: Faulstich W. (ed.) *Image, Imageanalyse, Imagegestaltung.* Bardowick, Wissenschaftler-Verlag, 7–12.

Ferguson, M. (1984) 'Building Theory in Public Relations: Inter-organisational Relationship.' Paper presented to Association for Education in Journalism & Mass Communication, Gainesville, FL. August.

Fill, C., Baines, P. and Page, K. (2010) *Marketing.* Oxford, Oxford University Press.

Fischer, L. (1982) *The Life of Mahatma Gandhi.* London, Granada.

Fombrun, C.J. (1996) *Reputation: Realising Value from the Corporate Image.* Boston, MA, Harvard Business School Press.

Fombrun, C.J. and Rindova, V. (1996) *Who is Top and who Decides? The Social Construction of Corporate Reputations.* New York, Stern School of Business.

Fombrun, C.J. and van Riehl, C. (2004) *Fame and Fortune: How Successful Companies Build Winning Reputations.* New Jersey, Financial Times/Prentice Hall.

Forbes, P.S. (1992) 'Applying Strategic Management to Public Relations.' *Public Relations Journal*, 248(3), 31–32.

Franck, G. (1998) *Ökonomie der Aufmerksamkeit. Ein Entwurf.* München, Carl Hanser Verlag.

Franklin, B. (2003) 'A Good Day to Bury Bad News?' In: Cottle, S. (ed.) *News, Public Relations and Power.* Sage, London, 45–62.

——(2004) *Packaging Politics: Political Communication in Britain's Media Democracy.* London, Arnold.

Freeman, D. (1957) *1948–1957. George Washington, A Biography.* New York, Scribners.

Freidson, E. (2001) *Professionalism. The Third Logic.* Cambridge, Polity Press.

French, J.R.P. and Raven, R. (2001) 'The Bases of Social Power.' In: Asherman, I.G. and Asherman, S.V. (eds) *The Negotiation Sourcebook.* Amherst, MA, HRD Press.

Fridkin, K.L. and Kenney, P.J. (2005) 'Campaign Frames – Can Candidates Influence Media Coverage?' In: Callaghan, K. and Schnell, F. (eds) *Framing American Politics.* Pittsburgh, PA, University of Pittsburgh Press.

Friedrich, C.J. (1961) 'Political Leadership and the Problem of Charismatic Power.' *Journal of Politics*, 23(1), 3–24.

Froehlich, R. and Ruediger, B. (2005) 'Framing Political Public Relations: Measuring Success of Political Communication Strategies in Germany.' *Public Relations Review*, 32, 18–25.

Froman, L.A. (1963) *People and Politics: An Analysis of the American Political System.* New York, Prentice Hall.

Gaber, I. (1998) 'A World of Dogs and Lamp-posts.' *New Statesman*, 19 June, 14.

——(2000) 'Government by Spin: An Analysis of the Process.' *Media Culture & Society*, 22, 507–18.

Galtung, J. and Ruge, M.H. (1965) 'The Structure of Foreign News.' In: *Journal of Peace Research*, 2(1), 64–91.

Gandy, O. (1982) *Beyond Agenda Setting: Information Subsidies and Public Policy*. Norwood, NJ, Ablex.

Gans, H. (1979) *Deciding What's News*. New York, Vintage Books.

Gardner, H. (1995) *Leading Minds – An Anatomy of Leadership*. New York, Basic Books.

Garner, B. and Short, J. (1998) 'Hungry Media Need Fast Food: The Role of the Central Office of Information.' In: Franklin, B. and Murphy, D. (eds) *Making the Local News: Local Journalism in Context*. London, Routledge, 170–83.

GCN (Government Communications Network) (2010) *Engage Handbook for the Communications Community*. London, Cabinet Office, www.wiki.comms.gov.uk/index.php/what_is_Engage ... %3F (accessed 5 November 2011).

Gerstle, J., Davis, D. and Dubanel, O. (1991) 'Television News and the Construction of Political Reality in France and the United States.' In: Kaid, L.E., Gerstle, J. and Sanders, K.R. (eds) *Mediated Politics in Two Cultures: Presidential Campaigning in the USA and France*. New York, Praeger, 119–43.

Gerth, H.H. and Mills, C.W. (1958) *From Max Weber: Essays in Sociology*. New York and Oxford, Oxford University Press.

Gibson, R. and Römmele, A. (2001) 'Changing Campaign Communications. A Party-centred Theory of Professionalised Campaigning.' *Harvard International Journal of Press and Politics*, 6(4), 31–43.

Gioia, D.A., Schultz, M. and Corley, K.G. (2000) 'Organizational Identity, Image and Adaptive Instability.' *Academy of Management Reviews*, 25(1), 63–81.

Gitlin, T. (1980) *The Whole World is Watching*. Berkeley, University of California Press.

Gomibuchi, S. (2004) 'Trust and Leadership.' *Political Science*, 56(2), 27–38.

Gotsi, M. and Wilson, A.M. (2001) 'Corporate Reputation: Seeking a Definition.' *Corporate Communications: An International Journal*, 6(1), 24–30.

Gould, P. (1998a) *The Unfinished Revolution. How the Modernisers Saved the Labour Party*. London, Abacus.

——(1998b) 'Why Labour Won.' In: Crewe, I., Gosschalk, B. and Bartle, J. (eds) *Political Communications. Why Labour won the General Election of 1997*. London, Frank Cass Publishers, 3–11.

——(2002) *What Permanent Campaign?* BBC online, news.bbc.co.uk/1/hi/uk_politics/2499061.stm (accessed 5 September 2007).

Graber, D. (1997) *Mass Media and American Politics*. Washington, DC, Congressional Quarterly Press.

Gracian y Morales, B. (2005) *Handorakel und Kunst der Weltklugheit*. Munich, dtv Beck.

Gray, D.E. (2009) *Doing Research in the Real World*. Sage, London.

Greenaway, J., Smith, S. and Street, J. (1992) *Deciding Factors in British Politics*. London, Routledge.

Gregory, A. (2000) *Planning and Managing Public Relations Campaigns*. London, Kogan.

——(2007) 'Public Relations and Management.' In: Theaker, A. (ed.) *The Public Relations Handbook*. London, Routledge, 60–79.

——(2011) 'The Strategic Communication Process in Government: A UK Perspective.' In: Moss, D. and DeSanto, B. (eds) *Public Relations. A Managerial Perspective.* London, Sage, 193–221.

Grender, O. and Parminter, K. (2007) 'Elections and Campaigning. From "My Vote" to "The Real Alternative": Selling the Liberal Democrats.' *The Political Quarterly*, 78(1), 108–16.

Greve, J. (1999) 'Sprache, Kommunikation und Strategie in der Theorie von Jürgen Habermas.' *Koelner Zeitschrift fuer Soziologie und Sozialpsychologie*, 51(2), 232–59.

Griffin, A. (2008) *New Strategies for Reputation Management*. London, Kogan Page.

Grunig, J.E. (2002) *Qualitative Methods for Assessing Relationships between Organisations and Publics.* Gainesville, FL, Institute for Public Relations.

Grunig, J.E. and Huang, Y.H. (2000) 'From Organisational Effectiveness to Relationship Indicators: Antecedents of Relationships, Public Relations Strategies, and Relationship Outcomes.' In: Ledingham, J.A. and Bruning, S.D. (eds) *Public Relations as Relationship Management: A Relational Approach to the Study and Practice of Public Relations.* Mahwah, NJ, Erlbaum, 55–69.

Grunig, J.E. and Hunt, T. (1984) *Managing Public Relations.* New York, Holt, Rinehart & Winston.

Grunig, J.E. and Repper, F.C. (1992) 'Strategic Management. Publics and Issues.' In: Grunig, J. (ed.) *Excellence in Public Relations and Communication Management.* Hillsdale, NJ, Lawrence Erlbaum Associates, 135–37.

Grunig, L.A., Grunig, J.E. and Dozier, D.M. (2002) *Excellent Public Relations and Effective Organisations.* Mahwah, NJ, Erlbaum.

Habermas, J. (1987) 'The Theory of Communicative Action.' *Lifeworld and System: A Critique of Functionalist Reason.* Vol. 2, Boston, Beacon Press.

Haley, J. (1969) *The Power Tactics of Jesus Christ and Other Essays.* New York, Grossman.

Hallahan, K. (1999) 'Seven Models of Framing: Implications for Public Relations.' *Public Relations Review*, 11(3), 205–42.

——(2010) 'Being Public: Publicity as Public Relations.' In: Heath, R.L. (ed.) *Handbook of Public Relations.* Los Angeles, CA, Sage, 523–45.

——(2011) 'Political Public Relations and Strategic Framing.' In: Strömbäck, J. and Kiousis, S. (eds) *Political Public Relations. Principles and Applications.* London, Routledge.

Hallahan, K., Holtzhausen, D., van Ruler, B., Vercic, D. and Sriramesh, K. (2007) 'Defining Strategic Communication.' *International Journal of Strategic Communication*, 1(1), 3–35.

Harris, L. (1963) 'Polls and Politics in the United States.' *Public Opinion Quarterly*, 27, 3–8.

Harrop, M. (1990) 'Political Marketing.' *Parliamentary Affairs: A Journal of Comparative Politics*, 43(3), 277–91.

Hart, R. (1998) *Seducing America: How Television Charms the Modern Voter.* Thousand Oaks, Sage.

Häussler, T. (2008) 'Person vs Argument? Die Personalisierung der politischen Berichterstattung in Grossbritannien und der Schweiz seit 1960.' *Zeitschrift für Kommunikationsökologie und Medienethik*, 1, 6–9.

Heffernan, R. (2006) 'The Prime Minister and the News Media: Political Communication as a Leadership Resource.' *Parliamentary Affairs*, 59(4), 582–98.

Henneberg, S. (1996) 'Second Conference on Political Marketing.' *Journal of Marketing Management*, 12(8), 23–31.

——(2002) 'Understanding Political Marketing.' In: O'Shaughnessy, N.J. and Henneberg, S. (eds) *The Idea of Political Marketing*. Westport, CT, Praeger Publishers, 93–170.

——(2006) 'Strategic Postures of Political Marketing: An Exploratory Operationalization.' *Journal of Public Affairs*, 6(1), 15–30.

Heseltine, M. (2000) *Life in the Jungle*. Philadelphia, PA, Coronet Books.

Hibbert, C. (1965) *Garibaldi and his Enemies*. London, Longman.

Holzer, W. (1996) 'Von Hexenmeistern und Media-Handwerkern. Politische Öffentlichkeitsarbeit in den USA – ein unheimliches Wesen.' In Bertelsmann Stiftung (ed.) *Politik überzeugend vermitteln. Wahlkampfstrategien in Deutschland un den USA*. Gütersloh, Bertelsmann.

House, R.J. and Howell, J.M. (1992) 'Personality and Charismatic Leadership.' *Leadership Quarterly*, 3(2), 81–108.

Howard, C.M. (2004) 'Working with Reporters: Mastering the Fundamentals to Build Long-term Relationships.' *Public Relations Quarterly*, 49(1), 36–39.

Hujer, M. (2003) 'Choreography made in Hollywood.' *Süddeutsche Zeitung*, 3 June, 3.

Hutton, G.J., Goodman, M.B., Alexander, J.B. and Genest, C.M. (2001) 'Reputation Management: The New Face of Corporate Public Relations.' *Public Relations Review*, 27(3), 247–61.

Imhof, K. (2010) 'Personalisierte Ökonomie.' In: Eisenegger, M. and Wehmeiher, S. (eds) *Personalisierung der Organisationskommunication*. Wiesbaden, Verlag für Sozialwissenschaften.

Immelman, A. (2002) 'The Political Personality of U.S. Presidential Candidate George W. Bush.' In: Feldman, O. and Valenty, L.O. (eds) *Political Leadership for the New Century: Personality and Behaviour Among American Leaders*. Westport, CT, Greenwood Press, 81–103.

Immelman, A. and Beatty, A. (2004) *The Political Personality of U.S. Presidential Candidate John Kerry*. Paper presented at the 28th Annual Scientific Meeting of the International Society of Political Psychology. Toronto, Canada, www1.csbsju.edu/uspp/Research/Kerry%20profile.html (accessed 4 May 2009).

Ingham, B. (2003) *The Wages of Spin. A Clear Case of Communications Gone Wrong*. London, John Murray Publishers.

Jackson, N. (2003) 'MPs and Web Technologies: An Untapped Opportunity?' *Journal of Public Affairs*, 3(2).

——(2010) 'Political Public Relations: Spin, Persuasion or Reputation Building?' Paper presented at the Political Studies Association annual conference, Edinburgh.

Jackson, N.A. and Lilleker, D.G. (2004) 'Just Public Relations or an Attempt at Interaction? British MPs in the Press, on the Web and in Your Face.' *European Journal of Communication*, 19(4), 507–33.

Jefkins, J. and Yadin, D. (1998) *Public Relations*. London, Prentice Hall.

Johnson, D.W. (2000) 'The Business of Political Consulting.' In: Thurber, J.A. and Nelson, C.J. (eds) *Campaign Warriors*. Washington, DC, Brookings Institution.

——(2001) *No Place for Amateurs*. New York, Routledge.

Jones, E.E., Gergen, K.J. and Jones, R.G. (1963) 'Tactics of Ingratiation among Leaders and Subordinates in a Status Hierarchy.' *Psychological Monographs*, 77(3), 1–20.

Jones, E.E. and Pittman, T.S. (1982) 'Toward a General Theory of Strategic Self-presentation.' In: Suls, J. (ed.) *Psychological Perspectives on the Self.* Hillsdale, NJ, Erlbaum, Vol. 1, 231–62.

Jones, N. (1999) *Sultans of Spin. The Media and the New Labour Government.* London, Cassell.

——(2001) *Campaign 2001.* London, Politicos.

Jun, U. (2004) *Der Wandel von Parteien in der Mediendemokratie. SPD and Labour Party im Vergleich.* Frankfurt am Main, Campus.

Kaase, M. (1994) 'Is there Personalisation in Politics? Candidates and Voting Behaviour in Germany.' *International Political Science Review*, 15(3), 211–30.

Kaid, L., Gerstle, J. and Sanders, K. (eds) (1991) *Mediated Politics in Two Cultures: Presidential Campaigning in the United States and France.* New York, Praeger.

Kavanagh, D. and Butler, D. (2005) *The British General Election of 2005.* Basingstoke, Macmillan.

Keith, R.J. (1960) 'The Marketing Revolution.' *Journal of Marketing*, 24(3), 35–38.

Kelley, S. (1956) *Professional PR and Political Power.* Baltimore, Johns Hopkins University Press.

Kershaw, I. (1991) *Hitler.* London, Longman.

Kirchheimer, O. (1965) 'Wandel des westeuropäischen Parteiensystems.' *Politische Vierteljahresschrift*, 6, 20–41.

Klapp, O.E. (1964) *Symbolic Leaders.* Chicago, Aldine-Atherton.

Kopfman, E. and Ruth-McSwain, A. (2012) 'Public Information Campaigns.' In Lee, M., Neeley, G. and Stewart, K. (eds) *The Practice of Government Public Relations.* Boca Raton, FL, CRC Press, 75–99.

Korte, K.R. and Froehlich, M. (2009) *Politik und Regieren in Deutschland.* Paderborn. Strukturen, Prozesse, Entscheidungen.

Kotler, P. and Bliemel, F. (1992) *Marketing Management: Analyse, planung, umsetzung und steuerung.* Stuttgart, Schaeffer-Poeschel.

Kotler, P. and Kotler, N. (1981) 'Business Marketing for Political Candidates.' *Campaigns and Elections*, 2, 24–33.

——(1999) 'Political Marketing: Generating Effective Candidates, Campaigns and Causes.' In: Newman, B. (ed.) *Handbook of Political Marketing.* Thousand Oaks, CA, Sage, 3–18.

Kotler, P. and Levy, S.J. (1969) 'Broadening the Concept of Marketing.' *Journal of Political Marketing*, 33 January, 10–15.

Kuhn, A. (1975) *Unified Social Science.* Homewood, IL, Dorsey Publishers.

Kypers, J.A. (1997) *Presidential Crisis Rhetoric and the Press in the Post-Cold War World.* Westport, CT, Praeger.

Leary, M.R. (1995) *Self Presentation: Impression Management and Interpersonal Behaviour.* Boulder, CO, Westview.

Le Bon, G. (1982) *The Crowd: A Study of the Popular Mind.* Marietta, Larin Corporation.

Ledingham, J.A. (2001) 'Government-community Relationships: Extending the Relational Theory of Public Relations.' *Public Relations Review*, 27, 285–95.

Ledingham, J. and Bruning, S. (1998) 'Relationship Management in Public Relations: Dimensions of an Organisation-public Relationship.' *Public Relations Review*, 24(1), 55–65.

——(2000) 'Background and Current Trends in the Study of Relationship Management.' In: Ledingham, J.A. and Bruning, S.D. (eds) *Public Relations as Relationship*

Management: A Relational Approach to Public Relations. Mahwah, NJ. Lawrence Erlbaum Associates.

Lees-Marshment, J. (2001) *Political Marketing and British Political Parties*. Manchester, Manchester University Press.

——(2004) *The Political Marketing Revolution. Transforming the Government of the UK*. Manchester, Manchester University Press.

——(2008) *Political Marketing and British Political Parties. The Party's Just Begun*. Manchester, Manchester University Press.

——(2009) *Political Marketing – Principles and Applications*. Routledge, London.

L'Etang, J. (2008) 'Writing PR History: Issues, Methods and Politics.' *Journal of Communication Management*, 12(4), 319–35.

Levi, M. and Stoker, L. (2000) 'Political Trust and Trustworthiness.' *Annual Review of Political Science*, 3, 475–507.

Lilleker, D.G. (2005) 'The Impact of Political Marketing on Internal Party Democracy.' *Parliamentary Affairs*, 58(3), 570–84.

——(2006) *Key Concepts in Political Communication*. London, Sage.

Lilleker, D.G. and Jackson, N. (2011) 'Political Public Relations and Political Marketing.' In: Strömbäck, J. and Kiousis, S. (eds) *Political Public Relations: Principles and Applications*. London, Routledge, 157–76.

Lilleker, D.G., Jackson, N.A. and Scullion, R. (2006) *The Marketing of Political Parties: Political Marketing at the 2005 UK General Election*. Manchester, Manchester University Press, 251–64.

Lilleker, D.G. and Negrine, R. (2006) 'Mapping a Market Orientation: Can we Detect Political Marketing Only through the Lens of Hindsight?' In: Davies, P.J. and Newman, B.I. (eds) *Winning Elections with Political Marketing*. New York, The Haworth Press, 33–58.

Lilleker, D., Negrine, R. and Stanyer, J. (2002) 'Politicians and Journalists: A Vicious Circle.' *Politics Review*, Autumn, 29–31.

Lindenmann, W.K. (1997) *Guidelines and Standards for Measuring and Evaluating PR Effectiveness*. www.instituteforpr.com/pdf/2002_Guidelines_Standards_Book.pdf (accessed 2 September 2012).

Lippmann, W. (1997 [1922]) *Public Opinion*. London, Free Press.

Liu, B.F. and Levenshus, A.B. (2012) 'Crisis Public Relations for Government Communicators.' In: Lee, M., Neeley, G. and Stewart, K. (eds) *The Practice of Government Public Relations*. Boca Raton, FL, CRC Press, 101–24.

Lloyd, J. (2004) *What the Media are Doing to Our Politics*. London, Constable.

Lock, A. and Harris, P. (1996) 'Political Marketing – Vive la difference.' *European Journal of Marketing*, 30(10/11), 21–32.

Maarek, P.J. (1995) *Political Marketing and Communication*. London, John Libby.

——(2011) *Campaign Communication & Political Marketing*. Chichester, Wiley-Blackwell.

Mair, P. (1998) *Party System Change. Approaches and Interpretations*. Oxford, Clarendon Press.

Major, J. (2000) *The Autobiography*. London, HarperCollins.

Maltese, J.A. (1994) *Spin Control: The White House Office of Communications and the Management of Presidential News*. Chapel Hill, NC, University of North Carolina Press.

Mandelson, P. (2011) *The Third Man*. London, Harper Press.

Manheim, J.B. (1994) *Strategic Public Diplomacy and American Foreign Policy: The Evolution of Influence*. New York, Oxford University Press.
Mannheim, J.B. (2011) *Strategy in Information and Influence Campaigns*. London, Routledge.
Manning, P. (2001) *News and News Sources: A Critical Introduction*. London, Sage.
Marcinkowski, F. (1998) 'Politikvermittlung durch Fernsehen und Hörfunk.' In: Sarcinelli, U. (ed.) *Politikvermittlung und Demokratie in der Mediengesellschaft*. Bonn, Westdeutscher Verlag, 165–83.
Marquand, D. (2004) *Decline of the Public. The Hollowing-out of Citizenship*. Cambridge, Malden.
Martinelli, D.K. (2012) 'Strategic Communication Planning.' In: Lee, M., Neeley, G. and Stewart, K. (eds) Boca Raton, FL, CRC Press, 143–56.
Marx, S. (2008) *Die Legende vom Spin Doctor*. Wiesbaden, Verlag für Sozialwissenschaften.
Mason, C.J. (1993) 'What Image do you Project?' *Management Review*, 82, November, 10–16.
Matalin, M. and Carville, J. (1994) *All's Fair. Love, War and the Running for President*. New York, Verlag.
Mattinson, D. (2010) *Talking to a Brick Wall*. London, Biteback.
Mauser, G.A. (1983) *Political Marketing: An Approach to Campaign Strategy*. Westport, CT, Praeger.
Mavondo, F.F. (2000) 'Marketing as a Form of Adaptation: Empirical Evidence from a Developing Economy.' *Marketing Intelligence & Planning*, 18(5), 256–72.
Mazzoleni, G. and Schulz, W. (1999) 'Mediatization of Politics: A Challenge for Democracy.' *Political Communication*, 16(3), 247–61.
McCombs, M. (2008) *Setting the Agenda. The Mass Media and Public Opinion*. Cambridge, Polity.
McElreath, M.P. (1997) *Managing Systematic and Ethical Public Relations Campaigns*. Madison, WI, Brown and Benchmark.
McKenna, R. (1991) 'Marketing is Everything.' *Harvard Business Review*, January, 65–79.
McNair, B. (1995) *An Introduction to Political Communication*. London, Routledge.
——(2000) *Journalism and Democracy*. London, Routledge.
——(2003) *An Introduction to Political Communication*. New York, Routledge.
——(2004) 'PR Must Die: Spin, Anti-spin and Political Public Relations in the UK, 1997–2004.' *Journalism Studies*, 5(3), 325–38.
——(2007) 'Theories of Government Communication and Trends in the UK.' In: Young, S. (ed.) *Government Communication in Australia*. Cambridge, Cambridge University Press, 93–110.
Meldrum, M. (1996) 'Critical Issues in Implementing Marketing.' *Journal of Marketing Practice: Applied Marketing Science*, 2(3), 29–43.
Merten, K. (1992) 'Begriff und Funktion von Public Relations.' *PR-Magazine*, 11/92, 35–46.
Meyer, C. (2005) *DC Confidential. The Controversial Memoirs of Britain's Ambassador to the U.S. at the Time of 9/11 and the Iraq War*. London, Weidenfeld & Nicolson.
Meyer, T. (2002) *Media Democracy – How the Media Colonises Politics*. Cambridge, Polity.
Meyer, T., Ontrup, R. and Schicha, C. (2000) *Die Inszenierung des Politischen. Zur Theatralität von Mediendiskursen*. Wiesbaden, Verlag für Sozialwissenschaften.

Meyrowitz, J. (1985) *No Sense of Place: The Impact of Electronic Media on Social Behaviour*. New York, Oxford University Press.

Michie, D. (1998) *The Invisible Persuaders*. London, Bantam Press.

Miller, D. (1994) *Don't Mention the War: Northern Ireland, Propaganda and the Media*. London, Pluto Press.

——(1997) *Capitalism. An Ethnographic Approach*. New York, Berg Publications.

Miller, D., Kitzinger, J., Williams, K. and Beharrell, P. (1998) *The Circuit of Mass Communication*. London, Sage.

Miller, R.S. (1992) 'The Nature and Severity of Self-reported Embarrassing Circumstance.' *Personality and Social Psychology Bulletin*, 18(2), 190–98.

Millon, T. (1986) 'Personality Prototypes and their Diagnostic Criteria.' In: Millon, T. and Klerman, G.I. (eds) *Contemporary Directions in Psychopathology*. New York, Guilford, 671–712.

Milne, R.S. and Mackenzie, H.C. (1954) *Straight Fight*. London, Hansard Society.

Mintzberg, H. (1975) 'The Manager's Job: Folklore and Fact.' *Harvard Business Review*, 53, 49–61.

——(1987) 'Crafting Strategy.' *Harvard Business Review*, July–August, 66–75.

Moloney, K. (2006) *Rethinking Public Relations*. Abingdon, Routledge.

Moloney, K. and Colmer, R. (2001) 'Does Political PR Enhance or Trivialise Democracy?' *Journal of Marketing Management*, 17, 957–68.

Moloney, K., Richards, B., Scullion, R. and Daymon, C. (2003) 'Mapping the Production of Political Communications: A Model to Assist in Understanding the Relationships between the Production and Consumption of Political Messages.' *Journal of Public Affairs*, 3(2), 166.

Morris, T. and Goldsworthy, S. (2008) *PR – A Persuasive Industry. Spin, PR, and the Shaping of the Modern Media*. London, Palgrave.

——(2012) *PR Today. The Authoritative Guide to Public Relations*. London, Palgrave.

Mortimore, R. and Gill, M. (2010) 'Implementing and Interpreting Market-orientation in Practice: Lessons from the UK.' In: Lees-Marshment, J., Stroembaeck, J. and Rudd, C. (eds) *Global Political Marketing*. London, Routledge.

Moss, D. (2011) 'A Managerial Perspective of Public Relations: Locating the Function and Analysing the Environment and Organisational Context.' In: Moss, D. and DeSanto, B. (eds) *Public Relations. A Managerial Perspective*. London, Sage, 23–56.

Mountfield Report (1997) *Report of the Working Group on the Government Information Service*. London, Cabinet Office.

Needham, C. (2005) 'Brand Leaders: Clinton, Blair and the Limitations of the Permanent Campaign.' *Political Studies*, 53(2), 543–361.

Negrine, R. (2007) 'Professionalisation of Political Communication in Europe.' In: Negrine, R., Mancini, P., Holtz-Bacha C. and Papathanassopoulos, S. (eds) *The Professionalisation of Political Communication*. Bristol, Intellect, 27–46.

——(2008) *The Transformation of Political Communication*. Basingstoke, Palgrave Macmillan.

Negrine, R. and Lilleker, D. (2003) 'The Rise of a Proactive Local Media Strategy in British Political Communication: Clear Continuities and Evolutionary Change 1966–2001.' *Journalism Studies*, 4(2), 199–211.

——(2004) 'The Rise of a Local Media Strategy in British Political Communication: Clear Continuities and Evolutionary Change 1996–2001.' *Journalism Studies*, 4(2), 199–211.

Nessmann, K. (2009) 'Kommunickationsmanagement für Personen. Beratungsmodelle, Konzepte und theoretische Sichtweisen.' In: Eisenegger, M. and Wehmeier S. (eds) *Personalisierung der Organisationskommunikation*. Wiesbaden, Verlag für Sozialwissenschaften.

Newman, B.I. (1994a) 'The Forces behind the Merging of Marketing and Politics.' *Wirtschaft und Politik*, 39(2), 42.

——(1994b) *The Marketing of the President – Political Marketing as Campaign Strategy*. Thousand Oaks, CA, Sage.

——(1999a) *The Mass Marketing of Politics. Democracy in the Age of Manufactured Images*. Thousand Oaks, CA, Sage.

——(1999b) *Handbook of Political Marketing*. Thousand Oaks, CA, Sage Publications.

——(2002) 'The Role of Marketing in Politics.' *Journal of Political Marketing*, 1(1), 1–5.

Newman, B.I. and Davies, P.J. (2006) *Winning Election with Political Marketing*. New York, Haworth Press.

Nimmo, D. (2001) *The Political Persuaders. The Techniques of Modern Election Campaigns*. New Brunswick, NJ, Translation Publishers.

Nolte, K. (2005) *Der Kampf um Aufmerksamkeit*. Frankfurt am Main, Campus Verlag.

Nolte, W.L. (1979) *Fundamentals of Public Relations*. New York, Pergamon.

Norris, P. (2000) *A Virtuous Circle: Political Communications in Post-industrial Democracies*. New York, Cambridge University Press.

Oborne, P. (1999) *Alastair Campbell, New Labour and the Rise of the Media Class*. London, Aurum Press.

Oborne, P. and Walters, S. (2004) *Alastair Campbell*. London, Aurum Press.

O'Cass, A. (2001) 'Political Marketing: An Investigation of the Political Marketing Concept and Political Market Orientation in Australian Politics.' *European Journal of Marketing*, 35(9/10), 1003–125.

Ohl, C.M., Pincus, J.D., Rimmer, T. and Harrison, D. (1995) 'Agenda Building Role of News Releases in Corporate Takeovers.' *Public Relations Review*, 21(2), 89–101.

Omar, M. (2005) *Managing and Sustaining Corporate Image, Identity and Reputation*. Edinburgh, Napier University.

Ormrod, R. (2005) 'A Conceptual Model of Political Market Orientation.' *Journal of Non-Profit and Public Sector Marketing*, 14(1), 47–64.

Ormrod, R.P. (2011) *Political Market Orientation: An Introduction*. www.econ.au.dk/fileadmin/site_files/filer_oekonomi/Working_Papers/Management/2011/wp11_01.pdf (accessed 9 September 2012).

Ormrod, R.P. and Henneberg, S. (2006) 'Are You Thinking what we're Thinking? Or are we Thinking what you're Thinking? An Exploratory Analysis of the Market Orientation of the UK Parties.' In: Lilleker, D.G., Jackson, N.A. and Scullion, R. (eds) *The Marketing of Political Parties*. Manchester, Manchester University Press.

——(2010) 'An Investigation into the Relationship between Political Activity Levels and Political Market Orientation.' *European Journal of Marketing*, 44(3/4), 382–400.

O'Shaughnessy, N.J. (1990) *The Phenomenon of Political Marketing*. London, Macmillan.

——(2001) 'The Marketing of Political Marketing.' *European Journal of Marketing*, 35(9/10), 1047–57.

O'Shaughnessy, N.J., Baines, B.R. and Ormrod, R.P. (2012) 'Political Marketing Orientation: Confusions, Complications, and Criticisms.' *Journal of Political Marketing*, 11(4), 353–66.

Osuagwu, L. (2008) 'Political Marketing: Conceptualisation, Dimensions and Research Agenda.' *Marketing Intelligence & Planning*, 26(7), 793–810.

Page, B. (1996) 'The Mass Media as Political Actors.' *Political Science & Politics*, 29 (1), 20–24.

Palmer, J. (2000) *Spinning into Control: News Values and Sources Strategies*. London, Leicester University Press.

——(2001) 'Smoke and Mirrors: Is that the Way it is? Themes in Political Marketing.' *Media, Culture and Society*, 24(3), 345–63.

——(2004) 'Secrecy, Communications Strategy and Democratic Values.' *Ethical Space*, 1(2), 31–39.

Papathanassopoulos, S., Negrine, P., Mancini, C. and Holtz-Bacha, C. (2007) 'Political Communication in the Era of Professionalization.' In: Negrine, R., Mancini, P., Holtz-Bacha, C. and Papathanassopoulos, S. (eds) *The Professionalization of Political Communication*. Intellect, Bristol, 9–26.

Parry-Giles, S.J. and Parry-Giles, T. (2002) *Constructing Clinton: Hyperreality and Presidential Image-making in Postmodern Politics*. New York, Peter Lang.

Pearson, M. and Patching, R. (2008) *Government Media Relations: A 'Spin' through the Literature*. Bond University, epublications.bond.edu.au/cgi/viewcontent.cgi?article=1243&context=hss_pubs (accessed 5 January 2013).

Phau, I. and Lau, K.L. (2000) 'Conceptualising Brand Personality: A Review and Research Propositions.' *Journal of Targeting. Measurement and Analysis for Marketing*, 9(1), 52–69.

Phillis Review (2004) 'An Independent Review of Government Communications.' www.cabinetoffice.gov.uk/publications/reports/communications_review/final_report.pdf and archive.cabinetoffice.gov.uk/gcreview/News/index.htm (accessed 8 November 2010).

Pitcher, G. (2003) *The Death of Spin*. Chichester, Wiley.

Plasser, F. and Plasser, G. (2002) *Global Political Campaigning*. London, Praeger.

Plasser, F., Scheucher, C. and Senf, G.M. (1999) 'Is there a European Style of Political Marketing.' In: Newman, B.I. (ed.) *Handbook of Political Marketing*. Thousand Oaks, CA, Sage, 89–112.

Pratt, M.G. (2003) 'Disentangling Collective Identity.' In: Polzer, J.T., Polzer, J. and Leon, D.J. (eds) *Identity Issues in Groups: Research in Managing Groups and Teams*. Bradford, Emerald Group Publishing, Vol. 5, 161–88.

Public Administration Select Committee (1998) *Sixth Report. The Government Information and Communication Service*. www.publications.parliament.uk/pa/cm199798/cmselectcmpubadm/770/77006.htm (accessed 4 February 2006).

Quinn, T. (2012) 'Spin Doctors and Political News Management: A Rational-choice "Exchange" Analysis.' *British Politics*, 7, 72–300.

Ratnam, K.J. (1964) 'Charisma and Political Leadership.' *Political Studies*, 12(3), 341–54.

Rawnsley, A. (2001) *Servants of the People. The Inside Story of New Labour*. London, Penguin.

——(2010) *The End of the Party. The Rise and Fall of New Labour*. London, Penguin.

Reber, B.H. and Cameron, G.T. (2003) 'Measuring Contingencies: Using Scales to Measure Public Relations Practitioner Limits to Accommodation.' *Journalism and Mass Communication Quarterly*, 80(2), 431–46.

Rennard, C. (2011) 'From Protest to Power.' In: Wring, D., Mortimore, R. and Atkinson, S. (eds) *Political Communication in Britain*. London, Palgrave.

Roberts, J.M. (1978) *The French Revolution*. Oxford University Press.

Robinson, C. (2010) 'Manifest Market Orientation in Political Advertising and the Achievement of Electoral Objectives.' 60th Political Studies Association Annual Conference, Edinburgh. www.psa.ac.uk/journals/pdf/5/2010/1127_1041.pdf (accessed 22 August 2012).

Robinson, E.J. (1969) *Public Relations Research and Survey Research: Achieving Organisational Goals in a Communication Context.* New York, Appleton-Century-Crofts.

Ronneberger, F. and Rühl, M. (1992) *Theorie der Public Relations.* Opladen, Westdeutscher Verlag.

Roper, S. and Fill, C. (2012) *Corporate Reputation. Brand and Communication.* London, Pearson.

Rose, R. (2001) *The Prime Minister in a Shrinking World.* Cambridge, Polity.

Rowan, D. (1998) 'A Short Guide to New Labour Speak.' *The Observer*, 13 September.

Ryan, C. (1991) *Prime Time Activism.* Boston, MA, South End Press.

Sampson, A. (2005) 'The Fourth Estate Under Fire.' *The Guardian*, 10 January, 2.

Sarcinelli, U. (2005) *Politische Kommunikation in Deutschland. Zur Politikvermittlung im demokratischen System.* Wiesbaden, VS Verlag.

Savigny, H. (2007) 'Focus Groups and Political Marketing: Science and Democracy as Axiomatic?' *British Journal of Politics and International Relations*, 9, 122–37.

——(2012) *The Problem of Political Marketing.* London, Continuum.

Saxton, K. (1998) 'Where Do Reputations Come From?' *Corporate Reputation Review*, 1(4), 393–99.

Scammell, M. (2007) 'Political Brands and Consumer Citizens: The Rebranding of Tony Blair.' *The Annals of the American Academy of Political and Social Science.* ann.sagepub.com (accessed 3 May 2009).

——(2008) 'Brand Blair: Marketing Politics in the Consumer Age.' In: Lilleker, D. and Scullion, R. (eds) *Voters or Consumers: Imagining the Contemporary Electorate.* Newcastle, Cambridge Scholars Publishing.

Schama, S. (1989) *Citizens: A Chronicle of the French Revolution.* New York, Viking Penguin.

Schechner, R. (2002) *Performance Studies: An Introduction.* London, Routledge.

Scheufele, D. (1999) 'Framing as a Theory of Media Effects.' *Journal of Communication*, 49(1), 103–22.

Schlenker, B.R., Weigold, M.F. and Hallam, J.R. (1990) 'Self Serving Attributions in Social Context.' *Journal of Personality and Social Psychology*, 58(5), 855–63.

Schlesinger, P. (1993) *Communication, Culture and Hegemony. From the Media to the Mediations.* London, Sage.

Schlesinger, P. and Tumber, H. (1994) *Reporting Crime. The Media Politics of Criminal Justice.* Oxford, Clarendon Press.

Schneider, H. (2004) *Marken in der Politik. Erscheinungsformen, Relevanz, identitätsorientierte Führung und demokratietheoretische Reflexion.* Wiesbaden, VS Verlag für Sozialwissenschaften.

Schnell, R., Hill, P. and Esser, E. (2005) *Methoden der empirischen Sozialforschung.* München, Oldenbourg Verlag.

Schudson, M. (1991) 'The Sociology of News Production Revisited.' In: Curran, J. and Gurevitch, M. (eds) *Mass Media and Society.* London, Arnold.

Schwartzenberg, R. (1977) *Politieke superstars. Vedettencultus in de politiek* [Political Superstars. Celebrity-cult in Politics]. Antwerpen, Belgium, Standaard Uitgeverij.

Schweiger, G. and Adami, M. (1999) 'The Nonverbal Image of Politicians and Political Parties.' In: Newman, B.I. (ed.) *Handbook of Political Marketing*. London, Sage, 347–64.
Schweitzer, A. (1984) *The Age of Charisma*. Chicago, Nelson-Hall.
Seitel, F. (2001) *The Practice of Public Relations*. Upper Saddle River, NJ, Prentice Hall.
Seldon, A. (2005) *Blair*. London, Free Press.
Sellers, P. (2010) *Cycles of Spin. Strategic Communication in the U.S. Congress*. Cambridge, Cambridge University Press.
Seymour-Ure, C. (2003) *Prime Ministers and the Media*. Oxford, Blackwell Publishing.
Shamir, B., House, R.J. and Arthur, M.B. (1993) 'The Motivational Effects of Charismatic Leadership: A Self-concept Based Theory.' *Organization Science*, 4(4), 577–94.
Sheafer, T. (2008) 'Charismatic Communication Skill, Media Legitimacy and Electoral Success.' *Journal of Political Marketing*, 7(1), 1–24.
Shenkar, O. and Yuchtman-Yaar, E. (1997) 'Reputation, Image, Prestige, and Goodwill: An Interdisciplinary Approach to Organizational Standing.' *Human Relations*, 50(11), 151–79.
Shepherd, M. (2008) 'Candidate Image and Electoral Preference in Britain.' *British Politics*, 3, 324–49.
Shils, E. (1965) 'Charisma, Order, Status.' *American Sociological Review*, 30(2), 199–213.
Shoemaker, P.J. and Reese, S.D. (1991) *Mediating the Message: Theories of Influences on Mass Media Content*. White Plains, NY, Longman.
Shoemaker, P.J. and Vos, T.P. (2009) *Gatekeeping Theory*. Abingdon, Taylor & Francis.
Simons, W.H. and Jones, J.G. (2011) *Persuasion in Society*. London, Routledge.
Sitrick, M. (1998) *Spin. How to Turn the Power of the Press to Your Advantage*. Washington, Regnery Publishing.
Smith, G. (2001) 'The 2001 General Election: Factors Influencing the Brand Image of Political Parties and their Leaders.' *Journal of Marketing Management*, 17(9–10), 989–1006.
——(2009) 'Conceptualising and Testing Brand Personality in British Politics.' *Journal of Political Marketing*, 8(3), 209–32.
Smith, G. and Hirst, A. (2001) 'Strategic Political Segmentation: A New Approach for a New Era of Political Marketing.' *European Journal of Marketing*, 35(9/10), 1058–73.
Smith, G. and Saunders, J. (1990) 'The Application of Marketing to British Politics.' *Journal of Marketing Management*, 5(3), 295–306.
Smith, R.D. (2012) *Strategic Planning for Public Relations*. London, Routledge.
Spinrad, W. (1991) 'Charisma: A Blighted Concept and an Alternative Formula.' *Political Science Quarterly*, 106(2), 295–311.
Staab, J.F. (1990) 'The Role of News Factors in News Selection. A Theoretical Reconsideration.' *European Journal of Communication*, 5(4), 423–43.
Stacks, D.W. (2004) 'Crisis Management: Toward a Multidimensional Model of Public Relations.' In: Millar, D.P. and Heath, L.H. (eds) *Responding to Crisis: A Rhetorical Approach to Crisis Communication*. Mahwah, NJ, Erlbaum.
Stephanopoulos, G. (1999) *All Too Human. A Political Education*. Boston. Little, Brown & Company.
Stockwell, S. (2007) 'Spin Doctors, Citizens and Democracy.' In: Young, S. (ed.) *Government Communication in Australia*. Cambridge, Cambridge University Press, 130–43.
Strauss, A.L. and Corbin, J. (1998) *Basics of Qualitative Research*. Thousand Oaks, CA, Sage.

Strömbäck, J. and Kiousis, S. (2011) 'Political Public Relations.' In: Strömbäck, J. and Kiousis, J. (eds) *Political Public Relations. Principles and Applications*. London, Routledge, 3–25.

Suchman, M. (1995) 'Managing Legitimacy: Strategic and Institutional Approaches.' *The Academy of Management Review*, 20(3), 571–610.

Sumpter, R. and Tankard, J.W. (1994) 'The Spin Doctor: An Alternative Model of Public Relations.' *Public Relations Review*, 20(1), 19–27.

Swanson, D. and Mancini, P. (1996) *Politics, Media and Modern Democracy: An International Study of Innovation in Electoral Campaigning and their Consequences*. Westport, CT, Praeger.

Szyszka, P. (1992) 'Image und Vertrauen. Zu einer weniger beachteten Perspektive des Image-Begriffes.' In: Faulstich, W. (ed.) *Image, Imageanalyse, Imagegestaltung*. Bardowick, Wissenschaftler-Verlag, 104–11.

Taylor, M. (2012) 'Using Monitoring and Evaluation to Measure Public Affairs Effectiveness.' In: Lee, M., Neeley, G. and Steward, K. (eds) *The Practice of Government Public Relations*. Boca Raton, CRC Press, 213–28.

Tedeschi, J.T. and Melburg, V. (1984) 'Impression Management and Influence in the Organization.' *Research in the Sociology of Organization*, 3, 31–58.

Tedesco, J.C. (2011) 'Political Public Relations and Agenda Building.' In: Strömbäck, J. and Kiousis, S. (eds) *Political Public Relations. Principles and Applications*. London, Routledge, 75–94.

Tench, R. (2009) *Exploring Public Relations*. Harlow, Essex, Parson.

Thatcher, M. (1993) *The Downing Street Years*. London, Harper Collins.

Theakston, K. (2010) *Gordon Brown as Prime Minister. Political Skills and Leadership Style*. PSA Conference Paper, www.psa.ac.uk/journals/pdf/5/2010/857_513.pdf (accessed 8 April 2012).

Thompson, J.B. (2000) *Political Scandal – Power and Visibility in the Media Age*. Cambridge, Polity Press.

Thurber, J.A. and Nelson, C. (2000) *Campaign Warriors*. Washington, DC, Brookings Institution.

Tiffen, R. (1989) *News and Power*. Sydney, Allen & Unwin.

Timmins, N. (1997) 'Blair Aide Calls on Whitehall to Raise its PR Game.' *Financial Times*, 9 October, 2.

Trux, W. (2002) 'Unternhmensidentiät, Unternehmenspolitik und öffentliche Meinung.' In: Birkigt, K., Stadler, M. and Funck, H.J. (eds) *Corporate Identity. Grundlagen, Funktionen, Beispiele. Landsberg am Lech*. Verlag Moderne Industrie, 65–76.

Tunstall, J. (1996) *Newspaper Power. The New National Press in Britain*. Oxford, Oxford University Press.

Turk, J.V. (1986) 'Information Subsidies and Media Content: A Study of Public Relations Influence on the News.' *Journalism Monographs. No. 100*. Columbia, SC. Association for Education in Journalism and Mass Communication.

Turnbull, N. (2007) 'Perspectives on Government PR.' In: Young, S. (eds) *Government Communication in Australia*. Cambridge, Cambridge University Press, 113–29.

Ulmer, R.R., Sellnow, T.L. and Seeger, M.W. (2007) *Effective Crisis Communication: Moving from Crisis to Opportunity*. Thousand Oaks, CA, Sage.

van Riel, C.B.M. and Fombrun, C. (2007) *Essentials of Corporate Communication*. Abingdon, Routledge.

Vidal, G. (1984) *Lincoln*. New York, Random House.

Walsh, K. (1994) 'The Marketing of Public Sector Services.' *Journal of Marketing Management*, 28(3), 63–71.

Wanta, W. (1991) 'Presidential Approval Ratings as a Variable in the Agenda Building Process.' *Journalism Quarterly*, 68(4), 672–79.

Waterman, R.W., Wright, R. and St Clair, G. (1999) *The Image-is-everything Presidency: Dilemmas in American Leadership.* Boulder, CO, Westview Press.

Watson, T. and Kitchen, P.J. (2008) 'Corporate Communication. Reputation in Action.' In: Melevar, T.C. (ed.) *Facets of Corporate Identity, Communication and Reputation.* London, Routledge, 121–40.

Watts, D. (1997) *Political Communication Today.* Manchester, Manchester University Press.

Weaver, D. (1996) 'Media Agenda Setting and Elections: Assumptions and Implications.' In: Paletz, D.L. (ed.) *Political Communication Research: Approaches, Studies, Assessments.* Norwood, NJ, Ablex, 176–93.

Weber, M. (1947) *The Theory of Social and Economic Organization.* New York, Free Press.

——(1968) *Economy and Society.* Guenther Roth and Claus Wittich (eds), vol. 3. New York, Bedminster Press.

——(1978) *Economy and Society.* Berkeley, CA, Free Press.

Webster, C. (1992) 'What Kind of Marketing Culture Exists in your Service Firm? An Audit.' *The Journal of Services Marketing*, 6(2), 54–67.

Whetten, D.A. and Mackey, A. (2002) 'A Social Actor Conception of Organisation and Identity and its Implications for the Study of Organisational Reputation.' *Business and Society*, 41(4), 393–414.

Williams, J.E., Saiz, J.L. and Munick, M. (1991) *Scaling the Adjective Check List for Psychological Importance.* Winston-Salem, NC, Wake Forest University.

Willner, A.R. (1984) *The Spellbinders – Charismatic Political Leadership.* New Haven, CT, Yale University Press.

Wilson, A. (2011) 'The Conservative Campaign.' In: Wring, D., Mortimore, R. and Atkinson, S. (eds) *Political Communication in Britain.* London, Palgrave.

Wilson, J.Q. (1989) *Bureaucracy: What Government Agencies Do and Why they Do it.* New York, Basic Books.

Windlesham, L. (1966) *Communication and Political Power.* London, Jonathan Cape.

Winter, D.G. (2004) 'Leader Appeal, Leader Performance, and the Motive Profiles of Leaders and Followers: A Study of American Presidents and Elections.' In: Jost, J.T. and Sidanius, J. (eds) *Political Psychology.* New York, Psychology Press, 124–38.

Wolcott, H.F. (1994) *Transforming Qualitative Data: Description, Analysis and Interpretation.* Thousand Oaks, CA, Sage.

Wolfsfeld, G. (1997) *Media and Political Conflict. News from the Middle East.* Cambridge, Cambridge University Press.

——(2003) 'The Political Contest Model.' In: Cottle, S. (ed.) *News, Public Relations and Power.* London, Sage.

Wray, J.H. (1999) 'Money and Politics.' In: Newman, B.I. (ed.) *Handbook of Political Marketing.* Thousand Oaks, CA, Sage, 741–58.

Wring, D. (1996) 'Political Marketing and Party Development in Britain – A Secret History.' *European Journal of Marketing*, 30(10), 92–103.

——(1999) 'The Marketing Colonization of Political Campaigning.' In: Newman, B.I. (ed.) *The Handbook of Political Marketing.* Thousand Oaks, CA, Sage.

——(2004) *Politics of Marketing the Labour Party: A Century of Stratified Electioneering*. Palgrave, New York.

Xifra, J. (2010) 'Linkages between Public Relations Models and Communication Managers' Roles in Spanish Political Parties.' *Journal of Political Marketing*, 9, 167–85.

Young, S. (2007) 'Introduction: The Theory and Practice of Government Communication.' In: Young, S. (eds) *Government Communication in Australia*. Cambridge, Cambridge University Press, xxiii–1.

Zoch, L.M. and Molleda, J.C. (2006) 'Building a Theoretical Model of Media Relations Using Framing, Information Subsidies, and Agenda Building.' In: Botan, C. and Hazleton, V. (eds) *Public Relations Theory vol. II*. Mahwah, NJ, Erlbaum, 279–310.

Index

Abels, H. 37
Aberbach, D. 37
Abrams, M. 63
access: exclusivity of 65; internal organization, access and 64–67; quality of access, quality of communications and 142–43; resource of 61–62, 64–67
adaptability: constant change, adaptability to 5; environmental change, adaptation to 62–63; expectations, adaptation of politicians to 2–3; public persona, adaptation and realignment with new demands 130–31, 135; strategic management models, need for flexible adaptation of 52
adverse developments, responses to 118
agenda-setting: framing issues and, critical nature of differentiation between 56; need for resources for 56–57; political communications management, agenda and frames in 58–61; research study 155–57; technicalities of 57
Ake, C. 38
Alessandri, Westcott 44n15
Althaus, M. 28
anticipation of issues 125
Arnold, S. *et al.* 52
artificial or constructed persona 82. 83–85, 136
audience identification 86–89
audience research 87
Austin, E.W, and Pinkleton, B.E. 46
authenticity, call for (and dangers of lack of) 83–85

Bagdikian, B. 61
Bagehot 3
Baines, P.R. 5
Baines, P.R. and Egan, J. 9
Baines, P.R. and Worcester, R.M. 12, 23
Baines, P.R. *et al.* 15
balance of power: communications managers and 22; strategic skills and 23
Balls, Ed 146
Balmas, M. and Sheafer, T. 56
Barber, J.D. 36
Barkham, P. *et al.* 4
Bartle, John 10, 27
Bass, B.M. 40
Bauer, H.H. *et al.* 11
Baumeister, R.F. 60
BBC 5 Live 97
Beattie, Jason 130, 136, 144, 149, 157; communications management in action 70, 80, 81, 83, 84, 88, 89; news, management of 108, 112, 117, 118, 123, 126–28
Beckett, A. 14
Beckett, Margaret 131
Bendix, R. 38
Benn, Hilary 76
Bennett, G.A. and George, A.L. 41, 58
Bennett, W.L. 19
Bentele, G. 23
Bentele, G. and Fähnrich, B. 32
Bentele, G. and Seeling, S. 15
Bernays, E. 18
'Big Society' idea 139–40
Bismarck, Otto von 40
Black, S. 17
Blair, Tony 3, 22, 27–30, 63, 64, 66, 155, 157; communications management in action 70, 72, 77–79, 85, 89, 90–94, 96, 98, 103–6; news, management of 107–11, 115, 116, 121, 123–25; public

persona of 72–73, 85; resources, management of 132, 136, 137, 140, 143, 144, 148
Blears, Hazel 71, 82, 90
Blick, A. 66
Blumler, J. and Kavanagh, D. 31, 60, 62
Blumler, J.G. and Gurevitch, M. 59
Blunkett, David 90
Boorstin, Daniel J. 2, 53, 60, 153
Botan, C. 65
branding 13–14, 15
Branigan, T. 66
Brettschneider, F. 33
Brewer, P. and Sigelman, L. 57
Brissenden, J.G. and Moloney, K. 18, 24, 43n3
Brogan, D.W. 39
Bromley, D. 33, 38, 41
Broom, G.M. 15, 45, 47, 50, 57
Brown, Gordon 3, 151, 153; communications management in action 70–73, 76, 77, 81, 84–85, 87–89, 91, 92, 95, 96, 100, 101, 103; news, management of 108, 109, 111, 113, 115, 119, 121, 122, 123, 126; public persona of 3, 81, 85, 103, 119, 132; resources, management of 129, 130, 131, 137, 140, 141, 142, 148, 149
Brown, T.J. *et al.* 42
Bryman, A. 40
Bucy, E.P. 34
Budge, I. 27
Burton, B. 55
Busby, R. 11, 36, 37
Bush, George W. 52
Butler, D. and Kavanagh, D. 30
Butler, P. and Collins, N. 10, 13, 28

Cable, Vince 71, 78, 80, 83, 94, 101, 105, 114, 130, 152
Callaghan, Jim 81
Cameron, David 2, 14, 64, 150, 151; communications management in action 70, 74, 75, 77, 81, 92, 95, 99, 102, 103, 105 106; news, management of 107, 112, 113, 117, 118, 122, 127; public persona of 102–3; resources, management of 132, 133, 137, 139, 146, 148, 151
Cameron, G.T. *et al.* 25
Campbell, Alastair 22, 27, 30, 60, 63, 64, 66, 70, 88, 98, 115, 143, 144
Campbell, Menzies 80, 118
Carroll, C. and McCombs, M. 26
Castells, M. 65
centralization 8, 32, 66–67, 144
channels of communication 87–88
charisma: charismatic leadership 38–39; charismatic public persona, features of 40–41; individuality and 38; public persona and 37–39, 40
Churchill, Winston 40
Clark, Ronald W. 40
Clarke, Kenneth 75, 80, 152
Clarke, P. and Evans, S. 59
Clegg, Nick 121, 122, 152
Clemente, M.N. 11
client satisfaction, concentration on 12–13
Clinton, Bill 23, 28, 30, 31, 124
C-MACIE model 46
Cohen, Nick 30
communications management in action 69–106, 121–25; audience identification 86–89; audience research 87; audiences, familiarity with 88; authenticity, call for (and dangers of lack of) 83–85; channels of communication 87–88; communications advisers, need for frankness in 137–38; communications and performance, connection between 152; content of public discourse, style and selection of 86; corporate and political communications, difference between 88; data, collection and analysis of 69–72; distinct publics, identification of 86; forward planning of policy announcements 94; ideal public persona 79–82; ideal public persona, definition of 81–82; leaks, fear of 93; media relations, approaches to 96–98; media relations, policy options and 106; New Labour, strategic approach to policies and communications 100; newspapers 87–88; official engagements 94–95; party leader's conference speech 89; personal behaviour, messages resulting from 100–101; personality and reputation management objectives, linking of 82–85; planning in opposition 95; policies and reputation, linking of 102–6; policy implementation, timing and 101–2; policy issues, ignoring those difficult to communicate 104; political reinvention 103–4; positioning

politicians 89–92; practitioner interviews (and evidence from) 69–72, 78–79, 86, 89, 93, 95; prime ministerial interference 95; public perceptions of politicians, identification and consolidation of 90–91; public persona, reconciliation with diverse strands of demands and expectations 86–87; public persona, remoulding of 85; reputation, control of 73; reputation, creation and safeguarding of 73–74; reputation, limits on shaping of 104–6; reputation, power of 72–73; reputation, relevance of 75–76; reputation management, central role of 74–75; reputation management, objectives of personality and, linking of 82–85; reputation management, planning process and 92–95; reputation management, recognition of relevance of 72–75; reputation management, use of research in 75–79; segmentation of audiences 87; strategic advice, resources for 98–100; strategic options, recognition of 95–101; strategic planning of media relations and images, intuition and 93; strategic reputation management 4–5, 5–6; systematic research, lack of interest in and resources for 77–79; target audiences 12, 88, 122; target audiences, conflicting stakes within 86; television 88; timing, considerations of 101–2; unplanned, reactive media relations 94; women's magazines 87; written plans 93–94
communications plans, problems with 154–57
communications professionals, functions, roles and skills of 65–66
communicative actions: deployment of 153–54; expertise of communicators, scrutinization of 144–48; leverage in dealing with journalists 114; shaping of narratives 110–12
communicative focus, restriction of 25
communicative styles, comparison of 107–10
comparative advertising 14–15
competitive advantage, maintenance of 62–63
Conboy, M. 55
Conger, J.A. and Kanungo, R.N. 39
Conservative Party 2, 26, 28, 30, 40, 65, 150, 151, 152; communications management in action 70, 71, 73, 74–75, 76, 77, 80, 82, 83–84, 87, 92, 95, 100, 103, 106; news, management of 109, 111, 113, 122, 125, 128; resources, management of 130–31, 132, 133, 139, 142, 147, 149
contingency planning: contingency theory 25; long-term contingency planning 120; policy gaffes in contingency situations 121; protection of perceptions and 119–21; short-term contingency planning 120–21
Cook, G. 10
Cook, T.E. 4, 18, 40, 58, 59
Coombs, W.T. 25
Cooper, Andrew 65
Corbin, J. 72
Cornelissen, J. 24, 26
Coulson, Andy 64, 98, 142, 146
crisis communications 156–57
Curtin, P.A. 56
Cutlip, S.M. and Center, A.H. 17
Cutlip, S.M. *et al.* 16

The Daily Mail 123, 128
The Daily Mirror 70, 87–88
The Daily Telegraph 145
Darling, Alastair 97
data, collection and analysis of 6; communications management in action 69–72; research study 6, 69–72
Davies, Mark 70, 77–78, 80–82, 86, 87, 94–97, 100, 105–6, 118–19, 122–23, 136, 138–39, 143, 145
Davies, N. 59, 60, 61
Davis, A. 57
Davis, Aeron 64
Davis, David 75, 76
day-to-day political communications, long-term perspectives and 110–11
de Landtsheer, C. 14
de Landtsheer, C. *et al.* 3
Deaver, Michael 2
Deeds, Bill 145
Delli Carpini, M.X. 57
Deng, S. and Dart, J. 12
Denver, D. *et al.* 2
Diamantopoulos, A. and Hart, S. 12
Diana, Princess of Wales 96, 103, 110
discipline, concept of 124
Dowling, G. 42
Dozier, D.M. *et al.* 20

dramatization 60–61
du Plessis, Erik 44n11

Eagly, A.R. *et al.* 35
The Economist 3
Edelman, M. 33
Edelmann, R.J. 53
editorial resources, limits on 59
Ehling, W.P. *et al.* 16
Eilders, C. 32
Eisenegger, M. 2, 39
Eisenegger, M. and Konieczny-Wössner, E. 33
Eisinger, R. 23
election campaigns, themes in 36–37
electoral system, oligopolistic aspect of 14
ENGAGE framework 46
Entman, R.M. 56
Erikson, E.H. 34
Esser, F. 31
Esser, F. and d'Angelo, P. 3
Esser, F. *et al.* 18, 19, 20, 21, 22, 23, 31
Eustice, George: communications management in action 70, 74, 77, 79, 82, 83, 84, 92, 95, 98, 99, 100, 102, 103, 105, 106; news, management of 107, 111, 112, 113, 114, 115, 116, 117, 121, 125; resources, management of 132, 133, 134, 137, 138, 139, 141, 144
Evening Standard 71
events: charismatic leadership and 39–41; consequences for reputation management 116–19; crisis management and 119; deficient planning and 118; emphasis of reporting events, influences on 56; prediction of 118–19
exclusivity: of access 65; journalistic goal of 144–45
exemplification 53

Farrell, D. and Webb, P. 62
Farrell, D.M. and Wortmann, M. 15
Faulstich, W. 16
Ferguson, M. 24, 25
Fill, C. *et al.* 11
Financial Times 71
Fischer, Louis 40
Fombrun, C.J. and Rindova, V. 42
Foot, Michael 80
Forbes, P.S. 45
Franck, G. 37
Franklin, B. 26, 27, 29, 30, 31, 64
Freeman, D. 39
Freidson, E. 62
French, J.R.P. and Raven, R. 36
Fridkin, K.L. and Kenney, P.J. 59
Friedrich, C.J. 38
Froehlich, R. and Ruediger, B. 18
Froman, L.A. 37

Gaber, I. 18, 19, 22, 27, 29
Galtung, J. and Ruge, M.H. 32
Gandhi, Mahatma 39–40
Gandy, O. 59
Gans, H. 55, 56
Gardner, H. 34
Garibaldi, Giuseppe 39, 40
Garner, B. and Short, J. 27
Geldof, Bob 14
Gerstle, J. *et al.* 56
Gerth, H.H. and Mills, C.W. 38
Gibson, R. and Römmele, A. 13
Gioia, D.A. *et al.* 42
Gitlin, T. 40, 56, 58
Goldsmith, Zac 14
Gomibuchi, S. 35
Gotsi, M. and Wilson, A.M. 41
Gould, Philip 2, 4, 5, 28, 29, 63, 66, 93
government communications units 63
GQ magazine 87, 139
Graber, D. 59, 60
Gracian, B. y Morales, B. 1
Gracian, Baltasar 1
Gray, D.E. 71
Greenaway, J. *et al.* 68n1
Greer, Shane 70, 73, 75, 81, 85, 92, 100, 104, 118, 119, 123, 139, 142, 143, 149
Gregory, A. 1, 16, 24, 46, 52
Grender, O. and Parminter, K. 22, 23, 25
Griffin, A. 24, 26
Grunig, J.E. 16, 17
Grunig, J.E. and Huang, Y.H. 16, 25
Grunig, J.E. and Hunt, T. 15, 16, 17, 20, 49, 50
Grunig, J.E. and Repper, F.C. 4
Grunig, L.A. *et al* 65
Grunig and Hunt's communications model 49–51
The Guardian 29–30, 70, 112, 123, 127, 149

Hague, William 30, 71, 73, 75, 80, 82, 84, 100, 107, 110, 133; public persona of 14, 131
Haley, J. 44n13

Hallahan, K. 56, 57
Hallahan, K. *et al.* 65
Harman, Harriet 73, 76
Harris, L. 66
Harrop, M. 9
Hart, R. 2
Häussler, T. 32
Have I Got News for You (BBC TV) 112, 138
Hazlewood, Richard 70, 86, 93, 97, 131, 138, 146, 148
Heffernan, R. 18, 22, 23, 24
Henneberg, S. 10, 11, 12, 13
Heseltine, M. 21
Hewitt, Patricia 71, 90, 97, 104
Hibbert, C. 39
Hill, David: communications management in action 70, 72, 74, 77, 83, 86, 89, 93, 94, 100, 106; news, management of 110, 111, 114, 121, 124, 126; resources, management of 134, 136, 137, 138, 143, 144, 145, 146
Hilton, Steve 139, 142
histrionic performance 52–53
Hitler, Adolf 40
Holzer, W. 28
House, R.J. and Howell, J.M. 40
Howard, C.M. 57
Howard, Michael 70, 73, 78, 79, 83, 99, 133
Hujer, M. 52
human hinterland 130
Hutton, G.J. *et al.* 25

ideal persona 79–82; definition of 81–82
ideal politician, definition of 33–37
identity and persona 85
image and reputation, centrality of 1–2
image and reputation, terminological clarification 41–43
image creation 2
image cultivation 2–3
Imhof, K. 32, 37
Immelman, A. 35
Immelman, A. and Beatty, A. 35
impression management: strategic communications 53–54; strategic reputation management 2
incumbents, powers of 59–60
The Independent 30
Ingham, Bernard 27, 44n10
ingratiation 53
instant-rebuttal units 22–23
interpretation, struggle over power of 59–60
intuition, reliance on 152–53

Jackson, N.A. 20, 25
Jackson, N.A. and Lilleker, D.J. 18, 20, 21, 24
Jefkins, J. and Yadin, D. 18
Jenkins, Greg 52
Johnson, Alan 76, 81, 86, 99
Johnson, Boris 80, 88; public persona of 74
Johnson, D.W. 20, 65, 66
Jonathan Ross Show (ITV TV) 87
Jones, E.E. 27, 30, 64
Jones, E.E. and Pittman, T.S. 53
Jones, E.E. *et al.* 36
Jones, Nicholas 145, 146, 147, 155; communications management in action 70, 72, 73, 74, 75, 80, 82, 83, 84, 85, 89, 93, 99, 103, 104, 106; news, management of 107, 108, 109, 112, 113, 115, 116, 122, 124, 127, 128
journalism: communicator and journalist, power balance between 29–30; exclusivity, journalistic goal of 144–45; narrative shaping, journalists and 110–12; political public relations and, liaison between 19; tabloid journalism, political connection with 145
Jowell, Tessa 121
Jun, U. 28

Kaase, M. 32
Kaid, L. *et al.* 68n3
Kavanagh, D. and Butler, D. 10
Keith, R.J. 12
Kelley, S. 63, 65
Kelly, Tom 70, 77, 84, 85, 88, 94, 97, 98, 99, 101, 111, 116, 117, 137, 141, 142, 143
Kershaw, I. 40
Kettle, Martin 70, 80, 81, 98, 109, 127, 128, 134, 136, 144, 152, 155, 157
Kinnock, Neil 85, 109, 134; public persona of 73
Kirchheimer, O. 10
Klapp, O.E. 36
Klein, Joe 44n12
Kopfman, E. and Ruth-McSwain, A. 20
Korte, K.R. and Froehlich, M. 24, 31
Kotler, P. and Kotler, P. 10

Kotler, P. and Levy, S.J. 10
Kotzaivazoglou's political marketing model 49
Kuhn, A. 49, 50
Kypers, J.A. 56

Le Bon, G. 17–18
leadership image 36
leaks, fear of 154; communications management in action 93
Leary, M.R. 2, 33, 36, 38, 39, 53, 60
Ledingham, J. and Bruning, S. 15, 25
Ledingham, J.A. 25
Lees-Marshment, Jennifer 4, 10, 12, 13, 15, 25, 26, 43n1, 45, 49, 62
legitimate authority 57–58
Lenin, Vladimir 40
L'Etang, Jacquie 163
Levi, M. and Stoker, L. 35
Liberal Democrats 80–81, 118, 131, 152
Lilleker, D.G. 10, 22, 34
Lilleker, D.G. and Jackson, N. 24, 25
Lilleker, D.G. and Negrine, R. 9, 12
Lilleker, D.G. *et al.* 9, 12
Lincoln, Abraham 34, 39
Lippmann, Walter 2, 32, 55
Liu, B.F. and Levenshus, A.B. 20, 21, 23, 25, 43n8
Livermore, Spencer 70, 77, 80, 81, 83, 85, 93, 102, 108, 117, 125, 126, 130, 132, 148, 151, 155
Lloyd, J. 60
local media experience 145
Lock, A. and Harris,P. 10, 11, 12, 13
long-term contingency planning 120
long-term relationship building 11–12
long-term reputation management 132–36

Maarek, P.J. 3, 4, 11, 15
McBride, Damian: communications management in action 71, 73, 76, 77, 78, 82, 83, 85, 86, 87, 88, 89, 90, 92, 97, 98, 99, 103; news, management of 109, 111, 112, 113, 114, 119, 120, 121, 123, 126, 128; resources, management of 132, 133, 134, 137, 140, 141, 142
McCombs, M. 55, 56, 57, 59
McElreath, M.P. 45, 46
McKenna, R. 12
McNair, Brian 18, 19, 27, 28, 43n9, 55, 56, 59, 60
Macrory, H. and Thorogood, Z. 82
Macrory, Henry 70, 74, 76, 87, 101, 102, 103, 106, 117, 122, 132, 136, 139, 146, 147, 148, 150, 151
Mair, P. 62
Major, John 27, 73, 96
Maltese, J.A. 19
Mandelson, Peter 28, 30, 59, 98, 108
Manheim, J.B. 59
Mannheim, J.B. 19, 21, 23, 24
Marcinkowski, F. 33
marketing: government communications, marketing approaches in 146; Kotzaivazoglou's political marketing model 49; marketing perspective within research study 9–10, 166; marketing strategies 9–10, 10–11, 11–12; media and marketing, role in shaping public persona 27; misunderstandings about political marketing 12; Newman's political marketing model 47–49; public relations and, distinction between 16; *see also* political marketing
Marquand, David 2, 3
Martinelli, D.K. 21, 25
Marx, S. 27, 28, 31
Mason, C.J. 6
Mattinson, D. 66
Mauser, G.A. 11
Mavondo, F.F. 9, 13
Mazzoleni, G. and Schulz, W. 40, 58
media: behaviour of, prediction of 125; fickleness of 114; intermediate role of 56; management of, decision-making 122–23; management of, style of 29–30; marketing and, role in shaping public persona 27; media advisers, operations freedom for 29; media attention, strategic perspectives to succeed in contest for 59; media capital 57–58; media-representative democracy 2; pivotal role of 56; political communications management practice and 55–58; politician's narratives, role in shaping 112
media relations: approaches to 96–98; complexities of 15; conditions for effectiveness in 123–24, 139; policy options and 106
Al-Megrahi case 140
Merten, K. 16
message delivery 21–22

message formulation 23–24
message framing 163
meta-communication 31
Meyer, Christopher 27
Meyer, T. 21
Meyer, T. *et al.* 53
Meyrowitz, J. 40
Michie, D. 61
Milburn, Alan 142
Miliband, David 71, 88, 129, 130, 145, 149
Miliband, Ed 108, 112, 128; public persona of 74, 104, 134
Miller, D. 10, 53, 64
Miller, D. *et al.* 68n1
Millon, T. 35
Mintzberg, H. 5, 155
Moloney, K. 20, 25
Moloney, K. and Colmer, R. 18, 19, 21, 22, 23
Moloney, K. *et al.* 22
Morris, T. and Goldsworthy, S. 16, 59
Mortimore, R. and Gill, M. 13
Moss, D. 5, 45, 65
Moss, D. and Mintzberg, H. 5
Mountfield Report (1997) 29, 66
Mowlam, Mo 79
mutual dependence 60

narrative: pivotal role of 111; shaping of 110–12
Neather, Andrew 71, 78, 97, 109, 113, 116, 117, 118, 119, 120, 132, 146
Needham, C. 13, 14
negative advertising 14–15
Negrine, R. 4, 7, 26, 54n1, 62, 63, 64, 66, 67
Negrine, R. and Lilleker, D. 21, 25
Nessmann, K. 33
New Labour 2, 4, 27, 30, 31, 59, 66, 131; ideological repositioning 158; reputation over time 132; strategic approach to policies and communications 100
Newman, B.I. 4, 9, 10, 13, 14, 15, 35; political marketing model 47–49
Newman, B.I. and Davies, P.J. 35, 36
news, management of 107–28; adverse developments, responses to 118; anticipation of issues 125; communications of politicians, management of 121–25; communications of politicians, role of expertise and resources in 110; communicative styles, comparison of 107–10; communicators and shaping of narratives 110–12; communicator's leverage in dealing with journalists 114; contingency planning and protection of perceptions 119–21; contingency situations, policy gaffes and 121; day-to-day political communications, long-term perspectives and 110–11; discipline, concept of 124; events, crisis management and 119; events, deficient planning and 118; events, prediction of 118–19; events and consequences for reputation management 116–19; journalists and shaping of narratives 110–12; long-term contingency planning 120; media, role in shaping politician's narratives 112; media behaviour, prediction of 125; media fickleness 114; media management decision-making 122–23; media relations, conditions for effectiveness in 123–24; misinterpretation and distortion of policy content by journalists 113–14; narrative, pivotal role of 111; narrative shaping 110–12; news agenda, control of 125–28; news agendas, categories of content 58–59; news reporting, consequences for public persona of 112–16; news reporting, pivotal role in shaping reputation 115–16; perceptions, contingency planning and protection of 119–21; personal communications, differences in quality of 107–9; political news reporting, entertainment in 114–15; practitioner interviews (and evidence from) 115–16; public persona, news reports and consequences for 112–16; reputation management, events and consequences for 116–19; rhetorical shortcomings 109; self-inflicted scandal 117–18; short-term contingency planning 120–21; stories, news value of 32; television debates, preparations for 122; unpredictable incidents, dealing with 116–18
newspapers 22, 55, 64, 87–88, 89, 116, 128, 147
Nimmo, D. 11
Nixon, Richard 53

'noise,' conditioning power of 161–62
Nolte, K. 53
Nolte, W.L. 17
Norris, P. and Palmer, J. 14

Obome, P. 30
Obome, P. and Walters, S. 21
O'Cass, A. 12
official engagements 94–95
Ohl, C.M. *et al.* 56
Omar, M. 42
opinion research, resources for commissioning of 150–51
Ormrod, R. 11, 12, 13
Ormrod, R.P. and Henneberg, S. 10, 11, 12
Osborne, George 85, 97
O'Shaughnessy, N.J. 4, 11, 12, 43n1
O'Shaughnessy, N.J. *et al.* 5, 10
Osuagwu, L. 9, 11, 14

Page, B. 22
Palmer, J. 57
Papathanassopoulos, S. *et al.* 32, 61, 62
Parris, Matthew 27
Parry-Giles, S.J. and Parry-Giles, T. 31
party leadership: conference speech 89; support for 2
Pearson, M. and Patching, R. 10, 30, 58, 60, 61
perceptions, contingency planning and protection of 119–21
personal attributes 34–35
personal behaviour, messages resulting from 100–101
personal communications, differences in quality of 107–9
personal media relations 4
personal relationship, variable of 160
personal reputation in politics, limitations in approaches to 166–67
personal reputation management, predictive model of 162
personality: desirable personality traits 35; reputation management objectives and, linking of 82–85; time and revelation of 136
personalization 3, 33
persuasion 16–17
Phau, I. and Lau, K.L. 13
Phillis Review (2004) 66–67
Pitcher, G. 43n4
Plasser, F. and Plasser, G. 62, 63
policies: contingency situations, policy gaffes and 121; forward planning of policy announcements 94; implementation of, timing and 101–2; issues within, ignoring those difficult to communicate 104; media relations, policy options and 106; misinterpretation and distortion of policy content by journalists 113–14; New Labour, strategic approach to policies and communications 100; reputation and, linking of 102–6; selection and content development of 66
political choreography 19–20
political communications management 7–8, 9–44; academic disciplines, usage of terms in 42; balance of power, communications managers and 22; branding 13–14, 15; charisma and individuality 38; charisma and public persona 37–39; charismatic leadership 38–39; charismatic public persona, features of 40–41; client satisfaction, concentration on 12–13; communications processes, functioning and outcomes of 24; communicative focus, restriction of 25; comparative advertising 14–15; contingency theory 25; corporate public relations, models of 25–26; desirable personality traits 35; election campaigns, themes in 36–37; electoral system, oligopolistic aspect of 14; environmental changes 21; events, charismatic leadership and 39–41; external circumstances 39–41; focusing events 21; ideal politician, definition of 33–37; image and reputation, terminological clarification 41–43; instant-rebuttal units 22–23; journalism and political public relations, liaison between 19; journalist and communicator, power balance between 29–30; journalist and marketer, contributions to communication 146–47; leadership image 36; literature on 10; long-term relationship building 11–12; market-orientated stance, espousal of 13; marketing and public relations, distinction between 16; marketing strategies 9–10, 10–11, 11–12; media

advisers, operations freedom for 29; media management, style of 29–30; media relations, complexities of 15; message delivery speed and variety 21–22; message formulation, systematic research and 23–24; meta-communication 31; misunderstandings about political marketing 12; models of public relations practice 20–21; Mountfield Report (1997) 29; negative advertising 14–15; new perspective in 159–62; news value of stories 32; personal attributes 34–35; personalization 33; persuasion 16–17; political choreography 19–20; political marketing 9–15; political public relations, redefinition of 17–26; political rebuttals, speed and immediacy of 28; popular preferences, transitory nature of 36; potential role for marketing in 11; professionalism in politics, ascendancy of 26–32; public profile 18–19; public relations and process of reputation management 15–17; public relations practice, models of 20–21; publicity and sophisticated communications management, recognition of value of 27–28; reactive approach, lack of forward planning and 21; relationships, role of construction of 24–25; reputation, notion of 26; reputation, personalization and celebrity politics 32–33; reputational objectives 33–37, 37–39; resources, organizational arrangements and 23–24; speed in media operations, relevance of 22–23; strategic skill, balance of power and 23; textbook concepts of 151–52; US campaigns, lessons from 28–29; visual impressions, significance of 14

political communications management practice 8, 55–68; access, resource of 61–62, 64–67; agenda and frames in 58–61; agenda-setting, framing issues and, critical nature of differentiation between 56; agenda-setting, need for resources for 56–57; agenda-setting, technicalities of 57; centralization 67; communications professionals, functions, roles and skills of 65–66; competition among journalists for political news 60; competitive advantage, maintenance of 62–63; dramatization 60–61; editorial resources, limits on 59; emphasis of reporting events, influences on 56; environmental change, adaptation to 62–63; exclusivity of access 65; expertise, resource of 61–63, 65; government communications units 63; incumbents, powers of 59–60; internal organization, access and 64–67; interpretation, struggle over power of 59–60; legitimate authority 57–58; literature, review of 67–68; media, intermediate role of 56; media, pivotal role of 56; media and 55–58; media attention, strategic perspectives to succeed in contest for 59; media capital 57–58; Mountfield Report (1997) 66; mutual dependence 60; news agendas, categories of content 58–59; newsworthy material, pressures for provision of 60; organizational arrangements 65; Phillis Review (2004) 66–67; policy selection and content development 66; political journalism, role of 55; political structures, resource of 61–62; power structures, resource of 62–63; professional strategists, reliance on advice from 62; pseudo-events 60; Public Administration Select Committee Report (1998) 66; ready-to-use media information 59; real events outside communicator's control, centrality of 57; resources, distribution and balance of 64; resources, pivotal role of 63–64; resources, power of 57; source attributes, questioning of 58; specialization 62; themes, media interpretation of 56

political judgement, bases for 150–51

political marketing 9–15; theory, concepts of 3–4

political news reporting, entertainment in 114–15

political positioning 89–92

political rebuttals, speed and immediacy of 28

political reinvention 103–4

political structures, resource of 61–62

politicians' narratives, shaping of 155–57

popular preferences, transitory nature of 36
Portillo, Michael 82, 99, 130, 131, 134, 153, 157
power structures, resource of 62–63
practitioner interviews (and evidence from): communications management in action 69–72, 78–79, 86, 89, 93, 95; news, management of 115–16; research study 7, 8, 68, 150–51, 152, 155–56, 157, 159–60, 162–63, 164–65, 168–69; strategic communications management process 48–49
Pratt, M.G. 42
Prescott, John 85, 86, 110, 117, 118
presentational prowess, need for 155
Price, Lance: communications management in action 71, 72, 77, 79, 80, 89, 90, 91, 93, 94, 95, 96, 98, 102, 103; news, management of 110, 115, 116, 124; resources, manegement of 129, 130, 135, 138, 139, 143, 144, 147, 149
prime ministerial interference: communications management in action 95; resources, management of 143–44
professional advice, quality and implementation of 136–40
professional communicators, pivotal role of 2–3
professional practice in communications management 52–54
professionalism in politics, ascendancy of 26–32
pseudo-events 60
Public Administration Select Committee Report (1998) 66
public feedback 146
public persona 2, 3, 8, 41, 75, 78, 96, 105, 110, 118, 150, 152–54, 161, 165, 167; adaptation and realignment with new demands 130–31, 135; artificial or constructed persona 82. 83–85, 136; Blair's persona 72–73, 85; Brown's persona 3, 81, 85, 103, 119, 132; Cameron's persona 102–3; charisma and 37–39, 40; creation and communication of 52, 133; Hague's persona 14, 131; ideal persona 79–82; identification and consolidation of 90–91; identity and persona 85; Johnson's persona 74; Kinnock's persona 73; limitations caused by 169–70; make-over attempts 153; media and marketing, role in shaping 27; Miliband's persona 74, 104, 134; news reports and consequences for 112–16; past record and 129–32; power and 2, 3; reconciliation of persona 86–87; reinvention of 157–58; remoulding of 85; Straw's persona 100; values, personification in 33, 154–55
public profile, political communications and 18–19
public relations: corporate public relations, models of 25–26; journalism and political public relations, liaison between 19; marketing and, distinction between 16; perspective within research study 26, 50–51, 165–66; political public relations, redefinition of 17–26; practice of, models of 20–21; reputation management process and 15–17

qualitative data, problems with analysis of 71–72
quality of advice, resources and 139–40
quality of communications: quality of access and 142–43; resource availability and 140–42
Quinn, T. 59, 60

Ratnam, K.J. 39
Rawnsley, Andrew 4, 30
ready-to-use media information 59
Reagan, Ronald 2
Reber, B.H. and Cameron, G.T. 25
Redfern, Simon 71, 86, 88, 92, 107, 108, 124, 129, 130, 134, 145, 147, 148, 149
Reid, John 90
relationships: construction of, role in communications management 24–25; long-term relationship building 11–12; trust, relationships of 138–39
Rennard, C. 10
reputation: building of, process of 45–52; concepts of 157; control of 73; creation and safeguarding of 73–74; limits on shaping of 104–6; notion of 26; personalization and celebrity politics 32–33; power of 72–73; relevance of 75–76
reputation management: central role of 74–75; dealing with challenges to 157–59; events and consequences for

116–19; long-term approach to 132–36; objectives of personality and, linking of 82–85; planning process and 92–95; recognition of relevance of 72–75; reputation shaping 4–5; reputational objectives 33–37, 37–39; research in, use of 75–79; resources as quality factor in 148–49
research study: agenda-setting 155–57; communications and performance, connection between 152; communications plans, problems with 154–57; communicative actions, deployment of 153–54; comprehensive planning, absence of or deficiency in 165; conclusion 164–69; crisis communications 156–57; data collection and analysis 6, 69–72; dynamic political setting 161–62; financial means, variable of 160–61; findings and discussion 150–59, 164–69; findings reviewed against current literature 167; focus of 163–64, 168; further research, recommendation for 169–70; initial assumption 1–2, 150; intuition, reliance on 152–53; leaks, fear of 154; limitations 162–64; management, variable of 161; managerial implications 159–62; marketing perspective 9–10, 166; message framing 163; 'noise,' conditioning power of 161–62; opinion research, resources for commissioning of 150–51; personal relationship, variable of 160; personal reputation in politics, limitations in approaches to 166–67; personal reputation management, predictive model of 162; political communications management, new perspective in 159–62; political communications management, textbook concepts of 151–52; political communications practice, lack of accord with current academic discourse 165–66; political judgement, bases for 150–51; politicians' narratives, shaping of 155–57; practitioner interviews (and evidence from) 7, 8, 68, 150–51, 152, 155–56, 157, 159–60, 162–63, 164–65, 168–69; presentational prowess, need for 155; professional background, variable of 161; public persona, make-over attempts 153; public relations perspective 26, 50–51, 165–66; qualitative data, problems with analysis of 71–72; reputation, concepts of 157; reputation management, dealing with challenges to 157–59; research design 6–7; selection of interviewees 163; strategic reputation management, feasibility of 154–55; strategic skill, Mannheim's contention about 23; systematic data analysis, dearth of research and 80, 152; tactical stratagems 153–54; terminology 41–43; theoretical implications 159–62, 167–69; time, variable of 161; training, variable of 161; variables, categorization of 160–61, 162; volatile media environment 161–62
resources: distribution and balance of 64; organizational arrangements and 23–24; pivotal role of 63–64; power of 57
resources, management of 129–49; 'Big Society' idea 139–40; cathartic moments, reputation change and 134; communications advisers, need for frankness in 137–38; communications staff. former journalists on 145–46; communicators and their expertise, scrutinization of 144–48; exclusivity, journalistic goal of 144–45; external experts and confidants, consultation with 137; human hinterland 130; internal communications and management structures 140–44; local media experience 145; long-term reputation management 132–36; marketing approaches in government communications 146; media relations, conditions for effectiveness in 139; Al-Megrahi case 140; past decisions, political mood changes and 130; past election campaigns, baggage of 129; past record, burden (and opportunity) of 129–32; past record, inheritance by association of 131–32; past record, value of 130; personality, time and revelation of 136; political communications, journalists' and marketers' contributions to 146–47; prime ministerial interference 143–44; professional advice, quality and implementation of 136–40; public

feedback 146; public persona, adaptation and realignment with new demands 130–31, 135; quality of advice 139–40; quality of communications, quality of access and 142–43; quality of communications, resource availability and 140–42; reputation management, resources as quality factor in 148–49; reputation management over time 132–36; sales, journalistic goal of 145; skilled communications staff, recruitment of 147–48; tabloid journalism, political connection with 145; trust, relationships of 138–39
rhetorical shortcomings 109
Richards, Paul 151; communications management in action 71, 73, 78, 82, 84, 85, 90, 92, 93, 94, 97, 99, 102, 104, 105; news, management of 108, 117, 118, 125; resources, management of 131, 134, 137, 139, 142, 147, 148
Roberts, J.M. 39
Robespierre, Maximilien de 39
Robinson, C. 13
Robinson, Edward 45
Ronneberger, F. and Rühl, M. 15
Roosevelt, Franklin D. 34, 44n13
Roper, S. and Fill, C. 42
Rose, R. 67
Rowan, D. 2
Rusbridger, Alan 29
Ryan, C. 56

Saatchi, Charles and Maurice 26, 43n9
sales, journalistic goal of 145
Salmond, Alex 88
Sampson, A. 22
Sarcinelli, U. 2, 33
Savigny, H. 10, 15, 23
Saxton, K. 26
Scammell, M. 27, 62
Schama, Simon 39
Schechner, R. 2
Scheufele, D. 56
Schlenker, B.R. *et al.* 53
Schlesinger, P. 59
Schlesinger, P. and Tumber, H. 59
Schneider, H. 13
Schnell, R. *et al.* 69
Schudson, M. 57
Schwartzenberg, R. 4
Schweiger, G. and Adami, M. 34, 35
Schweitzer, A. 37, 38
segmentation of audiences 87
Seitel, F. 24
Seldon, A. 66
selection of interviewees 163
self-inflicted scandal 117–18
Sellers, P. 43n6
Seymour-Ure, C. 18, 23, 67
Shamir, B. *et al.* 40
Sheafer, T. 58
Shenkar, O. and Yuchtman-Yaar, E. 41, 42, 44n15
Shepherd, M. 2
Shils, E. 40
Shoemaker, P.J. and Reese, S.D. 40
Shoemaker, P.J. and Vos, T.P. 58
Short, Clare 79
short-term contingency planning 120–21
Simons, W.H. and Jones, J.G. 57
Sitrick, M. 19
skilled communications staff, recruitment of 147–48
Smith, G. 5, 14
Smith, G. and Hirst, A. 11
Smith, G. and Saunders, J. 10, 13
Smith, Iain Duncan 71, 73, 83, 103, 104, 109, 130, 131, 136, 157
Smith, John 72, 136, 137
Smith, R.D. 4, 16, 45, 46, 47, 48, 51, 57
Smith's management model 46–47, 51
source attributes, questioning of 58
specialization 62
speed in media operations, relevance of 22–23
Spelman, Caroline 101, 104
spin doctors (and spin doctoring) 4–5, 19, 30, 43n3, 132, 156
Spinrad, W. 37
Staab, J.F. 58
Stacey, Kiran 71, 81, 83, 84, 85, 103, 104, 112, 118, 124, 126, 127, 128, 133, 134, 139, 144, 146
Stacks, D.W. 65
Stephanopoulos, G. 22, 28
Stevenson, Wilfred 71, 81, 84, 86, 87, 110, 113, 124, 125, 130, 132, 136, 141, 142
Stockwell, S. 19, 22
strategic advice, resources for 98–100
strategic approach, practical advantages of 6
strategic communications management process 8, 45–54; C-MACIE model 46; ENGAGE framework 46; exemplification 53; Grunig and Hunt's communications model 49–51;

histrionic performance 52–53; impression management 53–54; ingratiation 53; Kotzaivazoglou's political marketing model 49; management of political communications 52–54; Newman's political marketing model 47–49; planned communications programmes 45; practitioner interviews (and evidence from) 48–49; professional practice 52–54; reputation building, process of 45–52; Smith's management model 46–47, 51; strategic management models 45–52; strategic management models, flexible adaptation of, necessity for 52; visual presentation 53
strategic management models 45–52; flexible adaptation of, necessity for 52
strategic options, recognition of 95–101
strategic reputation management 1–7, 150–70; adaptability to constant change, core requirement of 5; communications management 4–5, 5–6; communications practitioners, performance of 5–6; debunking the strategy myth 150–70; expectations, adaptation of politicians to 2–3; feasibility of 154–55; image creation 2; image cultivation 2–3; images and reputation, centrality of 1–2; impression management 2; media-representative democracy 2; misleading appearances 2; party leadership, support for 2; personal media relations 4; personalization in politics 3; planning and strategy making in communications context 6; political marketing theory, concepts of 3–4; politics and political journalism, unpredictable nature of 5; professional communicators, pivotal role of 2–3; public persona, power and 2, 3; reputation shaping 4–5; spin doctors 4–5; strategic approach, practical advantages of 6; strategy myth? 1–7, 150–70; *see also* research study
strategic skills: Mannheim's contention about 23; in safeguarding public persona, need for 161
Straw, Jack 70, 80, 94, 96, 97, 105, 122, 123, 131, 138, 139, 145; public persona of 100
Strictly Come Dancing (BBC TV) 83
Strömbäck, J. and Kiousis, S. 16, 24, 65
Suchman, M. 20
Sumpter, R. and Tankard, J.W. 19
Swanson, D. and Mancini, P. 3, 4
systematic data analysis, dearth of research and 80, 152
systematic research, lack of interest in and resources for 77–79
Szyszka, P. 15

tabloid journalism, political connection with 145
tactical stratagems 153–54
target audiences 12, 88, 122; conflicting stakes within 86
Taylor, M. 24
Tedesco, J.C. 56
television 3, 33, 44, 53, 60, 80, 112, 116; communications management and 88–89; debates on, preparations for 122
Tench, R. 15, 45
terminology 41–43
Thatcher, Margaret 14, 26, 27, 73, 92, 115, 124, 139, 147
Theakston, K. 3
themes, media interpretation of 56
theoretical framework, dearth of 6–7
theoretical implications of research 159–62, 167–69
Thompson, J.B. 65
Thorogood, Zoë 71, 101, 102
Thurber, J.A. and Nelson, C. 62
Tiffen, R. 55
time: considerations of, communications management and 101–2; variable of 161
Timmins, N. 30, 67
Total Politics 70
training, variable of 161
trust, relationships of 138–39
Trux, W. 4
Tunstall, J. 43n7, 63
Turk, J.V. 56
Turnbull, N. 19

Ulmer, R.R. *et al.* 65
unplanned, reactive media relations 94
unpredictable incidents, dealing with 116–18
US campaigns, lessons from 28–29

van Riel, C.B.M. and Fombrun, C. 43
variables, categorization of 160–61, 162
Vidal, G. 44n13
visual impressions, significance of 14
visual presentation 53
volatility of: communications processes 50; media environment 5, 47, 52, 65, 154, 161–62, 166–67

Walsh, K. 12
Wanta, W. 57
Waring, Katie 71, 78, 83, 84, 87, 90, 94, 97, 101, 105, 113, 116, 130, 131, 138, 139, 146, 148
Washington, George 39
Waterman, R.W. *et al.* 2, 36
Watson, T. and Kitchen, P.J. 15, 43
Watts, D. 26
Weaver, D. 56
Weber, Max 37, 38, 39
Webster, C. 12
Whetten, D.A. and Mackey, A. 42
Williams, J.E. *et al.* 35
Willner, Ann Ruth 38, 39
Wilson, A. 10
Winter, D.G. 34, 37
Wolcott, H.F. 72
Wolfsfeld, G. 30, 57, 58
women's magazines 87
Wood, Nick 71, 87, 100, 131, 133, 134, 136, 145, 147, 149
Wray, J.H. 33
Wring, D. 4, 10, 13
written plans 93–94

Xifra, J. 20, 21, 43n5

Young, S. 26

Zoch, L.M. and Molleda, J.C. 57